Nationalism
and Sectionalism in
South Carolina
1852-1860

A Da Capo Press Reprint Series

THE AMERICAN SCENE
Comments and Commentators
GENERAL EDITOR: WALLACE D. FARNHAM
University of Illinois

Nationalism and Sectionalism in South Carolina
1852-1860

A STUDY OF THE MOVEMENT
FOR SOUTHERN INDEPENDENCE

By Harold S. Schultz

DA CAPO PRESS · NEW YORK · 1969

0272792

A Da Capo Press Reprint Edition

This Da Capo Press edition of
Nationalism and Sectionalism in South Carolina, 1852-1860,
is an unabridged republication of the first edition published in 1950.
It is reprinted by special arrangement with
Duke University Press.

Library of Congress Catalog Card Number 70-84190

Copyright, 1950, by the Duke University Press

Published by Da Capo Press
A Division of Plenum Publishing Corporation
227 West 17th Street
New York, N.Y. 10011

Printed in the United States of America

DUKE · UNIVERSITY · PUBLICATIONS

*Nationalism and
Sectionalism in South Carolina
1852-1860*

Nationalism and Sectionalism in South Carolina
1852-1860

A STUDY OF THE MOVEMENT
FOR SOUTHERN INDEPENDENCE

Harold S. Schultz

DURHAM, NORTH CAROLINA

DUKE UNIVERSITY PRESS

1950

PRINTED IN THE UNITED STATES OF AMERICA
BY THE SEEMAN PRINTERY, INC., DURHAM, N. C.

To Carol

PREFACE

EVERY piece of historical writing is a co-operative work. The historian, even when his subject is quite limited in scope, is indebted to innumerable persons and institutions, as a mere glance at the bibliography and footnotes to this book will show. To a host of unnamed coadjutors and benefactors—historians, biographers, editors, bibliographers, curators, librarians, copy-readers, statisticians, cartographers, genealogists, antiquarians, friends, neighbors, and relatives—I should like to express my gratitude for making this study possible. To those who have collected source materials for the history of South Carolina and the South, and to those who have written in these fields, I feel particularly indebted. Several university professors have given me invaluable information, suggestions, and criticism. Professors William T. Laprade and Charles S. Sydnor, who have done much to stimulate research in political and Southern history among graduate students at Duke University, have been most helpful.

The framework of the story told in this book is shaped more by a consideration for the factional alignments in South Carolina than for national issues. Each chapter is not simply a treatment of one of the leading issues, such as the Kansas-Nebraska Act, the slave trade, Cuba, or the John Brown raid. Instead, each chapter deals with a multitude of issues as they affected factional groupings in the state. The first chapter is both an introduction to the narrative and an exposition of political leadership in the decade of the fifties. The second chapter begins the narrative in the year 1852; and, in order to explain the situation in that year, the secession controversy of the previous two years is reviewed. Each of the following eight chapters is devoted to one year. These chapters contain accounts of such topics as presidential policies, legislative issues, agitation of the slavery question, political parties, prominent politicians, federal elections, and significant personal conflicts arising from sectional antagonism. They terminate with discussions of the leaders, policies, and strength of major factional groups in the state. The concluding chapter is a brief statement of the paramount issue in South Carolina politics in the decade before secession. This rather strictly narrative form of presentation was used because it seemed the most suitable medium for demonstrating the importance in politics of interacting and concurrent events.

It is my opinion that this book corroborates, more than it disproves or denies, the findings of those who have written on special aspects of the political history of South Carolina. However, I do believe that there has been a tendency among recent scholars to overestimate the strength of national Democracy and Unionism in South Carolina during the period of the Buchanan administration. That faction which can most conveniently be labeled National Democrats and which was organized under the leadership of James L. Orr, as far as I have been able to determine, at no time was able to control the legislature; and its position during the years after 1857 was one of gradual decline rather than increasing strength. Effective leadership and organization of moderate opinion during these years gave an appearance of much greater strength to the National Democrats than they actually possessed. National sentiment crystallized in the middle fifties, but I have found no evidence to indicate that it expanded thereafter.

In approach this book differs rather markedly from John G. Van Deusen's *Economic Bases of Disunion in South Carolina.* I have stressed the role of the slavery issue in South Carolina politics without attempting to decide the question of its motivation. Dr. Van Deusen viewed Northern hostility to slavery as merely the avowed reason for secession; the real motive he found "in bitter resentment over real or fancied economic wrongs, and the feeling that South Carolina would never be economically independent while she remained in the Union."

Inasmuch as the foregoing conclusion does not deny that slavery was the avowed reason for secession, it does not necessarily contradict the central theme of this book.

In principle the approach employed by Dr. Van Deusen is not objectionable. That expressed and conscious thought may be derived from unconscious, unrecognized, or unexpressed desires is a teaching of modern psychoanalysts that historians can hardly afford to ignore. But I am not convinced that the desire for economic independence was a strong influence in creating disunion sentiment in South Carolina. My doubt rests chiefly upon the failure of such an explanation to account for differences of opinion in the state on the question of disunion. It fails to tell us why certain parts of the electorate persistently and actively maintained an attitude of intense insurgency, while other parts were conciliatory and reluctant to adopt extreme measures. Why, for example, was disunion sentiment strongest in districts where the proportion of slaves to population was highest? Is one to assume that the desire for economic independence was strongest in those districts?

If the desire to make slavery secure was merely a psychic mechanism substituted for other ungratified desires—a hypothesis that I am willing to consider as a theoretical possibility— it seems to me that the "real" source of discontent will have to be found in conditions that impinged upon the white population in those areas where disunion sentiment was strongest. It might well be that special conditions within those areas created discontent and frustrations greater than in the districts where disunion sentiment was weakest. Theorctically, one might ultimately reach the conclusion that both the desire for economic independence and the desire to make slavery secure were substitutionary mechanisms that had their origins in underlying economic and social conditions.

What has been said above should serve as a word of caution to the reader who already believes that the antislavery movement was the main reason for secession. Such a reader will find much in this book that accords with his preconceptions. But I should like to point out that I have at no place declared explicitly that the antislavery movement was the main cause of the secession of South Carolina. This diffidence is not the result of doubts about the main theme of this book. I am thoroughly convinced that the antislavery movement was uppermost in the conscious thinking of South Carolina politicians during the 1850's. No other issue—the tariff, internal improvements, expenditures of the federal government, territorial expansion, economic reform—occupied the attention of the politicians so much as the slavery question. It is only because there still remains the theoretical possibility that the expressed thought of the public men may not have been a true reflection of their motivation that I have refrained from asserting that fear of the antislavery movement caused the secession of South Carolina.

HAROLD S. SCHULTZ

University of Vermont

CONTENTS

CHAPTER   PAGE

Preface vii

List of Maps, Table, and Figures xii

i. Leadership, 1850-1860 3

ii. Acquiescence, 1852 26

iii. Intransigence or Reconciliation, 1853 52

iv. Fear or Gratitude, 1854 58

v. Nativism or Slavery, 1855 75

vi. Isolation or Affiliation, 1856 87

vii. Extremism or Moderation, 1857 134

viii. Provocation or Nonaggression, 1858 150

ix. Defiance or Forbearance, 1859 178

x. Insurgency, 1860 200

xi. The Paramount Issue 231

Bibliography 234

Index 245

LIST OF MAPS, TABLE, AND FIGURES

PAGE

Map: Congressional and State Districts in South Carolina,
1852-1860 15

Map: Proportion of Slaves to Population in State Districts,
1860 89

Map: Resolution against National Convention in State House,
1856 104

Map: Resolution on Secession in State House, 1856 126

Map: Resolution on Slave Trade in State House, 1858 159

Table 1: Proportion of Slaves to Population in State Districts,
1860 91

Fig. 1: Members of Legislature for National Convention, 1855   90

Fig. 2: Resolution against National Convention in State House,
1856 105

Fig. 3: Resolution on Secession in State House, 1856 127

Fig. 4: Resolution on Southern Confederacy in State Senate,
1856 128

Fig. 5: Resolution on Slave Trade in State Senate, 1856 143

Fig. 6: Resolution on Slave Trade in State House, 1858 160

Fig. 7: Resolution on Slave Trade in State House, 1858 161

Fig. 8: Resolution on Slave Trade in State Senate, 1858 162

Fig. 9: Resolution on Slave Trade in State Senate, 1858 163

Fig. 10: Resolution on Slave Trade in State Senate, 1859 184

Fig. 11: Resolution on Southern Independence in State Senate,
1859 193

Fig. 12: Resolution on Secession in State House, 1859 196

Fig. 13: Resolution on Southern Confederacy in State House,
1859 197

Fig. 14: Resolution on Southern Confederacy in State House,
1859 199

Fig. 15: Members of Legislature for National Convention,
1855 and 1859 211

*Nationalism and
Sectionalism in South Carolina
1852-1860*

CHAPTER I

LEADERSHIP, 1850-1860

POLITICAL leadership in ante-bellum South Carolina was a patriotic duty. The citizens of the state, sensitive to internal decline and external danger, sought the best men the state could offer to conduct their political affairs. Any man who had extraordinary abilities for political leadership was solicited to take part in public life. Year after year notable citizens and leaders of rival factions urged James Henry Hammond to re-enter politics. When Calhoun was in private life for a short time in 1845, letters came from all over the South and South Carolina pleading with him to return to the Senate.[1] In a letter written in 1838, Calhoun expressed the argument of necessity and indispensability which was heard many times in the state:

It is vain to think of getting clear of politicks. However we may desire to free ourselves from it, we may be assured that it will not permit the separation to take place. If the capable and worthy retire, the designing, or worthless will take their place. Our destiny, and that of posterity is involved in our political institutions and the conduct of the Government; and if we do not attend to them chains and servitude will be our fate. There is no section of our country, in which the duty imposed on the enlightened and patriotic to devote their time and their talents to the country is so imperious as in ours. We are surrounded by invisible dangers, against which nothing can protect us, but our foresight and energy. . . . Our state has ever had its full share of talents and virtue and patriotism in the publick councils of the Union, and we must not in this crisis of our fate permit any diminution to take place.[2]

[1] John C. Calhoun to F. W. Pickens, Sept. 23, 1845, in the *South Carolina Historical Magazine*, VII (1906), 16-19.
[2] John C. Calhoun to James Henry Hammond, April 18, 1838, in J. Franklin Jameson (ed.), "The Correspondence of John C. Calhoun," *Ameri-*

The small population and wealth of the state accentuated the yearning for exceptional leadership in politics. Almost stable in population and wealth during the period from 1830 to 1860, South Carolina declined in relation to the other states in the Union. The political incidence of these conditions was a loss of representation in the federal Congress. From nine Representatives in 1832, the number dropped to seven in 1842 and to six in 1852. As early as 1826 the Charleston *Mercury* declared that the ability of the South Carolina Representatives alone could safeguard the interests of the state in the Union: "Superiority in talent may counterpoise superiority in numbers."[3]

Hope was transformed into reliance as experience showed that South Carolina could continue to exert an influence in national politics out of proportion to its resources and population. James Henley Thornwell, president of South Carolina College, wrote of his state in 1853: "A mere speck compared with several other States in the Union, her reliance for the protection of her rights, and her full and equal influence in Federal legislation, must be the genius of her statesmen and the character of her people."[4] In 1859 Stephen Elliott counseled the students of South Carolina: "Although you occupy but an inconsiderable space upon the map of the world; although your population is but limited, and is not likely very much to increase, yet you have that from the past which can lead you to a greatness higher than you have yet attained. It is useless for you to enter upon the race of physical greatness; you have neither

can Historical Association Annual Report for the Year 1899 (Washington, 1900), II, 395.

H. C. Williams wrote to J. H. Hammond, Jan. 23, 1860: "I am aware that public life has but little if any charm for you, but as you are a South Carolinian, you cannot and no other citizen of that state can on any private consideration . . . claim exemption from the duties which his country requires. The plea might avail with citizens of other states, not so with South Carolina, which has suffered no depreciation in her heroes and statesmen since the revolutionary period" (Hammond Papers, Library of Congress; unless otherwise indicated, all letters by or to James Henry Hammond hereinafter cited are from the Hammond Papers in the Library of Congress).

[3] Charleston *Mercury*, July 28, 1826, quoted by David Franklin Houston, *A Critical Study of Nullification in South Carolina* (New York, 1896), p. 49.

[4] James Henley Thornwell, *Letter to His Excellency Governor Manning on Public Instruction in South Carolina* (Columbia, 1853), p. 35.

the position nor the taste for it. . . . You must continue to be great as your fathers were, or you will not be great at all; great in statesmanship, great in oratory, great in the philosophy of law and government, great in council."[5] Congressman Lawrence Keitt wrote to Sue Sparks, July 11, 1855: "Our state is small in numbers and resources; yet around its head is the aureole of undying fame. Small as it is, it is classic ground, and has more weight in the federal councils than any state in the union. This it won by the intellect of its sons; it can only be kept by it."

Political leadership was also a social custom in South Carolina. The demand of the electorate for the most capable public men would hardly have been supplied had there been insufficient incentives to draw them into politics. The human desire to exercise power, while responsible for the entrance of many into public life, can hardly account for the unusually large number of talented men who took part in the politics of the state. The fecundity of the state as a breeder of politicians was partially the result of the fertilizing influence of social prestige. Politics was held in high esteem by the citizens of South Carolina, especially the upper class. It was a vocation and an avocation proper for the planter-gentleman. To those who had no aspiration for high places in government, politics provided an opportunity for public service and a diversion of recognized social standing. The sessions of the legislature at Columbia were always accompanied by a lively social life among the members of the legislature and their families, most of whom were drawn from the gentry. The functions of the governorship were more civic and social than political, and few men sought it who had not the means of entertaining lavishly.

Now and then a lonely litterateur, scholar, or merchant protested against the emphasis on politics. William Henry Trescot, a profound and lucid critic of his state, thought that the people rarely needed the politician. The business of the country was

---

[5] Stephen Elliott, *Annual Address before the Clariosophic and Euphradian Societies of the South Carolina College . . . Delivered Dec. 4, 1859* (Charleston, 1859), p. 12.

carried on by the capitalists, merchants, mechanics, and planters; the "hubbub of politics," he said, had little effect upon the daily life of the people.[6] A spokesman for the neglected literary group of Charleston complained to the readers of *Russell's Magazine* that the talent of the state was too much absorbed in politics.[7] John Belton O'Neall, for many years a judge on the highest court of appeals and prominent in the civic life of his community, insinuated that politics was the work the devil found for the idle hands of gentlemen.[8]

These were lonely voices in the South Carolina of the 1850's, and few heeded their admonitions. O'Neall pointed out that mechanics, merchants, and farmers were too busy making a living to indulge in the luxury of politics. But there were plenty of planters and lawyers to play the game, and in most elections a superfluity of candidates contended for office.

The participation of the planters and lawyers in politics was far from disapproved. Was not the existence of this planter class the very basis of Southern statesmanship? The Spartanburg *Carolina Spartan* expressed the predominant view in an editorial under the headline "Southern and Northern Statesmen." The North, this editorial asserted, produced inferior statesmen because it was a manufacturing and commercial region; its people were too busy making money to cultivate the traits requisite for statesmanship. The South, on the other hand, produced superior statesmen because of its agricultural economy and social organization; it had a class of people with leisure,

---

[6] [William Henry Trescot], "The Bench and Bar," *Russell's Magazine*, VI (Jan., 1860), 296.

[7] *Russell's Magazine*, I (April, 1857), 89.

[8] O'Neall wrote: "I regard politics as a sorry trade! I never have found the man whom it warmed, fed or clothed. But I know many . . . whom it has made naked, cold and hungry. Employment and attention to a man's own business is the best antidote to politics. The honest, laborious farmer, mechanic or merchant is no politician. He has enough to do at home" (from a letter published in the Newberry [S. C.] *Conservatist*, July 10, 1860).

Francis Lieber, professor at the South Carolina College, was disgusted with the preoccupation with politics. "Every son of a fool here is a great statesman meditating on the relations of State sovereignty to the United States government," he wrote in a letter to G. S. Hillard, May, 1851 (Thomas Sargent Perry [ed.], *The Life and Letters of Francis Lieber*, Boston, 1882, p. 254).

means, and inclination to undergo the training essential to political leadership.[9]

South Carolina politicians in the 1850's had strikingly similar backgrounds. Most of them had spent their childhood in much the same kind of homes, had gone to the same kind of schools, had studied at the same college, had prepared for the same profession, had engaged in the same occupation, had held the same offices, and had witnessed the same political events. With few exceptions they had been born in South Carolina in the era from 1800 to 1825. Most of them had at one time or another studied law. In private life they were lawyers or planters and often both. A few were journalists, teachers, merchants, or bankers. Many of them had begun their careers in the state legislature.[10]

[9] June 25, 1857.

[10] Data from the biographies of twenty-one men who served as U. S. Senators or Representatives or as governors during the period 1851-1860 were tabulated with the following results:

Year of birth
1786-1799 4
1800-1809 8
1810-1819 6
1820-1824 3
Place of birth
South Carolina 20
North Carolina 1
Higher education
South Carolina College 11
College of Charleston 1
University of North Carolina.............. 1
University of Virginia 1
Princeton 1
Yale 1
Harvard 1
United States Military Academy 1
self—in South Carolina 3
Law training 16
Occupations
planter 11
lawyer 7
lawyer-planter 2
professor 1
Offices held
legislature 17
judiciary 3
governor 8
attorney-general 1

The South Carolina College was particularly important in shaping the mind of South Carolina leadership. It was founded in the first decade of the century to provide a means of educating the young men within the state and to break down differences of opinion between the residents of the up and low country. During the presidency of Thomas Cooper, 1820-1834, the college became a center for the dissemination of State-Rights, free-trade, and proslavery views. Cooper was an ardent advocate of nullification and as early as 1827 declared that the time had arrived to calculate the value of the Union. Both as a teacher and a publicist he had great influence in bringing the leaders to accept what was later called the Calhoun or South Carolina doctrine. His pamphlet, *Consolidation*, written in 1824, was aptly called the "text book of South Carolina politics." Many men who later became prominent in politics attended the college during his presidency, and some survived to take an outstanding part in the events of the fifties. Senators James Henry Hammond and James Chesnut; Governors William Henry Gist, John Hugh Means, and Francis W. Pickens; Congressmen William Aiken, Milledge L. Bonham, and William F. Colcock; and others of less distinction attended the college during Cooper's regime.[11]

These same leaders of the fifties, whose long attachment to the state had developed in them a strong feeling of patriotism for South Carolina and whose education had provided them early in life with a theory of government and a rationale of their social institutions, had lived through a period of incessant

---

solicitor 2
comptroller-general 1
surveyor-general 1
mayor 1
U. S. Congress 16
port-collector 1
naval agent 1

[11] Edwin L. Green, *A History of the University of South Carolina* (Columbia, 1916); Maximilian La Borde, *History of the South Carolina College, from its Incorporation, Dec. 19, 1801, to Dec. 19, 1865, Including Sketches of Its Presidents and Professors. With an Appendix. Prefaced by a Life of the Author*, by J. L. Reynolds (rev. ed., Charleston, 1874); Dumas Malone, *The Public Life of Thomas Cooper, 1783-1839* (New Haven, 1926).

political tension and controversy. Few of them could remember a time when the people of South Carolina were satisfied with the position of their state in the Federal Union. Men like R. Barnwell Rhett, James Henry Hammond, Francis W. Pickens, and James H. Adams, while in their twenties or early thirties, had gained their first experience in the politics of insurgency at the time of the nullification crisis. Younger politicians, such as Milledge Bonham, Lawrence Keitt, James L. Orr, and James Chesnut, who had not yet finished college when the nullification ordinance was passed, had never known the meaning of good will in their federal relations.[12] During their generation the antislavery movement had been transformed from a cause of discontented cranks and reformers into a pressure group that had ominous possibilities of becoming a major political party. The younger men had experienced no great crisis before that of 1850, but they had lived in a perennial atmosphere of emergency. And some had taken part in abortive movements for secession, like that of 1844, which may have taught some of them the art of agitation.[13]

Everlasting attacks upon the slaveholders of the South and South Carolina had made the people irritable and restless under the existing federal government. In the face of attacks from the Northern antislavery agitators, the arguments, appeals, and slogans which had been formulated and popularized at the time of the nullification crisis were never allowed to die. A younger leader such as Keitt, Bonham, or Brooks heard the vocabulary of State Rights and Southern patriotism from childhood. All the expressions of appeal used to stir the people in 1850—all the talk about "resistance" and "submission," all the imprecations against a "consolidated empire," all of the denunciations

[12] In the U. S. House of Representatives, Dec. 16, 1859, Milledge Bonham said: "Though but a boy at the time of that disinterested struggle for the constitutional rights of a whole section [1832], I learned my first political lesson in that school. And I believe that struggle did more to disseminate throughout the South, a clear understanding and just appreciation of the doctrine of State rights than any event which has occurred since the days of Mr. Jefferson" (*Congressional Globe*, 36 Cong., 1 Sess., p. 166).

[13] Laura White, *Robert Barnwell Rhett: Father of Secession* (New York, 1931), p. 84.

of the "tyranny of the numerical majority," all of the cries for "constitutional rights"—had been, twenty years before, the word weapons of Turnbull, Hamilton, Cooper, McDuffie, and the other nullifiers. The authors had died, but their words were perpetuated by their spiritual progeny, by men like R. Barnwell Rhett.

The same leaders who had taught the younger generation of politicians the vocabulary of State Rights also taught them the beliefs and methods necessary for political advancement. In the decade 1820-1830 the Representatives and Senators were not sure that a militant defense of the interests of the state and a strict construction of the Constitution were necessary in order to stay in office. By 1833 they had no doubts; in that year ten of the eleven members of the South Carolina delegation were nullificationists. Never thereafter did an aspiring politician doubt that the voters of South Carolina demanded an advocacy of free trade. Nor did he ever doubt that slavery was a vital interest which had to be defended. Nor did he doubt that the electorate would insist upon a strict interpretation of the Constitution. The lessons were clearly before all aspirants to office. The politicians who had been carried over from the decade of the twenties to the next decade were those who had undergone a conversion. Like George McDuffie, who had begun his career in Congress by writing *A Defense of the Liberal Construction of the Powers of Congress*, officeholders who were at one time indifferent to free trade and State Rights became unswerving supporters of the doctrine of state interposition or nullification.[14]

As a contest between South Carolina and the federal government, the success of nullification was debatable. But in terms of political power within the state the decision was final and apparent to all. As an organized party the opposition to nullification completely disintegrated. Its most distinguished leaders, with few exceptions, retired to private life or left the state.

[14] Three monographs are especially useful for the nullification period: David Franklin Houston, *A Critical Study of Nullification* (New York, 1896); Chauncey Samuel Boucher, *The Nullification Controversy in South Carolina* (Chicago, 1916); Frederic Bancroft, *Calhoun and the South Carolina Nullification Movement* (Baltimore, 1928).

All important offices of the state were denied them.[15]   The rule of the state after 1832 was clearly in the hands of the nullifiers, who were under the spell of Calhoun.

For almost two decades John C. Calhoun was master of South Carolina politics.[16]   From 1832, when he captured control of the State Rights group from rival organizers, until his death in 1850, his supremacy was never seriously threatened.   Other political leaders of importance in the state were associates, not rivals, of Calhoun.

Calhoun's success in eliminating rivals and unifying opinion of the state behind his policies was remarkable.   A year after his death every prominent member of the South Carolina delegation in Congress was known to have been his loyal supporter. Only one, Barnwell Rhett, who was a devoted disciple, had ever opposed him publicly on a single issue.   In private life, on the other hand, there were capable and orthodox men like William C. Preston, Waddy Thompson, Henry L. Pinckney, and Francis W. Pickens, whose retirement from office was largely the consequence of Calhoun's disfavor.

The concentration and centralization of leadership which characterized the Calhoun regime disintegrated rapidly during the 1850's.   It is, of course, impossible to know to what extent impersonal causes were responsible for this breakdown of one-man domination.   Perhaps in the face of basic economic changes and party reorganizations neither Calhoun nor any other man

[15] Gaillard Hunt, *John C. Calhoun* (Philadelphia, 1908), p. 196; J. H. Hammond to J. C. Calhoun, May 31, 1840, in J. Franklin Jameson (ed.), "The Correspondence of John C. Calhoun," II, 825.

[16] The most useful biographies of Calhoun for the purposes of this chapter were Gaillard Hunt, *John C. Calhoun*, and William M. Meigs, *The Life of John Caldwell Calhoun* (2 vols.; New York, 1917).   Biographical sketches of Calhoun, Rhett, Hammond, Pickens, Preston, Thompson, and Pinckney are in the *Dictionary of American Biography*.   The relationships of Calhoun to Rhett, Pickens, and Hammond were studied in the biographies of Calhoun, and in Elizabeth Merritt, *James Henry Hammond, 1807-1864* (*Johns Hopkins University Studies in Historical and Poltiical Science*, Vol. XLI, No. 4, Baltimore, 1923); Laura A. White, *Robert Barnwell Rhett: Father of Secession*; Jameson's edition of Calhoun's correspondence; and "Correspondence Addressed to John C. Calhoun, 1837-1849," edited by Chauncey S. Boucher and Robert P. Brooks and published in the *Annual Report of the American Historical Association for the Year 1929* (Washington, 1930).

could have preserved the same degree of political unity in South Carolina in the fifties that existed in the forties. Yet, regardless of the underlying impersonal forces that may have fostered division within the state, the importance of the removal of Calhoun's personal leadership cannot be ignored in any serious speculations upon the reasons for the altered alignments of the fifties.

If the centralization of the period before 1850 had been rooted in a permanent political organization, Calhoun might have been able to appoint a successor capable of forestalling contention among the various leaders. Without the discipline of an established organization, however, and unable to agree that any one among them was pre-eminently qualified to direct the politics of the state, the politicians of the fifties were left without a supreme command. There were still many able men in South Carolina, but there was no individual who could match Calhoun's success in uniting public opinion and commanding deference from rival leaders.[17]

At the time of Calhoun's death the three outstanding candidates for succession to the position of highest leadership in the

[17] Alfred Huger wrote to William Porcher Miles, June 1, 1860: "While Mr. Calhoun lived, the only lesson either taught or comprehended, from the parish schools to the senate chamber, was to obey orders! We did this implicitly and kept up the appearance of a solid column! We were drilled in the lock step, but the instruction was merely mechanical—nothing was said of the theory for keeping the limbs in motion and preparing facilities for marching, but the tramp was loud and strong, and every man supposed himself a soldier. Well, our great chief, for he was essentially great, is among the dead, and he has left no one to administer upon his political estate. The better part of society acquired the habit of following, and lost the habit of thinking" (Miles Papers, University of North Carolina; unless otherwise indicated, all letters by and to William Porcher Miles hereinafter cited are in the Miles Papers, University of North Carolina).

"Malachi," in one of a series of articles on South Carolina's policy, said in a letter published in the Charleston *Courier*, Jan. 7, 1856: "The dominant party governed the State to the exclusion of their opponents, and with Mr. Calhoun as their leader, the State was a unit subject to his dictation. The question of what was right or proper, or expedient, was not so much considered as was the question of what was Mr. Calhoun's opinion. His great intellect overshadowed the State, and like the great oak, everything which grew under it became weak."

For Benjamin F. Perry's comments on Calhoun's domination of South Carolina, see Benjamin F. Perry, *Reminiscences of Public Men* (Philadelphia, 1883), pp. 49, 61, 298.

state were Barnwell Rhett, Francis W. Pickens, and James
Henry Hammond.[18] Each of these men had been at one time
or another closely associated with Calhoun. Similar courses that
brought the three men equal advancement never converged to
form either lasting friendships or political alliances among any
of them. While Calhoun lived, their relationships to each
other were cordially cool. Of equal ambition and ability, each
man knew that promotion to second in rank could be made
only with the preference of Calhoun. Ingratiating toward Calhoun but uneasy toward his rivals, each found it difficult to be
an admirer of the others. Once the cohesive force of Calhoun's
predominance was removed, the obstructions to harmonious association were vastly multiplied.

Nominally Barnwell Rhett succeeded to the first place in
South Carolina politics, for he was elected to fill Calhoun's seat
in the Senate. In reality, however, Rhett possessed neither the
power in South Carolina nor the influence in Washington to fill
Calhoun's place for long. Although elected by 65 per cent of
the total votes on the final balloting of the legislature,[19] his
popularity quickly waned.

Rhett was an avowed secessionist, and the fundamental
postulates of his argument ruled out discussion with the North.
In Washington he could only try to make secessionists of the
other Southern Congressmen and Senators. The rest of the
South, however, was willing to accept the Compromise of 1850,
and the elections held in the fall of 1851 demonstrated con-
clusively that secession was not desired. So when Rhett attended
the Congress which assembled in December, 1851, he was re-
buffed sharply in his attempts to convert Southern members to
his views. Vigorously but vainly he defended himself against

---

[18] Brief sketches of the life of Robert Barnwell Rhett were written by
Laura A. White for the *Dictionary of American Biography* and by Nathaniel
W. Stephenson for the *Encyclopedia of Social Sciences*. A book-length biography of Rhett is Laura A. White, *Robert Barnwell Rhett: Father of Secession*.
Francis Butler Simkins wrote the sketch of Francis W. Pickens in the *Dictionary of American Biography*. A sketch of Hammond's life, by J. G. de R.
Hamilton, is in the *Dictionary of American Biography*. A monographic biography of Hammond is Elizabeth Merritt, *James Henry Hammond, 1807-1864*.
[19] Charleston *Courier*, Dec. 19 and 20, 1850.

several Southern Senators who spitefully flaunted reports of his unpopularity in the South.[20]   Although his position in the Senate was hardly tenable, he did not resign until April, 1852, when the South Carolina convention met and declined to secede.[21]   By this time Rhett was scorned by his opponents and abandoned by most of his erstwhile followers.   He was even denied the privilege of speaking to a caucus of the group which stood for his own views.[22]

Rhett never regained power in South Carolina during the remainder of the decade.   He held no public office, nor was he seriously considered for any.   Distrust, even among the extremists, did not die out.   Discussing Rhett's qualifications for the Senate, the Spartanburg *Carolina Spartan*, August 13, 1857, indicated that public apprehensions had abated little since the time of his resignation:

> Notoriously unpopular in the state, an avowed disunionist *per se*, he would neither exert strength at home nor conciliate support abroad. We admit him a man of talent, but regard him a man without influence—and therefore totally unsuited for the only purpose for which his presence is desired at Washington.   No dogmatist is suited for diplomacy or statesmanship. . . .   Give us, say we, a man who knows when to advance, when to recede without yielding gained ground, and ready at all times to be governed by circumstances.

Only another movement for secession could restore public esteem for Rhett, but, ironically, his own reputation prevented his working publicly for such a movement.   His sphere of influence was limited to a restricted circle of personal friends and to the editorials of his newspaper, the Charleston *Mercury*.   But

[20] White, *Rhett*, pp. 125-128; *Congressional Globe*, 32 Cong., 1 Sess., Appendix, pp. 42, 53, 61, 64; *Congressional Globe*, 32 Cong., 1 Sess., pp. 640-647; Charleston *Courier*, Dec. 22, 1851; Charleston *Mercury*, March 11, 1852; Columbia *South Carolinian*, March 6, 1852; Camden *Journal*, March 12, 1852.
[21] White, *Rhett*, pp. 132-133; Perry, *Reminiscences of Public Men with Speeches and Addresses* (Greenville, S. C., 1889), pp. 396-397; the Columbia *South Carolinian*, May 10, 1852, printed correspondence between Governor John Hugh Means and Barnwell Rhett relative to the latter's resignation from the U. S. Senate.
[22] A. P. Aldrich to J. H. Hammond, May 3, 1852.

even the influence of the *Mercury* was diminished by his association with it. John Heart, business manager and co-owner of the *Mercury* until 1858, told A. P. Aldrich that "the paper had lost ground because it was supposed to be, and was called the Rhett organ."[23]

Men like Rhett represented the most extreme leaders in the state. They were the reckless men who would have seceded in the face of any cost, danger, or risk. They were the men who were most alarmed by the menace of abolition, who trembled with anger when the word was mentioned. Many of them had, for the greatest part of their adult lives, talked fervently and fitfully of honor and patriotism, of Southern civilization, chivalry, and heroism. They were the men of South Carolina who seemed temperamentally incapable of living peacefully under the same government with the people of the North. They were the fire-eaters.

CONGRESSIONAL AND STATE DISTRICTS IN SOUTH CAROLINA,
1852-1860

[23] A. P. Aldrich to J. H. Hammond, April 22, 1858.

The struggle which took place in South Carolina during the year following the Compromise of 1850, was, in part, between two groups of people with different temperaments. It was a conflict between the "heroic" and the practical, between the impetuous and the cautious, between the hotheads and the coolheads. In political training and doctrine, in social standing and class allegiance, in conceptions of ultimate goals many of the leaders who wanted South Carolina to secede unconditionally were strikingly similar to those who believed that secession must be contingent upon the support of other Southern states. Both groups saw the menace of antislavery agitation, and both saw the risks of secession. But the advocates of independent action faced the menace and turned their backs to the risks, while the advocates of concerted secession stood sideways with their eyes on both.

The fire-eater evinced few of the qualities commonly attributed to the office-seeking politician. Doctrinaire and uncompromising, he showed neither the desire nor the ability to dissimulate or to reconcile conflicting interests or points of view. Matters of constitutional principle or personal honor were not to be compromised, and always sensitive to violations of either, he found himself in frequent controversies. The fire-eater found Congress an uncomfortable place. He had either to reconcile himself to taking no part in the proceedings, or he had to play the part of the vigilant sentinel. Since his own disposition and beliefs precluded his exerting influence on national legislation, he spent much of his time defending the honor of his state and section.

Archetypical of the South Carolina fire-eater was Lawrence Keitt, who represented the Third Congressional District from 1853 to 1860.[24] The "Harry Hotspur of the South," as one writer dubbed him, was only twenty-nine years old when he took his seat in December, 1853. Like most South Carolina politicians his path of advancement included attendance at South Carolina College, the practice of law, and membership

[24] There is a brief sketch of Keitt's life by Robert L. Meriwether in the *Dictionary of American Biography*, X, 294.

in the state legislature. In college he had "a reputation for talents which, perhaps, would have given him a higher mark on the College rolls but for the fact of general and desultory reading."[25] While in the state House of Representatives from 1848 to 1852, he was one of those who clamored for immediate secession.

Power with me [Keitt wrote to the woman who became his wife] must be won by superiority, at least by haughty self-independence and assertion and not by dexterous trimming and whinning [*sic*] submission. It must be the power of leading, not following. I'd sooner write my own political epitaph than hold that power which is held by him who whiffles, whines, and crouches homage. I'll be submissive to one purer than myself, never to an equal, much less an inferior.[26]

Keitt's forte was oratory. His speeches were bombastic, spirited, colorful, heated—perfect reflections of his own intense nature. His was not the argument of a Calhoun—cold, plain, logical. Rather it was that of a McDuffie—hot, embellished, impassioned. He was told in Washington that he "had established a new style of elocution—imaginative, declamatory, and yet somewhat logical."[27] In the morning Keitt invoked "thunder and lightning," in the afternoon, "Heaven and Hell."[28] Republicans and members from his own section whom he considered traitors to the South were the objects of his wrath. Even a friendly commentator admitted that he was a little "highfalutin," and that some of his early speeches in Congress were marked by the "wild extravaganzas" of a "fervid, youthful imagination." But whatever his idiosyncrasies, declared this writer, Keitt was "a chivalrous, dashing fellow."[29] A newspaper correspondent gave this description of Keitt:

The convulsions, the starts, the spasms of his manner, give to his speaking a strong spell of interest. . . . An intensely Southern

[25] Obituary in the Charleston *Courier*, June 6,1864.
[26] Lawrence M. Keitt to Sue Sparks (n.d.), in Duke University Library.
[27] Lawrence M. Keitt to Sue Sparks, July 11,1855, in Duke University Library.
[28] From an anecdote in the Lancaster *Ledger*, July 6, 1853.
[29] Newberry *Rising Sun*, March 21, 1860.

feeling seems the prevailing peculiarity of his character. The rights of the South and the defence of her interests seems [*sic*] never absent from his thoughts. If he has the most dry and abstract subject to speak upon he will contrive to interweave an episode upon the slavery question. He has, too, a fund of restless propensity, which seems quite beyond his power to control. This over-weening vivacity is conspicuous in his whole manner and movement.[30]

Even in South Carolina, which was regarded as the haven of Southern extremists, few fire-eaters attained places in Congress. Not more than two of the six congressional districts would steadfastly sustain the hotspurs in office. A considerable portion, probably most, of the newspapers disapproved of electing men like Keitt and Rhett to high offices. The Newberry *Rising Sun*, a paper with a reputation for disunion proclivities, said: "It is not the hot and hasty *Hotspur* that carries the day as a statesman; that is calculated, by any means, to promote the interest of the nation. Such men may flash their lightning and roll their thunder for a time but the stormy feeling soon subsides, and they eventually calm down, gentle as a lamb, and learn to nod and smile and shrug with art."[31] The Spartanburg *Carolina Spartan*, in an editorial of August 27, 1857, made a similar comment: "Hotspurs may coruscate in the annals of chivalry, but the brilliancy of their deeds will always be clouded with defeat on the pages of history. The high mettled racer is beautiful to look upon by those devoted to the sports of the turf; but plain practical men prefer the heavy built draft horse, with bone and muscle adapting him to profit in every day operations of life." The Edgefield *Advertiser*, in an editorial aimed at the *Mercury*, questioned the wisdom of "ultraism." The worthy motives of the Charleston paper were not doubted. "Yet," the author wrote, "there is surely something slightly morbid in the despairing tone, the deep-seated alarm which moves our distinguished contemporaries at this time."[32] The Spartanburg *Express*, which was not unconditionally in favor of

[30] Sumter *Watchman*, June 30, 1858.
[31] March 21, 1860.
[32] June 24, 1857.

either the Union or a Southern confederacy, sarcastically re-
marked that it was amusing "to witness the tall pretensions and
blustering bravado of some of our politicians and newspaper
editors, who are eternally pouring a flood of abuse upon everything that squints of Yankeedom; and unceasingly ranting about
State Rights, Southern Rights and Southern Union." "Why,"
it asked, "why this unremitting and unending cry of wolf, wolf
—these constant and frothy speeches about invaded rights?"[33]

Politicians of South Carolina had long recognized that the
reputation of their state for extremism was an obstacle to its
leading the South. As early as 1844 Francis W. Pickens wrote
that whenever South Carolina moved first, there were thousands
who fell back under the everlasting charges of South Carolina
ultraism and South Carolina disunion. Calhoun found it expedient to encourage Mississippi to take the apparent initiative
in the calling of the Nashville Convention of 1850, and at that
convention the South Carolina delegates were aware of great
hostility toward their state. Pro-Union leaders in Georgia, in
1850 and 1851, denounced South Carolina "dictation."[34]

In 1852 the great majority of the leaders in the state agreed
that the first task of South Carolina statecraft was to secure the

[33] Spartanburg *Express* (n.d.), quoted by the Pickens *Keowee Courier*,
July 10, 1858.

[34] Francis W. Pickens to John C. Calhoun, May 16, 1844, in Boucher and
Brooks (eds.), "Correspondence," p. 228; Philip May Hamer, *The Secession
Movement in South Carolina, 1847-1852* (Allentown, Pa., 1918), pp. 8, 26,
41, 68; Chauncey Samuel Boucher, "The Secession and Co-operation Move-
ments in South Carolina, 1848 to 1852," *Washington University Studies*, V,
No. 2 (April, 1918), 84, 102; David Duncan Wallace, *The History of South
Carolina* (4 vols.; New York, 1934), III, 121; John C. Calhoun to James
H. Hammond, Dec. 7, 1849, in Jameson (ed.), "The Correspondence of John
C. Calhoun," p. 775. For Georgia's hostility to South Carolina in 1850 and
1851, see Richard H. Shryock, *Georgia and the Union in 1850* (Durham,
N. C., 1926), pp. 304-305, and George V. Irons, "The Secession Movement
in Georgia, 1850-61" (doctoral dissertation, Duke University, 1936, in Duke
Library), pp. 77-79. Governor W. B. Seabrook wrote to Governor G. W. B.
Towns, of Georgia, Oct. 8, 1850, that he was fully "aware of the jealousy
against So. Ca. among a certain class of politicians in the Southern States"
(letter in Library of Congress). Daniel Wallace, special representative for
Governor W. B. Seabrook in Mississippi in 1849, found widespread distrust
and suspicion of South Carolina among Mississippi politicians (Daniel Wallace to W. B. Seabrook, Oct. 20, Nov. 7, 1849, in Library of Congress). The
Columbia *South Carolinian*, May 3, 1852, referred to the "inveterate habit of
ridiculing and depreciating the high spirit" of South Carolina.

co-operation of the other Southern states. Most of them admitted, too, that their reputation for extremism was the greatest obstruction to the accomplishment of that objective. Since the fire-eaters were largely responsible for this reputation, they were the least fit to provide the kind of leadership needed in the early fifties. The dilemma of Rhett was the dilemma of most fire-eaters. Only by abnegation of public leadership could they further the movement for Southern unification.

After the failure of secession, the state lacked any outstanding leader and any outstanding program. Not a single public man or editor of any prominence thought that there was the slightest possibility of continuing to argue the question of secession. On the other hand, it was difficult to turn to a hearty participation in national politics, for the state had officially proclaimed in a solemn ordinance that it was in the Union against its will. Under the circumstances there was little else to do but acquiesce, take part in national politics perfunctorily, try to harmonize the antagonistic elements in the state, and await developments in the rest of the South.

During the lull after 1852 prudent leaders from the faction that had supported concerted secession gradually took the initiative in sponsoring a policy of participating in Southern and national politics. They were more trusted in the South because they had advocated a more conciliatory policy during the struggle over secession. They were therefore in a better position than their opponents to carry out the course which every important leader in the state agreed was necessary. James L. Orr was the leader of this group.

The political success of James L. Orr was anomalous.[35] By all the popular precepts and traditions current in ante-bellum

[35] There are several encyclopedic sketches of Orr's life: *Dictionary of American Biography,* XIV, 61; *Cyclopedia of Eminent and Representative Men of the Carolinas* (2 vols.; Madison, Wis., 1892), I, 112-117; U. R. Brooks, *South Carolina Bench and Bar* (Columbia, 1908), pp. 186-187; *The National Cyclopedia of American Biography* (New York, 1888), IV, 593; *The Cyclopedia of American Biographies Comprising the Men and Women of the United States Who Have Been Identified with the Growth of the Nation* (Boston, 1903), XVIII, 78-79; obituary in Charleston *News and Courier,* May 7, 1873; W. H. Topping, "Hon. James L. Orr, of South Carolina,"

South Carolina he should not have attained widespread influence in South Carolina politics. He was born in the up-country district of Anderson, whereas most of the famous leaders of the state were from Charleston, the low-country parishes, Edgefield, or Abbeville. He was the son of a merchant; most of the politicians had fathers who were planters or lawyers. He attended the University of Virginia, not the South Carolina College. Added to these ostensible handicaps, he had none of the abilities which had traditionally brought success to the ambitious of his state. He was not an orator. He spoke well but not eloquently. His appeal was neither emotional nor intellectual, merely practical. He was not a constitutional theorist. Unlike most of his colleagues in Congress, he seldom invoked the Constitution to support his argument; rather, he usually rested his arguments on grounds of policy. He had no reputation as a writer; no treatises on the merits of slavery, no disquisitions on government are credited to him. He was a good lawyer and little more.

His whole life history was a record of ambition for public office; yet he did not employ the methods commonly used in South Carolina at that time to secure it. He made no attempts to float into office on the rising tide of Southern patriotism; he never attempted to reap prestige by militant defense of slavery. He was the champion of no cause, gladiator in no battle, chauvinist for no nation, prophet of no republic. He would have made all of South Carolina a little less doctrinaire, a little more opportunistic, a little more like himself.

Orr was a party politician, probably the first to achieve distinction in South Carolina. He gained the support of his constituents by treating them as personal friends. He enlisted lieutenants by judicious use of a meager patronage. He reaped Northern support in Congress by avoiding sectional disputes as far as possible and by making personal friends with party leaders. As Speaker of the House he "commanded respect for his

National Democratic Review, I (April, 1856). The personality traits which made Orr a successful politician are commented upon by a man who knew him for thirty years in Benjamin F. Perry, *Reminiscences of Public Men* (1883), pp. 179-188.

force and impartiality, and attracted attention from the fact that he was the least fiery" of the South Carolinians.[36] He had the ability of a party leader to dissimulate, compromise, and conciliate. According to one commentator, his judgment was "ripe" and "discriminating," his administrative talents of the highest order, and his tact "wonderful in the extreme for governing masses of men."[37] Another South Carolina journalist wrote:

> His statesmanship is of that spacious kind that keeps its own counsel, and elaborates in secret thought the proper course on all occurring measures. Thus attack and opposition are not invited until after decision, and his mind is untrammelled by advice and undistracted by opposing views. A careful adherence to this system of tactics has given him reputation at home and abroad.[38]

In his professions of doctrine Orr agreed with his fellow South Carolinians. He did homage to the supremacy of the State Rights of South Carolina; he rendered obeisance to Southern Civilization. He seldom departed from the South Carolina delegation in his vote on congressional legislation. He was not an enthusiast for a Southern confederacy, nor was he an enthusiast for the Federal Union either. If his policy was one designed to keep the Union intact, it did not exclude the possibility of secession.

The great difference between Orr and the leaders who favored isolation from national politics was his belief in the efficacy of party organization. "No man now living in this Union," he told his constituents, "has power to accomplish any great measure or policy without the aid of party, and if you desire influence in a party, it is only to be attained by affiliating heartily in its organization."[39] If Orr had any program, that sentence was its keynote.

His policy of affiliation with the Democratic party was a departure from previous practice. Under Calhoun the state had co-operated with the party but had never become a part of

---

[36] Washington [D. C.] *States and Union*, Aug. 14, 1860.
[37] Newberry *Rising Sun*, March 21, 1860.
[38] Spartanburg *Carolina Spartan*, March 19, 1859.
[39] Pickens *Keowee Courier*, Aug. 28, 1858.

the machinery. South Carolinians had been independent, not organization, Democrats. In 1856, for the first time, as a result of Orr's leadership, the state sent a delegation to the national convention. And in 1860 Orr led another delegation to the national convention, which met, significantly, in South Carolina. Orr, as promoter of the new policy, was singled out by the fire-eaters for the butt of many attacks. They charged him with vaulting personal ambition, said he was more concerned about spoils than the interests of the state, censured him for speaking at Democratic meetings in the North, accused him of inconsistencies, and represented him as a menace to the old South Carolina traditions.

The first centers of support for the Orr program were Charleston and his own Fifth Congressional District, the same localities which had opposed unconditional secession most stubbornly in 1851. Gradually he built up a following in all the state districts with the exception of the low-country parishes. He had a number of able and experienced lieutenants to assist in creating this first real party organization in the state: Benjamin F. Perry, John D. Ashmore, and James Farrow in his own congressional district; Preston Brooks, Francis W. Pickens, and Arthur Simkins in the Fourth; Franklin Gaillard and John Smith Preston in the Sixth; W. D. Porter, A. G. Magrath, George N. Reynolds, and T. Y. Simons, Jr., in the Second Congressional District.

The extension of the new organization frightened the fire-eaters. They knew that they were up against an organization with capable leadership. R. B. Rhett, Jr., editor of the *Mercury*, wrote privately in January, 1858: "During the last few years, in the stagnation that has followed the failure of the secession movement, a spoils party has sprung up here. . . . It is strong, especially in Charleston and the up-country. It is organized, and has skillful, energetic and successful leaders. It is sustained, too, by wealth, and unless met and vanquished, must ultimately triumph."[40]

[40] R. B. Rhett, Jr., to J. H. Hammond, Jan. 5, 1858.

Despite Orr's accomplishment, the defeated proponents of separate secession, who were the chief advocates of isolation from national party politics, continued to have a share of political power in the state. James Hopkins Adams, John Hugh Means, Robert W. Allston, and William Henry Gist were the governors from 1854 to 1860. Lawrence Keitt, John McQueen, and Milledge Bonham were in Congress. In the legislature there were probably as many former secessionists as co-operationists. But for about four years after 1852 these leaders were faced with greater difficulties than the more cautious leaders in formulating the federal policy of the state. They could not continue to summon the voters to meet impending dangers because the weary people were impervious to their appeals. Furthermore, they had been forced to accept the decision that South Carolina could not secede alone; that is, they were forced to subscribe to a course in which they did not have their hearts.

Between the declared upholders and opponents of the Orr program was an amorphous aggregation of individual politicians who were either noncommittal, neutral, independent, indifferent, undecided, vacillating, or ambivalent with regard to controversial issues in the state. Associated with neither of the two major factions, they were frequently claimed by both. Among the most prominent leaders in this category were Senators James Henry Hammond and James Chesnut.

Seemingly the cleavage between the group that advocated secession by individual states and the group that favored co-operative action by the slaveholding states had been removed by the failure of secession in 1852. The advocates of separate secession had professed, and without doubt sincerely, a belief that co-operation of the Southern states was necessary and that they were willing to work for it. All factions had declared that harmony in the state was the great desideratum. And, in truth, the issue of separate versus concerted secession never again divided the leaders. Removal of this issue, however, did not reconcile the two groups of leaders. Few of those who had stood for unconditional secession by separate states ever worked in harmony with those who would support secession only if made jointly with other slaveholding states.

Within several years after the death of John C. Calhoun the structure of South Carolina leadership changed greatly. There continued to be many able men in public life, but no leader stood above all the rest. James L. Orr had more personal influence than any other single leader, but he was never able to command support from even a majority of the politicians. The relationships of the leaders to one another fell into a pattern of three main parts. One group of politicians clustered about James L. Orr and was fairly well organized under him. A second group was composed of men who persistently and actively opposed Orr. These men held common views on most political issues, but they were not united into a single body; they were divided into several cliques and never recognized the pre-eminence of any single leader. Between these two fairly distinct sets of leaders was the remainder, a small and fluid conglomeration of nondescripts.

CHAPTER II

ACQUIESCENCE, 1852

A S THE year 1852 opened, the citizens of South Carolina were living under a federal government whose leading officials stood for policies toward which they were hostile or indifferent. The President was Millard Fillmore, a New York lawyer and politician, who had been elevated to the Presidency upon the death of Zachary Taylor in July, 1850. More conciliatory than Taylor, he had gained the good will of pro-Union Southerners when he placed the administration behind the compromise legislation of 1850. The Congress then in session was predominantly in harmony with the President on the question of the slavery dispute. Elected after the passage of the compromise measures, most members of the House had approval from their constituents for the settlement. Congress and the President, with his cabinet of compromise Whigs, exemplified a policy which all responsible leaders in South Carolina had denounced for almost two years.

When South Carolinians turned their attention to the states of the Lower South for whose support they had urgently appealed in 1850 and 1851, they perceived even more poignant symbols of the defeat suffered by their policy. In Mississippi, which had at one time shown a willingness to join South Carolina in resistance to compromise, Henry S. Foote, a swashbuckling, daring, vainglorious champion of the Union, was governor. The change in the composition of the Mississippi delegation in Congress also told a story of defeat for the South Carolina course. In September, 1850, every member of the delegation except one had opposed the compromise measures. In January, 1852, every member except one supported them as an adequate settlement of the sectional conflict. In Georgia and Alabama, too, the governors and members of Congress were committed to support the Compromise.

In 1852 South Carolina alone, of all the Southern states, was unreconciled to the legislation passed in 1850 with the hope of providing a permanent settlement of the slavery dispute. Most responsible leaders of the state woud have preferred to have a Southern confederacy, but this goal they now realized was unattainable because of Southern opinion. Doomed to failure also was the alternative course of secession by South Carolina alone, which had been advocated by a large number of leaders for more than a year. Dissatisfied with their condition in the Union but powerless to effect a change, most leaders believed that only a policy with the purpose of restoring harmony in the state could be constructive.

The division in the state which these leaders were eager to eradicate had arisen after the passage of the compromise measures in September, 1850.[1] It resulted from a difference of opinion as to the proper course to follow in case the other Southern states accepted the Compromise. Until the state of opinion in the other Southern states was made clear, disagreement was not great. But when the organization of strong Union parties in Mississippi, Alabama, and Georgia in the fall of 1850 indicated that a policy based on the secession of these states could not be advocated with promises of certain success, some leaders proposed secession by South Carolina alone. Even before the

---

[1] The following account of the secession controversy in South Carolina during the period Oct., 1850, to April, 1852, is based primarily upon these authorities: C. S. Boucher, "The Secession and Co-operation Movements in South Carolina, 1848 to 1852," pp. 1, 5-136; P. M. Hamer, *The Secession Movement in South Carolina, 1847-1852*, pp. 73-143; Lillian Adele Kibler, *Benjamin F. Perry, South Carolina Unionist* (Durham, N. C., 1946), pp. 246-277; Merritt, *Hammond*, pp. 101-108; Benjamin F. Perry, *Reminiscences of Public Men* (Philadelphia, 1883), pp. 13-14, 134, 160-163, 227, 287, 289, 310; Perry, *Reminiscences of Public Men with Speeches and Addresses* (Greenville, S. C., 1889), pp. 389-397; Nathaniel W. Stephenson, "Southern Nationalism in South Carolina in 1851," *American Historical Review*, XXXVI (Jan., 1931), 314-335; White, *Rhett*, pp. 103-134. The Edgefield *Advertiser*, March 18, 1852, had a historical summary of the conflict between the co-operationists and secessionists. The Columbia *South Carolinian*, April 26, 1852, briefly explained the origin and organization of the secessionist party in South Carolina.

Georgia state convention, in December, 1850, rejected secession and accepted the Compromise, a number of prominent men had come out for immediate secession by South Carolina. This form of state action was not acceptable to another group of leaders, who advocated secession only upon the condition that it be achieved in concert with the states of the Lower South.

The legislature of 1850 followed a course that was largely in accord with proposals made by members who wanted co-operation with other states. An act was passed that called for a Southern congress to meet at Montgomery, Alabama, in January, 1852.[2] This same act provided for a state convention to meet at an unspecified date to ratify or reject any measures adopted by the projected congress. Delegates to the state convention were to be elected in February, 1851, while delegates to the proposed Southern congress were to be elected later in the same year, in October.

During the first five months of 1851, the leaders in favor of immediate secession conducted an intense campaign of propaganda which proved effective in winning public opinion to their side. The total vote in the election of delegates held in February was not heavy, but a large majority of the men elected were in favor of immediate secession. The secession agitation reached its peak in May, when a convention of local Southern Rights Associations met in Charleston. This convention adopted resolutions which stated that support of other Southern states was desirable but not indispensable. The secession leaders at this time were confident that they would achieve their objective.

Most of the leaders of this faction were ready to establish an independent republic of South Carolina if necessary. Undoubtedly, some of them thought that such a republic would be merely the precursor of a Southern confederacy. Once their state had seceded and the federal government tried to coerce it, the other states of the South would be compelled to side

[2] *Journal of the House of Representatives of the State of South Carolina, Being the Annual Session of 1850* (Columbia, 1850), p. 279; *Journal of the Senate of South Carolina, Being the Annual Session of 1850* (Columbia, 1850), p. 202.

with them. Perhaps Georgia preferred to stay in the Union, but it was in the power of South Carolina to prevent that state from making a choice between the Union and a Southern confederacy. It could force Georgia to choose between coercing a sister Southern state and withdrawing from the Union. The chances of being left alone were not inconsiderable, but even isolation was preferable to staying in the Union. From their point of view, when a people's institutions, interests, and way of life are menaced, a safe course cannot always be followed. They were convinced that the antislavery movement would continue to grow until abolition became an accomplished fact. If there were obstacles in the way of an independent state of South Carolina, they were of little consequence when compared to the dangers of the antislavery movement. South Carolina, like other small countries in the world, could prosper and defend itself as an independent republic. Were not the people of South Carolina a courageous and heroic people who would not submit to degradation without a struggle? Sentimental bonds with the other Southern states should not deter the state from going its way alone. The first allegiance of every citizen was to his own state government. Aware of the conflict between State Rights and Southern nationalism, the ardent secessionists gave greater weight to the value of the former. Maxcy Gregg, a manager for the secession party, regarded "consolidation with Georgia and Tennessee . . . as only not quite so great an evil as a consolidation with New York and Ohio."[3]

From May until October, 1851, the co-operation leaders were engaged in a severe counterattack against the secessionists. Starting in Charleston and Greenville, the co-operation leaders gradually organized support throughout the state. Each day that went by in the summer of 1851 converts were gained to oppose the separate secession of South Carolina.

Some of the leaders of this party, such as Benjamin F. Perry, were opponents of concerted as well as separate secession, but most of them confessedly wanted to join the other states in the establishment of a Southern confederacy. The

[3] Maxcy Gregg to J. H. Hammond, March 29, 1852.

paramount and immediate purpose of all the leaders was the negative goal of defeating the secessionists. More cautious, these leaders saw the many disadvantages and dangers of single secession. It was very easy to talk in glorious terms of an independent republic of South Carolina, but what would happen if the federal government blockaded the coast of the state and trade was diverted from Charleston to Wilmington or Savannah? And how could the coastal towns be protected from naval bombardment? And what was to happen to their claims to a common share in the territories of the United States? These were the questions of common sense which the co-operationists asked South Carolina voters in the summer of 1851.

Some of the leaders had come to have a sort of nationalistic feeling for the South. They felt that every problem of South Carolina was held in common by the other Southern states, that related interests, institutions, and blood bound them to direct their destiny into a common channel. To these men, separate secession was not only foolhardy, it was utterly unpatriotic.

By the end of the summer, all hope of securing the support of any other state had completely disappeared. The success of compromise candidates for governor in the states of Georgia, Alabama, and Mississippi demonstrated that South Carolina would never attend the Southern congress proposed by the legislature of 1850.

Although the call for a congress to meet in January, 1852, was not answered by the other Southern states, the election of delegates was not canceled. Both the secessionists and co-operationists were willing to hold this election as a test of opinion; it would decide whether the voters of the state wanted to secede or remain in the Union. The election resulted in a defeat of the secessionists. They carried only one of the seven congressional districts and polled a total popular vote of 17,471 as against 24,909 by co-operation candidates.

The leaders of the secession party immediately accepted the outcome as a repudiation of their proposed course, and the Central Committee of the Southern Rights Association recommended that its members cease agitating for secession. They did not, however, accept the results as an indication that the voters were opposed to all forms of protest against their condition in the Union and attempted to hold the co-operationists to their vows of resistance. Their strategy following the October defeat was to split the co-operation party by entering into a coalition with all the co-operation leaders who were strongly in favor of disunion or some form of resistance.[4]

Two main difficulties stood in the way of a successful execution of this maneuver. First, it was hard to conceive, even in a theoretical way, of a program upon which the co-operation "resisters" and the secessionists could unite. Secondly, none of the leaders of co-operation who reputedly favored resistance were eager to take the initiative in urging public support for such a move.

As a solution to the first problem, Maxcy Gregg, manager for the secession faction, turned to a program which had been formulated by James Henry Hammond during the previous spring. It provided for a course short of secession and in advance of any step yet taken by the state, and amounted substantially to breaking off political relations with the federal government. No presidential electors were to be chosen; no delegation was to be sent to Congress; no appropriations from the federal government were to be accepted; and citizens of the state were to hold only local civil offices under the federal government. Other measures provided for an imposition of a double tax on property in South Carolina owned by persons who resided more than one month in a year outside the slaveholding states, and for legislation for the encouragement of manufacturing, internal improvements, agriculture, and direct trade with foreign countries.[5]

As a solution to the second problem, Maxcy Gregg turned to the author of this plan. No other man, perhaps, was in a better position to assume leadership of the state in the winter of 1851-1852. Hammond, a man of great wealth, high social standing,

[4] A. P. Aldrich to J. H. Hammond, Nov. 26, 1851.
[5] J. H. Hammond to W. G. Simms, April 29, 1851; A. P. Aldrich to J. H. Hammond, Nov. 10, 11, 14, 1851.

and recognized integrity, had not taken a public part in the contest between the factions. Although opposed to the secession of South Carolina alone, he agreed with the secessionists that something should be done to prevent the Union and submissive wing of the co-operation party from gaining control of the state.[6] "For myself," he wrote in November to his friend Gilmore Simms, "I think it *all important* that South Carolina should at this juncture make a *forward movement*. . . . And I know of no such movement that can be made so safe, so sure, so sustainable & in fact unassailable as that indicated in my plan. It will keep the flag flying and do harm to nobody."[7] In spite of his great confidence in his plan, Hammond would not take the lead in promoting it. Maxcy Gregg, John Cunningham, and James Jones, of the secession faction, pleaded with him to assume the leadership, but he always refused.[8]

Gregg and his friends made no headway in gaining support for the plan among the co-operationists. A. P. Aldrich, a close friend of Hammond and associated with the leaders of the co-operation party, discussed it with members of the legislature but had no success in convincing the co-operationists that it was a measure in accord with their policy.[9]

The co-operationists proposed no alternative plan as a substitute for that presented by the secessionists. To the demands of the secessionists that they take the lead in formulating measures of resistance, they did not respond. Unlike the secessionists, they did not interpret the election as obligating them to undertake new measures of resistance.[10] A caucus of the co-operation party held on November 27 adopted resolutions that placed emphasis on the election as a defeat of separate secession.

[6] J. H. Hammond to John Cunningham, Nov. 14, 1851; J. H. Hammond to W. G. Simms, Nov. 21, 1851.

[7] J. H. Hammond to W. G. Simms, Nov. 21, 1851.

[8] James Jones, Oct. 26 and Nov. 16, and John Cunningham, Nov. 10, 1851, to J. H. Hammond; J. H. Hammond to John Cunningham, Nov. 14, 1851.

[9] Lewis M. Ayer, Dec. 1, and A. P. Aldrich, Nov. 26, 28, Dec. 9, 1851, to J. H. Hammond.

[10] L. M. Ayer, Dec. 1, and A. P. Aldrich, Nov. 26, 1851, to J. H. Hammond.

The election had decided that the right of secession was "fundamental and indisputable," but the exercise of it by a single state without the concurrence and support of other states was not the appropriate remedy for their grievances. In the future, declared these resolutions, any attempt either directly or indirectly to accomplish separate secession would be in contravention to the declared will of the people. These resolutions also declared that the people maintained a "deep and indignant sense" of their grievances and dangers, and were determined to remove and avert them by attempting to promote concerted action with the other Southern states.[11]

According to these resolutions, all causes which had separated those who advocated separate secession from those who advocated co-operative secession had been removed, and both factions should unite in pursuing the line of policy which the people of the state had marked out. This was no invitation for merging the two organizations, however, for the co-operationists, in the next breath, resolved to maintain their organization intact. The co-operationists were letting the public know that they believed that their policy was just that "line of policy" marked out by the people of the state. The implication was clear. Unity of opinion and organization was to be obtained by supporting the co-operationists.

One question remained to be disposed of by the legislature of 1851. Should the state convention be called? The act providing for a convention had stated that it was to pass on measures adopted by the proposed Southern congress. But since that congress had never progressed beyond the thoughts of hopeful South Carolinians, the original purpose of the convention was now void. There was hardly any other pressing need for the convention to meet. Even the secessionists, who had a majority of delegates for the convention, admitted that public opinion would not permit secession. Then what could the convention do? Anything, said the secessionists, anything that would prevent "abject submission" by South Carolina. They could offer

[11] Charleston *Courier*, Dec. 1, 1851.

no practical proposals acceptable to all factions in the state, but they did not stop talking about "true resistance."

Most of the co-operation leaders preferred not to set a date for the convention to meet. Among those who opposed convoking the convention were Langdon Cheves, oldest of South Carolina's active statesmen, former Speaker of the House, and one-time president of the United States Bank; R. W. Barnwell, former president of the South Carolina College; Congressman Armistead Burt; and C. G. Memminger, Chairman of the Committee on Ways and Means of the state House of Representatives. James L. Orr was willing for the convention to meet, if the secessionists disbanded their organization and promised that no measures would be proposed with the intention of bringing about secession. But the party was far from united. Some co-operationists, such as James Chesnut, Isaac W. Hayne, and A. P. Aldrich, thought the secessionists should be conciliated and hoped that the convention might be able to restore harmony in the state.[12]

The secessionists, who had a majority in the legislature, were determined that the convention should be called. Governor John Hugh Means, a leader of the secessionists, made no mention of the convention in his message, but he clearly spoke their mind. He emphasized the need for the state to protect its interests and institutions, which he insisted were as much in peril as they had ever been. The responsibility for framing a plan of action he placed squarely upon the shoulders of those who had defeated secession.[13] Through resolutions presented to the legislature by Lawrence Keitt and William Henry Gist the secessionists reiterated their belief that the state should adopt measures of protest and retaliation. Once more they gave the secessionists' interpretation of the recent election: the people had decided against secession, but not for "submission."[14] With the aid of some co-operationists, the secessionists were able to put

[12] A. P. Aldrich to J. H. Hammond, Nov. 26, 28, 1851.

[13] Message of November 25, 1851, *Journal of the House of Representatives* (Columbia, 1851), pp. 14-22.

[14] *Journal of the House* (1851), pp. 68-69; *Journal of the Senate* (Columbia, 1851), p. 73; Charleston *Courier*, Dec. 4, 11, 1851.

through a bill setting the fourth Monday in April as the date for the convention to meet. In the House, where opposition to calling the convention was strongest, about 65 per cent of the members voted for the bill.[15]

The convention was to meet in April. What that convention would do, what it could do, no one knew with certainty. The men who opposed its meeting, of course, were against its doing anything. Most of the co-operationists and some of the secessionists had voted to call the convention as a means of restoring harmony in the state, while most of the secessionists wanted the convention to meet in order to take definite action to safeguard what they considered their rights and interests and to preserve their position of insurgency. With the state so divided on the question of the purpose of the convention, many leaders were beginning to realize, as the year 1852 opened, that the convention would do little more than talk.

That part of the secessionist party under the influence of the Gregg clique continued to advocate the Hammond plan. Every provision was modified and qualified in an attempt to find some common ground upon which both the secessionists and co-operationists could stand. But Gregg's was a hopeless assignment. The delegation in Congress showed no enthusiasm for resigning. Public opinion would not permit taxation of Northern products and was opposed to nonintercourse. In order to get support of the opposing faction, Gregg found that he had to emasculate just those forceful provisions that he and other men in favor of action demanded.[16]

The secessionists were paralyzed by the antagonism between two desires. On the one hand, they were eager to prove the sincerity of their declarations that they had abandoned the cause of separate secession and wanted to conciliate and co-operate with the other Southern states. On the other hand, proud men that they were, they craved to fulfil their previous promises to resist the federal government. In the abstract there was per-

---

[15] *Journal of the House* (1851), p. 118; *Journal of the Senate* (1851), pp. 38, 45, 49, 73, 83.
[16] A. P. Aldrich, April 20, and Maxcy Gregg, March 29, 1852, to J. H. Hammond.

haps no insoluble conflict between these desires. But in the South of 1852 they could not be reconciled. State resistance and conciliation of the other slaveholding states were impossible, for any move by South Carolina could serve only to arouse more hostility to it in the rest of the South.

The secession press evinced little enthusiasm for the approaching convention. Some journals feared that the discussion of what the convention should do was serving the purpose of the co-operation party. The Camden *Journal* accused the Charleston *Southern Standard*, a leading organ of the co-operationists, of keeping up the agitation in order to ruin all chances for disunion forever.[17] The *Black River Watchman*, of Sumter, made a similar charge and published an editorial of the *State Rights Republican* which was said to show the intentions of the co-operationists to keep up the agitation in order to profit in the next election.[18] The object of the co-operationists in preserving their organization, said the Newberry *Sentinel*, was "to keep it in readiness for a political warfare in the state."[19] The Columbia *South Carolinian* also suspected the co-operationists of having ulterior motives in keeping their organization active.[20]

The apathetic state of public opinion led to the conviction that the convention would result only in the humiliation of South Carolina. The Sumter *Black River Watchman* declared that the vitality of both separate and co-operative secession had disappeared in South Carolina, which had become a land where federalism was in the ascendancy.[21] The Edgefield *Advertiser*, in a caustic editorial, said that South Carolina was a byword for "enraged impotency" and was considered "a fretful community of childish Hotspurs, who live by the stimulus of an occasional quarrel, in which the tongue and pen are the only weapons to be apprehended."[22] The Camden *Journal* predicted that the

[17] Camden *Journal*, Jan. 6, 1852.
[18] Sumter *Black River Watchman*, Feb. 7, 1852.
[19] Undated editorial quoted by the Columbia *South Carolinian*, Jan. 21, 1852.
[20] Columbia *South Carolinian*, Jan. 6, 10, 30, Feb. 4, March 2, April 24, 1852.
[21] Sumter *Black River Watchman*, April 17, 1852.
[22] Edgefield *Advertiser*, Feb. 12, 1852.

proceedings of the convention would be ridiculous: "South Caro-lina—glorious little Palmettodom—will sneak into the *rear* rank and do some tremendous *talking*."[23]

By the fourth Monday in April, even the most optimistic merely hoped that the convention would do no harm. The convention was an embarrassing incident.[24] Long before it met, editors and politicians had seen that it would be an easy subject for ridicule from the outside. It could do nothing to bring fame to the ambitious. No one who strongly desired a success-ful political career had anything to gain by being prominently associated with its deliberations. So the secessionists were man-aged by obscure men who were either incapable, inexperienced, or unambitious. Manager for the co-operationists was seventy-six-year-old Langdon Cheves, whose advanced age precluded aspirations for the future and whose impeccable reputation inspired respect.[25]

The convention was in session from April 26 to April 30.[26] As a matter of courtesy, the governor was elected chairman on the first day. A year before, John Hugh Means would have seen nothing but glory ahead. In May, 1851, he had written: "There is now not the slightest doubt that the next Legislature will call a convention together at a period during the ensuing year, and when that convention meets the state will secede."[27] Now, actually presiding over the promised convention, he could only deplore the embarrassing conditions under which the dele-gates met and urge them to harmonize their differences. The

[23] Camden *Journal*, Jan. 6, 1852.

[24] A. P. Aldrich to J. H. Hammond, April 20, 1852; public letter of A. W. Dozier in Sumter *Black River Watchman*, May 1, 1852; John H. Means to R. B. Rhett, May 7, 1852, in Charleston *Courier*, May 10, 1852. In his message to the legislature, Nov. 23, 1852, Means said: "Perhaps there never was a body assembled under circumstances of so much embarrassment" (*Senate Journal*, p. 29).

[25] A. P. Aldrich to J. H. Hammond, May 3, 1852.

[26] The proceedings of the convention were published in the *Journal of the State Convention; together with the Resolution and Ordinance* (Columbia, 1852), and in some of the newspapers, such as the Charleston *Courier*, April 27—May 3 and the Columbia *South Carolinian*, April 28—May 1, 1852.

[27] J. H. Means to J. A. Quitman, May 12, 1851, quoted in J. F. H. Claiborne, *Life and Correspondence of John A. Quitman* (2 vols.; New York, 1860), II, 133.

great questions of their wrongs had been forgotten amid wran-
glings as to the remedy, he declared. So long as the state was
divided, "the fanatical and fiendish spirit of abolition" would
move forward toward the accomplishment of its objective. The
task of the delegates was a delicate one, but they must rise above
petty party strife. "Upon the Union of our State," he said, "I
solemnly believe, depends our *destiny*."[28]

The real deliberations of the convention did not take place
during the public sessions. Caucuses and consultations were
held by both groups, and attempts to bring secessionists and
co-operationists behind a common program were entrusted to
committees appointed to represent them.[29] The committees of
conference met several times but accomplished nothing. The
Gregg group of secessionists wanted to withdraw the congressional delegation, take no part in the forthcoming presidential
election, and hold the state in readiness for secession. Later,
the secessionists proposed that the legislature be empowered to
secede upon approval by two thirds of the members. But the
co-operationists rejected all of these suggestions.[30]

A majority of the delegates did their best to keep up the
appearance of unity in the convention. A committee of twenty-
one, composed of twelve co-operationists, eight secessionists, and
one Unionist, was appointed to draft resolutions to recommend
for adoption by the convention. Lengthy debate on the committee's report was discouraged by tabling without discussion any
proposed amendments. The majority, it seemed, intended to
preserve the appearance of harmony even if they had to silence
every fire-eater in the convention.

Although the co-operationists had opposed such a move, a
group of secessionists decided to propose that the convention
grant the legislature the power to secede. A Charleston phy-
sician, John Bellinger, introduced their motion. The cold water
of Southern indifference had silenced many of the fire-eaters
in South Carolina, but the voice of this novice in politics was

[28] *Journal of the State Convention*, pp. 9-10.
[29] *Ibid.*, p. 14; B. F. Perry, *Reminiscences* (1889), pp. 389-397; Charleston *Courier*, April 29, May 1, 3, 1852.
[30] A. P. Aldrich to J. H. Hammond, April 28, 1852.

not yet drowned out. Dismayed because the co-operationists and some secessionists had come to the convention to do nothing, he cried out that the tame submission of the other Southern states furnished no excuse for hesitation. So much the more reason for South Carolina to act! If they were satisfied to proclaim for the hundredth time their "threadbare doctrines," consolidation would have achieved its greatest victory; it would have slain its last, its most determined foe. Why reaffirm their doctrines? That had been done many times before. The purpose of his proposal, he said, was to introduce federal issues into the elections for the legislature. If the legislature possessed the authority to secede, every candidate would be compelled to state his views on federal relations. To those who complained that this would cause incessant agitation, this irrepressible fire-eater retorted: "Let us have anything rather than a corpse-like coldness and stillness in the body politic."[31]

The extreme fire-eaters were not in control of this convention, and Bellinger's proposal was tabled by a vote of 96 to 60. For most of the delegates, secessionists as well as co-operationists, nothing was so much desired as peace and quiet.

A few other members tried to offer amendments to the majority report of the committee of twenty-one. Edmund Rhett wanted a limited nullification of that section of the Constitution which provided that the citizens of each state should be entitled to all the privileges and immunities of citizens of the several states. If his motion had carried, the state would not have applied this section of the Constitution to the citizens of Vermont and Massachusetts. Silenced by the convention, he protested hotly against the practice of laying motions on the table without debate. But his resolution was placed on the table, and a count of the vote was refused him.[32]

[31] *Ibid.*; Perry, *Reminiscences* (1889), p. 393; *Journal of the State Convention*, p. 16; Charleston *Courier*, May 1, 3, 22, 1852.

[32] *Journal of the State Convention*, p. 17; A. P. Aldrich to J. H. Hammond, May 3, 1852. Also tabled without discussion were James H. Adams's motion to adjourn *sine die* and A. V. Toomer's motion to call a Southern congress.

Two members from the committee of twenty-one, Benjamin F. Perry and Maxcy Gregg, presented minority reports to the convention.   Representative of the two extremes in the state, neither of these reports had the endorsement of any other member of the committee.

Benjamin F. Perry was one leader of the co-operation party who had opposed any kind of secession.   Commonly termed a Unionist, he probably would have favored disunion on certain conditions.   If faced with a choice between slavery and the Union, according to his own words, he would have chosen the former.   Slavery, said Perry, was moral, correct, and a blessing to the Negroes, and "absolutely necessary for the continued peace and prosperity of the slave-holding states."   It would be defended and maintained forever at any and all hazards.   Perry proposed that the convention endorse the "Georgia platform," a set of resolutions passed by the convention of that state in 1850.   In his report he told why he favored a conciliatory policy: the impracticability of separate secession, the unwillingness of the other Southern states to meet South Carolina in a congress, and the recent indications that the federal government was ceasing its aggressions against the South were sufficient reasons for the state to refrain from revolution.[33]

Gregg's report, which presented the view of a few dissident secessionists, briefly reviewed the division which had arisen among the people as to the proper method of redressing their grievances.   He opposed the report of the committee, he stated, because it proposed no mode of action.   He believed that the state should hold to a position that would guard it against the corrupting influence of the federal government and that would keep it prepared for eventual secession.[34]

The dominant purpose of the other members of the committee of twenty-one was to present a report which would com-

[33] Perry, *Reminiscences* (1889), pp. 13-14; *Journal of the State Convention*, pp. 23-24; Charleston *Courier*, May 3, 1852; Columbia *South Carolinian*, May 1, 1852; Camden *Journal*, May 7, 1852.

[34] Perry, *Reminiscences* (1889), p. 393; *Journal of the State Convention*, p. 25; Charleston *Courier*, May 3, 1852; Columbia *South Carolinian*, May 1, 1852; Camden *Journal*, May 7, 1852.

mand an overwhelming support in the convention. Chairman Langdon Cheves defended all the acts of this committee as motivated by the sole desire of promoting harmony. Only because discussion might inflame and aggravate differences had the committee followed the practice of excluding debate by moving to table all proposed amendments. The report submitted by the committee represented a compromise between conflicting opinions. It was not the one he individually preferred, nor was it likely to be the first choice of any delegate; but it was the only report acceptable to a large majority of the convention.[35]

The convention did the only thing it could do; the only thing sober-minded people expected under the circumstances. It followed the counsel of Cheves and adopted, by a vote of 136 to 19, the resolutions and ordinance submitted by the committee. An authoritative body representing the State of South Carolina thus declared by an overwhelming vote: (1) that secession was a legal right of the states; (2) that withdrawal from the Union was fully justified by violations of the Constitution and encroachments upon the reserved rights of the states; and (3) that the decision of South Carolina to remain in the Union was made for reasons of expediency alone.[36]

There were no fireworks and parades when the convention passed this declaratory ordinance—no shouting, no oratory, no bluster, no prophecies of great things to come. The newspapers of the rest of the country did not discuss its proceedings, and journalists in South Carolina seemed to squirm when they told of the deeds of this sovereign convention. A few undaunted editors tried to show that the convention had accomplished something,[37] but they were not convincing to those who had expected much more at one time. "The Report and Ordinance are too pitiful for comment," wrote James Henry Hammond.

[35] Charleston *Courier*, May 3, 1852.

[36] *Journal of the State Convention*, pp. 18-19; Charleston *Courier*, May 1, 1852; A. P. Aldrich to J. H. Hammond, May 3, 1852.

[37] Cheraw *Gazette* (n.d.), quoted by the Columbia *South Carolinian*, May 7, 1852; Charleston *Mercury*, May 1, 4, 1852; Edgefield *Advertiser*, May 6, 13, 1852; Laurensville *Herald* (n.d.), quoted by Columbia *South Carolinian*, May 11, 1852; Columbia *South Carolinian*, May 4, 5, 1852; Camden *Journal*, May 4, 11, 1852.

"Means, Bellinger and the rest could not cram them down any man's throat for glory."[38]

Most of the leaders of the state would have been happy to forget this convention of 1852. They thought of it as a great humiliation and could say no more in praise of it than that it had brought the contending factions into harmony. But they measured the results of the convention by the side of their earlier hopes, and disappointment inevitably followed. In reality, the ordinance of 1852 was quite significant, for in unmistakable language the rulers of South Carolina had solemnly pronounced their unqualified approval of the doctrine of legal secession and had expressed their grave discontent with the place of their state in the Federal Union.[39]

However discontented they may have been, the rulers of South Carolina neither seceded nor broke off relations with the federal government in 1852. Whether they liked it or not, they were constrained to take part at least perfunctorily in that government. The custom offices were still collecting revenue; the Post Office Department was still distributing the mails; the federal courts were holding trials; and the Army was maintaining forts in the state. In Congress the members of the South Carolina delegation were having to decide how they would debate and vote on legislation, some of which vitally concerned their own constituents.

The Senators and Representatives from South Carolina who attended the first session of the Thirty-second Congress, which lasted from December, 1851, to August, 1852, had no desire to enter zealously into its proceedings. They all had expressed the greatest dissatisfaction with their condition in the Union, and some had favored immediate secession. The problem of the factional division in South Carolina was more important to them than any pending federal legislation.

[38] J. H. Hammond to W. G. Simms, May 14, 1852.

[39] An editorial of the Columbia *South Carolinian*, May 4, 1852, stated: "This distinctive assertion of sovereignty may appear superfluous; yet, invested as it is with all the vitality, power, and supremacy of an organic law of the State, and supported with so much unanimity by men of both parties, [it] is the most important enactment ever perfected by the people of South Carolina since the adoption of the Federal Constitution."

Only a backwash of the sectional and slavery dispute made an appearance in this Congress. A safe majority of the members wanted to avoid the slavery controversy, and the House passed by a vote of 103 to 74 resolutions which pledged termination of the slavery agitation and proclaimed the Compromise of 1850 a final settlement of the sectional conflict. The six South Carolina Congressmen voted with fourteen other Southern members and fifty-four Northern members against these so-called "finality" resolutions. Senators Rhett and Butler spoke against similar resolutions in the Senate, where they were never brought to a vote.[40]

The South Carolina delegation was virtually unanimous in opposing the main legislation passed by this Congress. A river-and-harbor bill was severely denounced by the Senators. Butler made a number of short speeches against various bills granting public lands to aid in the construction of railroads and ship canals. Only James L. Orr spoke for bills that granted alternate sections of land to states to aid railroad construction. All the members urged economy when they spoke on appropriation bills. But aside from Butler's constant protests against appropriations for the benefit of local or special interest groups, the South Carolina members took little part in the debates on the floor. William F. Colcock, John McQueen, Armistead Burt, Daniel Wallace, and William Aiken were almost silent, while Joseph A. Woodward and James L. Orr, whose remarks were more numerous, made no lengthy speeches.[41]

The unanimity of the delegation in opposing all legislation except that which was absolutely necessary for operating the federal government was recorded in the votes on several bills. No member of the delegation voted for the resolutions declaring the Compromise of 1850 a final settlement of the slavery issue; none voted for a homestead bill which passed the House; none voted for bills granting public land to states for the con-

[40] *Congressional Globe*, 32 Cong., 1 Sess., pp. 35-36, 51, 61, 94-96, 116, 654-656, 983; Appendix, pp. 42, 44-48, 53, 61-64.
[41] *Congressional Globe*, 32 Cong., 1 Sess., pp. 945-946, 953-954, 1142, 1164, 1512, 1513, 1552, 1656, 1784, 1785, 1861, 1863, 2422; Appendix, pp. 272-274, 981, 985, 1101, 1140, 1006-1008.

struction of canals; none voted for bills making appropriations for the improvement of rivers and harbors; and none supported resolutions favorable to repeal of the fugitive-slave laws. Only James L. Orr voted to grant public lands to states for aid in the construction of railroads.[42]

The lassitude which possessed the South Carolina members during this drawn-out and monotonous session was dispelled when the honor of their state was impugned. Whenever their state constitution, leaders, or institutions were disparaged or attacked, some member of the delegation came to the defense of the state. These efforts to defend the reputation of South Carolina were naturally of no importance to national legislation, but they reveal a great deal about the temper of the South Carolina members and what they thought their constituents expected of them.

In the Senate, when the South Carolina constitution was attacked, it was Butler who spoke for his state. Henry Stuart Foote of Mississippi and Samuel Houston of Texas had asserted that the government of South Carolina, because of undemocratic provisions in its constitution, was controlled by a small oligarchy. In his reply Butler avoided defending the South Carolina constitution as "democratic" but suggested that it was in accord with the "republican" theory of government. "I am one of those who believe that the United States is an organized confederacy of republics," he declared. "I am not one of those who believe that it is a wild democracy."[43]

During this same debate Senator Foote had complimented Butler as a leader of the co-operation party in South Carolina, while at the same time making invidious remarks about the secession leaders of the state. Butler would not accept this kind of praise. In South Carolina he differed with the secessionists, he told the Senate, but in Congress he could not allow that difference to prevent his doing justice to a group of men who were "as high in spirit" and "as pure in motive" as any "who ever adorned the pages of history."[44]

[42] *Ibid.*, pp. 983, 1351, 1814, 2232, 2329, 2349, 2438.
[43] *Ibid.*, pp. 55, 69, 136, 2156, 2228.
[44] *Ibid.*, pp. 93-95; Appendix, pp. 53, 58.

In the House, William Aiken defended his state against what he considered false statements made by Charles Durkee in a printed speech. This Representative from Wisconsin had told the story of a hanging in Charleston of a Negro who allegedly slapped his master for violating the chastity of his wife.[45]

The reactions of people to minor occurrences often provide the best index of their truest feelings. Nothing, perhaps, so well demonstrated the immunity of South Carolinians to prevailing national opinion in 1852 as their attitude toward the American tour of a Hungarian patriot who had led an unsuccessful revolt in his native land four years before. From the day of his arrival in New York, December 5, 1851, Louis Kossuth's visit was marked by a whirlwind of receptions, banquets, interviews, and speeches. But South Carolina was adamant to the Hungarian's charms and inclined to criticize harshly the "Kossuth Mania." The press indicated that South Carolinians had special reasons for opposing intervention in the domestic affairs of a government and warned that Kossuth was fanning to a flame "that rampant democracy" in the North which threatened to "sweep with a fury totally destructive of the South." In Congress, no South Carolina member voted in favor of providing the committee that received Kossuth, and Senator Butler spoke against printing his letter thanking the American people for their hospitality. When enthusiasm for Kossuth waned in the North and it became certain that there would be no departure from the traditional foreign policy of nonintervention, at least two South Carolina newspapers credited the "conservative influence" of the South in national politics with having saved the country from a dangerous blunder.[46]

Eighteen fifty-two was an election year; but for the rulers of South Carolina, convinced as they were of their impotency

---

[45] *Ibid.*, pp. 2156, 2228.

[46] *Ibid.*, pp. 200, 587; "Kossuth and Intervention," *Southern Quarterly Review*, VI (July, 1852), 221-235; Darlington *Flag*, Jan. 8, 1852; Charleston *Evening News* (n.d.), quoted by Camden *Journal*, Feb. 20, 1852; Charleston *Mercury*, Jan. 26, 28, 1852; Edgefield *Advertiser*, Jan. 29, July 7, 1852; Columbia *South Carolinian*, Jan. 22, Feb. 17, 1852; Camden *Journal*, Jan. 16, 20, April 6, 1852; Sumter *Black River Watchman*, Feb. 21, 1852.

in the Federal Union, the question of who was to occupy the Presidency seemed of little importance. The voters knew well enough that the candidate of neither party could support the policy which their state had endorsed in a solemn ordinance. The officeholding politicians, who might have had something to gain in the way of administration favors by attending the convention, had been isolated from national party politics by the events of the previous two years. As after the nullification period, South Carolina had few ties with either party.[47]

These were not the times to break away from the traditional practice of not sending a delegation to the national convention of the Democratic party; perhaps there were some who felt that representation could do no harm, but more positive appeals were needed before responsible politicians could undertake to lead such a movement. The Charleston *Mercury* and the Camden *Journal*, which represented the view of most former secessionists, thought representation in these conventions was injurious to the cause of the South. Party politicians invariably sacrificed the interests of their section in order to obtain the nomination of a man who could command the support of both sections. Such compromise candidates were more dangerous to the South than the abolitionists, these newspapers argued, because their methods were insidious. The election of an out-and-out abolitionist would be a blessing, for it might provoke the South to act to protect its interests. The sooner Seward was President the better, declared the Camden *Journal*.[48]

[47] The Edgefield *Advertiser*, May 20, 1852, stated: "It is a source of much gratification, and reflects great and additional honor upon our State that she stands aloof from this contest for federal honors and federal spoils. Be the President who he may, her sons expect little or nothing at his hands." The Greenville *Mountaineer* (n.d.), quoted by the Columbia *South Carolinian*, May 3, 1852, said that it was impossible for South Carolina "to mingle actively in the canvass without dishonor." The Columbia *South Carolinian*, March 24, 1852, stated: "Thus far our position is that of indifference to the squabble—perhaps believing that it is no sort of consequence who will be elected President, or which party will have the distribution of the spoils. . . . The spirit of undying hostility to the institutions of the South is as clearly perceptible now as it ever has been. It cannot be laid by the political priests of either party."

[48] C. S. Boucher, "Secession and Cooperation," p. 137; Charleston *Mercury*, March 15, April 15, May 3, 17, 31, June 10, 1852; Edgefield *Adver-*

The arguments of these opponents of the convention changed little after the Democrats nominated Franklin Pierce. They continued to assert that the outcome of the presidential election was of little consequence to South Carolina. They also took the position that any participation in the campaign was a breach of the declared policy of the state. Several newspapers rebuked James L. Orr when he made a speech in Congress in praise of Pierce.[49]

None of these journals wanted the electoral vote to be withheld from the Democratic candidate. They usually conceded that the record of Pierce, although not a prominent one, was as "sound" as that of any Northern man. But they insisted that a campaign should not be conducted in the state, that Pierce should be thought of only as a choice of evils, that popular demonstrations for the purpose of ratifying the Democratic nominations were uncalled-for. The *Mercury* would not let its readers forget that Pierce was pledged in his platform to support legislation which South Carolina had declared sufficient grounds for disunion.[50]

tiser (n.d.), quoted by *Mercury*, July 3, 1852; Greenville *Southern Patriot* (n.d.), quoted by Columbia *South Carolinian*, April 10, 1852; Unionville *Journal* (n.d.), quoted by Columbia *South Carolinian*, June 21, 1852; Camden *Journal*, Jan. 26, April 16, 1852; Columbia *Carolina Times*, Jan. 8, 1852; Columbia *South Carolinian*, Jan. 12, 16, 23, March 4, 30, May 3, 4, 29, June 5, 1852; Sumter *Banner*, April 13, 1852; Sumter *Black River Watchman*, March 28, 1852.

[49] *Congressional Globe*, 32 Cong., 1 Sess., Appendix, pp. 658-660; Charleston *Mercury*, June 1, 10, 15, 18, 26, July 9, 10, Oct. 25, 1852; Edgefield *Advertiser*, June 30, 1852; Unionville Journal (n.d.), quoted by Columbia *South Carolinian*, June 21, 1852; Columbia *South Carolinian*, July 15, 1852.

[50] Charleston *Mercury*, June 1, 10, 15, July 12, 13, Oct. 25, 1852; Edgefield *Advertiser*, June 24, July 14, Aug. 18, Sept. 22, 1852; Camden *Journal*, June 15, 1852; Columbia *South Carolinian*, June 6, 12, 14, 23, July 10, 15, Aug. 26, 1852; Sumter *Banner*, June 29, July 20, 1852; Sumter *Black River Watchman*, June 26, July 17, 1852.

In a public letter Senator A. P. Butler recommended that South Carolina vote for Pierce, but he flatly stated that the Presidency could not provide a defense for the South nor achieve a reformation of the federal government (A. P. Butler to I. W. Hayne, Aug. 7, 1852, printed in Charleston *Courier*, Aug. 13, Camden *Journal*, Aug. 17, Columbia *South Carolinian*, Aug. 14, 1852).

The Columbia *South Carolinian*, July 10, 1852, said that there was no opposition to Pierce in South Carolina.

Nevertheless, avowals that South Carolina had something at stake in the presidential election and in national politics began to appear after the Democratic nomination. Proponents of active support for Pierce rested their arguments on a realistic evaluation of the situation as it was in the summer of 1852. South Carolina was still in the Union and would cast its electoral vote for either the Democratic or Whig candidate. Pierce was universally approved in South Carolina and would certainly receive the electoral vote of the state. There was, therefore, no valid reason why public testimonials in behalf of Pierce should be suppressed.[51]   James L. Orr said that he differed with the *Mercury* only as to the manner of responding to this question: "Shall South Carolina cast a *cheerful* vote for Pierce and King, as I believe she ought, or shall it be cast grudgingly, and with a snarl, as you desire?"[52]

At the Charleston meeting which ratified the Democratic nomination, Christopher G. Memminger went beyond the position held by most of the speakers, who contented themselves with merely eulogizing the career of Pierce. Memminger advocated promoting the Democratic candidacy upon the grounds of the advisability of giving up the position of insurgency which the state had maintained for two years and more. He proposed that both factions abandon their proposed measures, which had resulted only in a division in the state, and adopt the policy of the rest of the South. The people of the other Southern states, who differed with both factions in South Carolina, thought that their wrongs could be redressed in the Union, that there were conservatives in the North with whom they could unite to defend the Constitution. If South Carolina adopted this policy, and if it succeeded, the state would gain all that it wanted with-

[51] Speeches of W. D. Porter, Charles Macbeth, and A. G. Magrath at a Charleston political meeting, June 16, 1852, quoted by Charleston *Courier*, June 17, 1852; Charleston *Mercury*, June 15, 1852; Charleston *Evening News*, June 9, 10, 15, 18, 1852; Charleston *Southern Standard* (n.d.), quoted by Sumter *Banner*, July 20, 1852; Marion *Star* (n.d.), quoted by Sumter *Banner*, July 27, 1852; Pickens *Keowee Courier* (n.d.), quoted by Camden *Journal*, Aug. 3, 1852.
[52] Letter by James L. Orr dated June 21, 1852, in Charleston *Mercury*, June 26, 1852.

out a fierce struggle. If the policy failed, South Carolina could resume its old position and would have a fair claim to the co-operation of the other Southern states.[53] This statement by Memminger embodied the course which a number of former co-operation leaders were soon to follow. The objective of this course differed from that professed by most co-operation leaders in the recent controversy for it looked toward co-operation upon the terms of the other Southern states rather than those of South Carolina. It was the forerunner of a tendency toward reconciliation with Northerners friendly to the South.

As the months went by in 1852, South Carolina, which shared the national prosperity of that year, was becoming weary of agitation and glad to turn to practical problems of economic and educational amelioration. By the fall of 1852 the attention of most citizens in the state was directed toward agriculture, the banking system, railroad construction, the public schools, and foreign trade.[54]

As the year closed, the political and economic condition of the nation and of South Carolina appeared most unfavorable to the cause of those chronic insurgents who wanted to keep the people's emotions constantly mobilized for disunion. Yet these leaders did not fail to find sufficient evidence of Northern hostility to the South to justify a continued adherence to their course.[55] If the election of Pierce was interpreted by some as

[53] Charleston *Courier*, June 17, 1852.

[54] Edgefield *Advertiser*, Feb. 12, 1852; Camden *Journal*, June 11, 1852; correspondence of the *Courier*, Nov. 23, in Charleston *Courier*, Nov. 25, 1852; pseudonymous writer ["A"] in the Charleston *Courier*, March 1, 1852; pseudonymous writer ["Pacificator"] in the Charleston *Courier*, Nov. 16, 1852.

The Darlington *Flag*, Jan. 29, 1852, said: "At no period in the history of South Carolina has there ever been more general and wide-spread prosperity among the people, or brighter prospects for the future improvement of the State in wealth and intelligence, than at present." The Lancaster *Ledger*, May 27, 1852, said: "Probably our people are more prosperous now, than they have ever been, and by judicious, well directed exertion, will continue to prosper." Governor John H. Means, in his message to the legislature, Nov. 23, 1852, said that "a rich and abundant harvest" would be found everywhere in South Carolina except in those areas where the "desolating effects" of a "disastrous and unprecedented flood" were felt (*Senate Journal*, 1852, pp. 18-30, *House Journal*, 1852, pp. 16-29).

[55] The Edgefield *Advertiser*, Feb. 12, 1852, said that "a faithful deline-

proof that the North had no interest in the antislavery movement, men like Governor John H. Means were not impressed.

Material for the Governor's message was furnished by Harriet Beecher Stowe, whose story about Uncle Tom was published that year. Said Governor Means in his November message: "Agitation still goes on with ceaseless activity. Every element which can be made to operate on public opinion is put in action against our institutions. Even that powerful weapon, the literature of the country, is employed to direct its polished but poisoned shafts against them."[56] There was no mention by name of any author or any book, but the readers of South Carolina newspapers must have understood the meaning of the allusion. The editor of the Sumter *Black River Watchman* predicted: "This great and unparalleled success in the sale of an abolition novel designed to excite horror of slavery will call a host of writers to take the field in this new crusade against Southern institutions, and to reap a rich harvest of money and reputation by availing themselves of popular prejudices. The poison will thus be still more widely diffused, and will manifest its effects in the legislation of the country."[57]

Governor Means admitted in his message that Congress had done nothing in the last session against which they could complain, but he declared that permanent cessation of hostile acts against their institutions could not be expected. Future aggressions would occur, he predicted, and they would convince the people of the other Southern states that their institutions were not safe in the Union.[58]

---

ation of that government's past enormities and its tendency to despotic rule" should be kept "before the rising generation." The Columbia *South Carolinian*, Aug. 26, 1852, said: "We have no hope, in placing these matters [happenings in the North which showed hostility to South and slavery] before our readers, to be able to effect anything in the way of disturbing the dreary apathy of the South, or to awaken any feeling or sentiment of resistance to these aggravated insults. We record them as a portion of the history of the present day, and enter them as a plea of justification on the part of those who, like ourselves, have no faith in the finality of compromises or in the platforms of political parties."

[56] *Senate Journal* (1852), p. 29.
[57] Camden *Journal*, Oct. 26, 1852.
[58] *Senate Journal* (1852), pp. 29-30.

In December, 1852, the relationship of South Carolina to the nation and political conditions within the state were little different from what they had been in January. The same President was in the White House; the same Congress controlled by the same party was in its second session. In the neighboring states of the Lower South the same governors were in office. Within the state, during the twelve-month period, there had been no great shifts in power among the various factions. Neither of the old factions had gained a predominant power, but the co-operationists had maintained their prestige and influence more effectively than the secessionists, whose agitation suffered a denouement in the April convention. The slight but steady drift away from insurgency within the co-operation group had further weakened the secessionists.

Former co-operationists were elected by the legislature to the two most important vacant offices. John Lawrence Manning, a planter of moderate views, replaced John Hugh Means as governor, while Josiah J. Evans, a former judge, was elected to the Senate.[59] These men were elected, not because of their opinions on current issues, but because they were in harmony with the spirit of the times. Many new members were elected to the legislature in the October election, but federal questions had little to do with determining the selection of the candidates.[60]

The trend of events had gone against insurgency in 1852, but the leaders of the old secession party did not cease to believe that the citizenry should be mobilized against the threat of the Northern antislavery movement. In spite of widespread apathy, they did not permit the people to pass over any sign of Northern hostility to the South. As the year 1852 closed, this deep-seated conviction on the part of the extremists that the sectional conflict would resume its old intensity was the greatest obstacle to reconciliation with the North.

[59] *Ibid.*, pp. 64, 77, 130; Charleston *Mercury*, Dec. 18, 1852; Camden *Journal*, Dec. 7, 1852.

[60] Remarks of James Simons, Speaker of the state House of Representatives, Dec. 20, 1852, in *House Journal* (1852), p. 204; Charleston *Courier*, Oct. 13, 1852.

CHAPTER III

INTRANSIGENCE OR
RECONCILIATION, 1853

IN 1853 the question of the Compromise of 1850 disappeared
from public discussion in South Carolina. The malcontents,
largely the erstwhile secessionists, had continued throughout
1852 to try to hold all leaders to an avowed opposition to any-
one who accepted those measures as satisfactory. They had tried
to create the impression that there was no significant distinction
between compromisers and abolitionists. In 1853 they no longer
were able to denounce everyone who had stood for the Compromise. Public opinion in the rest of the country was too strongly
committed to the settlement for the extremists to continue to
make an issue of it in South Carolina. If they had held to their
position, almost every responsible leader outside their state
would have necessarily been considered an enemy. Still not
converted to a belief in the finality of the Compromise, they
nevertheless were forced temporarily to stop talking about it.

The revival of the antislavery agitation, which irreconcilables
such as Governor Means had predicted, did not occur in 1853.
On the contrary, the first ten months of the Pierce administration provided verification for those who had argued that protection of their interests was still possible in the Union. The
precise policy of the administration was not clearly defined during that period, but the nation and South Carolina had scattered
evidence of what could be expected from the administration.
Pierce's inaugural address and his message to Congress were
reassuring to South Carolinians. His avowal of a strict interpretation of the Constitution, his denunciation of slavery agitation, his acknowledgment of "Southern Rights," his demand for
economy in government, his belief that the federal government

should neither interfere with nor subsidize private business, his desire for tariff revision, and his willingness to be guided by precedents in his statecraft were sufficient to acquit him before a tribunal of even the most persistent insurgents. To no feature of Pierce's domestic policy did any large part of the South Carolina press object, and the politicians, whether intransigent or acquiescent, generally praised the new administration.[1]

Pierce's foreign policy, which called for a vigorous defense of American rights and interests and the exaltation of democracy throughout the world and which frankly proclaimed a goal of territorial and commercial expansion, did not appeal to the South Carolina press. No important journal showed enthusiasm for acquiring new territories, and several opposed the use of violence or force in our relations with foreign governments.[2]

The only forthright criticism of the President arose from his use of the patronage in New York. Pierce attempted to reward all factions within the party that had supported him in the campaign of 1852; the records of applicants for office were to be considered only since the convention of that year, and any Democrat who had expressed his adherence to the party platform was to be considered eligible for presidential favors. Because Southern leaders and proslavery "Hards" of New York objected to giving places to any Democrats who had shown antislavery tendencies, the execution of this policy proved difficult.

[1] Roy F. Nichols, *Franklin Pierce: Young Hickory of the Granite Hills* (Philadelphia, 1931), pp. 232-236, 276, 298-300; James Ford Rhodes, *History of the United States from the Compromise of 1850*, I, 385-387, 419-425; C. S. Boucher, "South Carolina and the South on the Eve of Secession, 1852-1860," *Washington University Studies, Humanistic Series*, VI, No. 2 (April, 1919), 86; Charleston *Courier*, March 8, Dec. 10, 1853; Charleston *Evening News*, March 4, 1853; Charleston *Mercury*, March 8, 9, Nov. 14, Dec. 10, 1853; Edgefield *Advertiser*, March 16, April 13, Sept. 28, Nov. 10, Dec. 14, 1853; Sumter *Black River Watchman*, March 18, 1853; speech of Lawrence Keitt, Jan. 19, 1854, in *Congressional Globe*, 33 Cong., 1 Sess., Appendix, p. 130; Sumter *Banner* (n.d.), quoted by Camden *Journal*, Nov. 15, 1853. The Greenville *Mountaineer* (n.d.) said that the newspapers in South Carolina, without exception, were supporting the Pierce administration (quoted by Camden *Journal*, March 22, 1853).
[2] Charleston *Evening News*, Jan. 9, March 28, April 30, May 17, 1853; Charleston *Mercury*, Jan. 1, March 24, April 5, 23, 26, May 2, 30, June 4, 8, 12, July 23, 26, Dec. 16, 29, 1853; Edgefield *Advertiser*, Jan. 5, June 22, Sept. 28, 1853.

The two South Carolina Senators, with four other Democrats, voted against confirmation of an antislavery "Barnburner" as Subtreasurer of New York, while the President's removal of a Collector of the Port of New York who had refused to give places to antislavery "Barnburners" and to "Softs" who wanted to propitiate the antislavery wing of the party caused a slight murmur of criticism from the South Carolina press. The Charleston *Mercury*, however, ostentatiously declined to favor any faction in the New York controversy. The whole affair was presented as just another example of the strife caused by the scramble for spoils, and it argued that the South could not trust any of the New York factions to support its interests.[3]

Federal patronage was not great in South Carolina, and outside Charleston there were few offices which offered remuneration sufficient to cause highly competitive office-seeking. The practice of proscribing either the heads of departments or subordinates, because of their party affiliations, had never taken root in South Carolina; and most of the forty-six men employed in the customhouse had been there through several administrations.[4] Since there was only one national party vested with power in the state and since all factions in that party had supported the Democratic candidate, Pierce did not discriminate between the secessionists and co-operationists. Places were offered to men who had expressed the greatest contempt for the federal government, and men who had advocated isolation from federal politics accepted places under a government toward which they had been openly hostile. William F. Colcock resigned from Congress to become Collector of the Port of Charleston; James Gadsden was appointed minister to Mexico; and Edwin De Leon, who had edited an extreme Southern Rights newspaper in Washington, was given the lucrative office

[3] Nichols, *Pierce*, pp. 216-220, 227, 247-257, 286-292; Rhodes, *History of the United States*, I, 387-389, 400; Boucher, "South Carolina and the South on the Eve of Secession," p. 86; Washington correspondence of the *Courier*, April 2, in Charleston *Courier*, April 7, 1853; Charleston *Mercury*, June 15, Sept. 5, 27, Oct. 12, 25, Nov. 14, 17, 1853; Edgefield *Advertiser*, Oct. 26, 1853; Sumter *Watchman*, Oct. 28, 1853.

[4] Pseudonymous writer ["Fiat Justitia"] in Charleston *Courier*, April 15, 1853; W. P. Miles to James Buchanan, Feb. 20, 1857.

of Consul-General in Alexandria, Egypt. These three men were secessionists in 1851. The places assigned to co-operationists were perhaps of an inferior rank to those that went to the secessionists. B. C. Pressley, who had edited a leading organ of the co-operationists, was made Assistant Treasurer of the United States in Charleston; Francis Burt became an auditor in the Treasury Department; and Thomas Evans was appointed United States District Attorney for Charleston.[5]

In 1853 President Pierce was widely commended in South Carolina. Few leaders in the state were in a position to observe at close hand his weaknesses as an executive, and the politicians had not yet been affected by his inability to control the party leaders. South Carolinians simply thought that a President who held constitutional views similar to their own was deserving of approbation.

The tendency to ignore national issues, which had become noticeable in the closing months of 1852, became much more pronounced in 1853. The legislature devoted its attention to purely state affairs. In his message Governor John Lawrence Manning, eschewing federal questions, said that everyone knew that South Carolina adhered to the principle of State Rights, to a strict construction of the Constitution, to a tariff for revenue only, to economy in government, and to a "stern and impartial administration of the laws and enforcement of all its constitutional obligations."[6] In the congressional elections this year, none of the candidates campaigned on any platform or pretended to represent any party or faction. In the three districts where

[5] Boucher, "South Carolina and the South on the Eve of Secession," p. 86; *Register of Officers and Agents, Civil, Military, and Naval, in the Service of the United States, on the thirtieth September, 1853* . . . (Washington, D. C., 1853), pp. 10, 12, 19, 26, 111, 257; Lancaster *Ledger*, March 16, 23, 1853; Charleston *Courier*, April 2, 9, May 17, 26, 1853; Camden *Journal*, March 22, 29, 1853; Sumter *Black River Watchman*, June 3, 1853; New York *Herald* (n.d.), quoted by Camden *Journal*, July 19, 1853; pseudonymous writer ["Spring Hill"] in Sumter *Watchman*, Feb. 20, 1856; J. H. Hammond to W. G. Simms, May 17, 1853.

[6] Message of November 29, 1853, in *House Journal* (1853), p. 30, in *Senate Journal* (1853), p. 27.

elections were contested, personal factors were more important than issues in determining the outcome.[7]

The South Carolina delegation that went to the Thirty-third Congress in December had six Representatives, one less than it had under the previous apportionment. Three of these, Lawrence Keitt, Preston Brooks, and W. W. Boyce, were newly elected. The introduction of these new members reduced the average age of the delegation by seven years. Most friendly to the administration was thirty-one-year-old James L. Orr, who was rumored in November to be its candidate for the Speakership.[8] In the Democratic caucus Orr received a "respectable vote" which would have been larger had the South Carolina delegation been present.[9]

During the opening month of Congress all signs pointed to a continuation of the pacific proceedings of the preceding Congress and the execution of an administration policy that would command Southern support. The President's message, bulging with optimism, assured the American people that adherence to the policies and principles of the founding fathers would bring unprecedented national glory and prosperity. The Democratic party, which had swept the spring and fall elections, had an even greater majority in both houses than in the Thirty-second Congress. The defeat of the administration candidate for printer to the Senate caused a slight scare among administration leaders, but it had no permanent effect upon their ability to control Congress. Senator Josiah J. Evans sided with the forces that opposed the administration candidate, but it is unlikely that he did so because of any hostility to President Pierce. In the House, Gerrit Smith and Joshua Giddings failed to introduce the slavery question into a debate on a minor bill. The bills

[7] Lancaster *Ledger*, Feb. 9, 1853; Edgefield *Advertiser* (n.d.), quoted by Columbia *South Carolinian*, Feb. 11, 1853; Camden *Journal*, March 8, 1853; letter of Francis W. Pickens to H. A. Jones, J. Martin, and C. H. Allen, Feb. 1, 1853, in Charleston *Mercury*, Feb. 19, 1853.

[8] Charleston *Courier*, Nov. 2, 24, 28, Dec. 6, 1853.

[9] Charleston *Courier*, Dec. 9, 1853.

for organizing the territory of Nebraska that were in committees gave no indication of causing trouble.[10]

Before Congress met, a correspondent of the Charleston *Courier*, writing from Washington on November 29, had said that Thomas Hart Benton would introduce a bill to organize Nebraska and that Senator David R. Atchison would propose an amendment to the Missouri restriction as it applied to that territory. "Thus we have material enough for exciting discussion in Congress," he temperately predicted.[11] As the year 1853 closed, this prescient hint as to the future had been forgotten, if it had even been noticed. Events were not sustaining it. It appeared to be just one more stillborn prognostication from a Washington correspondent.

A year had gone by since Governor John H. Means had promised the citizens of South Carolina that the slavery agitation would be revived with redoubled fury. A year had gone by, and still there were few signs to confirm his fearful prophecies. What did malcontents like Means think of the future during 1853? Were they still convinced that the slavery agitation would revive? Or were they beginning to wonder if they had been mistaken? It is certain that they talked less frequently and less positively of the day when the sectional dispute would once more make its appearance. But it is doubtful whether many of the old insurgents were yet converted to a belief in permanent peace between the North and the South. Much more time was needed before they would openly admit that the proponents of reconciliation had been correct in their assumptions. When a Democratic organ in Washington roseately predicted an era of good feelings for the Pierce administration, the *Mercury* exploded: "Humbug! rubbish! President Pierce will, on the contrary, have a hard time of it for the next four years; will be very glad to get out of office, and be as ready as Solomon to pronounce it vanity and vexation of spirit."[12]

[10] Nichols, *Pierce*, pp. 255, 279, 286, 292, 298-300, 302, 307, 315, 317; Charleston *Mercury*, Dec. 17, 1853.

[11] Charleston *Courier*, Dec. 2, 1853.

[12] Charleston *Mercury*, March 8, 1853.

CHAPTER IV

FEAR OR GRATITUDE, 1854

IN 1854 the slavery agitation was renewed. The South Carolina irreconcilables, after two years of waiting, could say to their conciliatory friends, we told you so. On January 10, the *Mercury* said: "We had confidently anticipated the revival of the slavery agitation this winter; and though we had supposed it would take another turn, we were not mistaken in supposing that abolitionism would seize the first opportunity to prove that its venom was as intense as ever." The *Mercury* thus referred to the reaction of Northern public opinion to the Nebraska Bill.

On January 4, 1854, the Chairman of the Senate Committee on Territories, Stephen A. Douglas, of Illinois, had reported a bill to organize a territorial government for the Nebraska region.[1] Bills for organizing the great stretch of territory west of Iowa, Missouri, and Arkansas had been introduced in previous Congresses and had suffered defeat, largely because New England members opposed continuation of the westward movement of population and Southern members desired to forestall the entrance of additional free states into the Union. But a number of forces were pressing for organization of the territory. Pioneering farmers of the surrounding states were eager to move in and begin tilling the rich agricultural lands; real estate speculators saw a good chance to make money; railroad pro-

[1] The account of the Kansas-Nebraska Bill given here is based upon these authorities: Avery Craven, *The Coming of the Civil War* (New York, 1942), pp. 325-337; George Fort Milton, *The Eve of the Conflict: Stephen A. Douglas and the Needless War* (New York, 1934), pp. 97-154; G. F. Milton, "The Kansas-Nebraska Act," *Dictionary of American History*, III, 197-198; Nichols, *Pierce*, pp. 319-324; J. G. Randall, *The Civil War and Reconstruction* (New York, 1937), pp. 129-133; Rhodes, *History of the United States*, I, 424-498; Theodore Clarke Smith, *Parties and Slavery, 1850-1859* ([*The American Nation: A History*, Vol. XVIII] New York, 1906), pp. 94-108.

moters from the great Middle West wanted an organized government to make more attractive a Northern route for the much discussed transcontinental railroad. Stephen A. Douglas was personally interested in securing a Northern transcontinental railroad that would terminate in Chicago, where he had real estate investments, and politically he had to respond to the demands of his Midwestern constituency. But how could he get an organizing bill through Congress with only the support of his own section?

A sure way to get the Southern vote was to include some feature in the bill that would appeal to proslavery feelings. Why not repeal that part of the Missouri Compromise legislation which had excluded slavery from the territories north of the line 36°30'? Southern politicians had long maintained that such an exclusion of slavery from the territories was a violation of the Contsitution. Furthermore, such action could really do no harm to Northern interests, since climate and soil would, just as effectively as any legislative act, prevent slavery in that region.

The first bill introduced by Douglas, on January 4, opened the territory to slavery but did not specifically repeal the Missouri restriction. This bill simply stated that the question of slavery in the territory would be governed by the same principle that had been applied to Utah and New Mexico in the compromise legislation of 1850. Those two territories had been organized with the proviso that slavery was to be neither established nor excluded by Congress and that the inhabitants themselves should decide whether they should have slavery when they drew up a constitution and applied for admission into the Union. In short, jurisdiction over slavery in the territories had been transferred from Congress to the people of the territories themselves. This principle of home rule in the territories Douglas called popular sovereignty, and he maintained that Congress in 1850 had solemnly accepted it as the just principle upon which to solve the conflict between the sections.

There was immediate confusion as to the correct interpretation of the slavery provision of the bill of January 4. Did it actually repeal the Missouri Compromise restriction? Some Southerners preferred an explicit repeal, and on January 23 Douglas presented a revised draft. The Senate bill in its final form provided for the organization of two territories—Nebraska and Kansas. Slavery was to be neither established nor prohibited, but when appyling for admission as states the said territories were to be "received . . . with or without slavery, as their constitutions may prescribe." The Missouri Compromise law was declared "inoperative and void."

The calculations of Douglas and his friends in regard to probable Southern support for the bill proved sound. The extent of Northern opposition, however, was greater than they had counted upon. As soon as Douglas introduced his first bill in January, antislavery politicians, journalists, publicists, and preachers began to protest against its passage. Within three months five Northern legislatures passed resolutions protesting against repeal of the Missouri Compromise, while only one approved it.

Most of the arguments about the bill advanced in state legislatures, press, pulpit, country store, and city bar had their prototypes in the Senate debate which lasted from January 30 to March 3. It was a bitter, impassioned, tumultuous debate between Douglas and his supporters on the one side and such outstanding antislavery orators as Chase, Sumner, Seward, and Wade on the other. The arguments of the latter may have had great effect on Northern public opinion, but they did not change the votes of many Senators. The bill passed by a vote of 37 to 14. In the House the opposition was much greater, and not until May 8 was the administration, through clever parliamentary maneuvering, able to force the bill to consideration. On May 22 the bill passed the House by a vote of 113 to 100.

Although the South Carolina Representatives and Senators voted for the bill, they had no part in its drafting and were not outstanding in the debate. Senator Andrew Pickens Butler was the first of the delegation to speak on the bill. He spoke on

February 24 and 25, over three weeks after the Senate debate began and a little more than a week before it ended. Butler had not intended to participate in the debate but changed his mind because of many letters which he received from South Carolina. His speech was largely a rebuttal to arguments and charges made against slavery and the South during the course of the debate. Vowing to the Senate that he would not use his tongue "as a rasp to exasperate sectional differences," he expressed regret at the style and temper of several men who had spoken against the bill. Replying to Benjamin F. Wade and Salmon P. Chase, he lampooned the idea of Negro equality and, returning to the same theme later, prophesied direful consequences from abolition. Like Calhoun in 1850, Butler warned that the slavery agitation, if continued, could end only in disunion. Denying the inferiority of Southern to Northern "civilization," he sarcastically attacked the "isms" of the North, of which feminism was the most ridiculous to this chivalric-minded South Carolinian.

In later years a schism developed between the supporters of the Kansas-Nebraska Bill over the meaning of popular sovereignty. But even when the bill was before Congress, the legislators were not ignorant of ambiguities in the doctrine as expressed in the proposed legislation. Butler, in his speech, stated the view of the leaders of that wing of the party who frequently termed themselves Southern or State Rights Democrats. In voting for the bill he was not, Butler said, committing himself "to any such doctrine as that of the uncontrolled sovereignty of the people of the Territories." It was his view that neither Congress nor territorial governments could do anything "inconsistent with the separate and combined sovereignties of the States."

Nothing in Butler's speech indicated that he thought that either Kansas or Nebraska would ever come into the Union as slave states. Although he thought that slavery was constitutionally permissible in those territories, he agreed with Webster that the "laws of God" would govern the employment of slave labor there.   The grounds upon which he supported the bill he stated in the following words:

> I am willing to take this bill as it is.   I am willing to take it, even upon the assumption that no slaves will go into Nebraska or Kansas.   I am willing to take it upon the ground that, if you adopt it, it will take a festering thorn from the side of the South.   I am willing to take it upon the ground that by it the sentiments of honor are regarded.   Even if I were perfectly certain that the bill would operate injuriously to the South, with the convictions on my mind that the Missouri Compromise is unconstitutional, I should be bound to vote for the bill.[2]

Butler's colleague, Josiah J. Evans, "was strongly tempted to say something" on the bill but, convinced that he "could add nothing to the argument," did not speak.[3]   In the House, three of the six Representatives delivered prepared addresses.   Preston Brooks spoke on March 15; Lawrence Keitt, on March 30; and W. W. Boyce, on May 20.   These three men, like Butler, devoted most of their time to explaining why the Missouri Compromise line should be abolished, not to reasons why the territories of Nebraska and Kansas should be organized.   They argued that the 1820 line was unconstitutional, unjust, and a perennial source of friction between the North and South.   None of the three expressed any hope that repeal would result in making Kansas or Nebraska a slave state.   Their interpretation of the doctrine of popular sovereignty was similar to Butler's, although Brooks was equivocal, and Boyce was hardly explicit. Keitt made it clear that he did not countenance "squatter sovereignty"—that interpretation of the Douglas doctrine which held that a territorial legislature could exclude or permit slavery.[4]   Not until the people of a territory drew up a state

[2] *Congressional Globe*, 33 Cong., 1 Sess., Appendix, pp. 232-240.

[3] Perry, *Reminiscences* (1883), p. 121.

Josiah J. Evans wrote to J. H. Hammond, Dec. 7, 1857: "The only recommendations the Kansas-Nebraska Act ever had 'to me was the repeal of the Missouri restriction and the assertion of the right of a slave holder to go into any territories.   I never had a reasonable hope of making it permanently a slave state."

[4] Throughout the remainder of the decade South Carolinians commonly used the term "squatter sovereignty" to designate what they considered the incorrect interpretation of popular sovereignty.

constitution and applied for admission into the Union could the inhabitants prohibit slavery, Keitt contended.

The three South Carolina Representatives spent a great deal of time replying to the objections which had already been advanced in the debate. Repeal was not a violation of good faith, said Boyce, for the 1820 legislation was not a compact between the North and the South. Preston Brooks, taking up the objections one by one, denied that it was the original policy of the United States to exclude slavery from the territories; that the slave states had theretofore enjoyed the benefits of the legislation of 1820; that there was a natural antagonism between free and slave labor; that foreign immigrants in the territories were desirable; that slavery was immoral; that the question of the morality of slavery was relevant to the discussion. The opposition to repeal the South Carolinians traced to the antislavery feelings of the North, which were being so vigorously expressed when they spoke. Boyce analyzed this antislavery feeling. He said that it rested upon moral fanaticism, love of power, and love of place. Moral fanaticism he considered the basic danger of the movement. "These moral manias are social tornadoes which sweep over the surface of society at intervals of history," Boyce declared. "History is full of them; they are the melancholy blot and blur of many a page. They are the only passions that admit of no settlement. They must run their course; it is the law of their nature."[5]

Except for the Charleston *Evening News*, which argued that the Douglas bill conferred upon the territorial legislatures the power to exclude slavery, the South Carolina press gave support to the arguments advanced by the delegation in Congress. There was little enthusiasm for the bill.[6] "Much Ado about

[5] *Congressional Globe*, 33 Cong., 1 Sess., Appendix, pp. 371-375 [Brooks], pp. 463-468 [Keitt], pp. 723-726 [Boyce].

[6] C. S. Boucher, "South Carolina and the South on the Eve of Secession," pp. 97-98; Craven, *Coming of the Civil War*, pp. 348, 352-353; Kibler, *Perry*, p. 280; Lancaster *Ledger*, March 29, 1854; Charleston *Evening News*, Jan. 27, Feb. 22, March 23, April 20, June 6, Nov. 20, 1854; Charleston *Mercury*, Jan. 10, 20, 23, 26, Feb. 6, 8, 14, 21, March 7, 11, 16, 21, 23, May 15, 29, 1854; Edgefield *Advertiser*, Jan. 25, Feb. 22, March 8, April 13, Sept. 28, Oct. 26, 1854. The Charleston *Evening News*, one of the few

Nothing" was the title of an editorial on the bill in the Edgefield *Advertiser*, which asked to "be excused from going into
ecstasies over the mere abstract renunciation of gross error."[7]

If South Carolina failed to glory in the passage of the
Kansas-Nebraska Act, one good reason was the revival of the
slavery agitation caused by it.   The deeds and words of the
antislavery leaders of the North had a magnetic attraction for
the wary of the state; they were condemned before Northern
friends were praised; the fear of the enemy was greater than
the love of the ally.   From its editorial of January 10, the
Mercury played upon the theme that the Kansas-Nebraska Bill
marked the reappearance of the predicted drive against slavery.
The reports of Congress and Northern journals were culled for
evidences of hostility to slavery and the South.   "They all unite
in proclaiming renewal of the war to the death upon the South,
and her institutions," said the *Mercury* on June 3.   All indications by which reasonable men could judge, according to the
Edgefield *Advertiser*, showed that there existed in the North
"a permanently rooted hostility" to the South.[8]   " Never in
the history of this country," declared the Sumter *Banner* on
June 7, 1854, "has the anti-slavery party of the North been so
violently excited and rampant as at this time."

The settlement of Kansas was not a major factor in the
antislavery agitation this year.   Once the Kansas-Nebraska Act
was passed, the flow of immigrants to the region swelled.   In
the summer months, pioneers and adventurers from both proslavery Missouri and the free states of the Northwest entered
the territory.   Settlers from the East were not numerous in

---

newspapers in the South to denounce the bill, said on April 5, 1854: "For
two months we have been denouncing the principles of the Nebraska bill, and
exposing the glazing by which it has been attempted to be palmed off on the
South as a Southern measure."

[7] Edgefield *Advertiser*, Feb. 22, March 8, 1854.

[8] Edgefield *Advertiser*, Sept. 28, 1854.

In his message to the legislature, Nov. 27, 1854, Governor Manning said:
"Events are transpiring in portions of this Confederacy which are well calculated to arrest the attention and excite the vigilance of the Southern people.
The results of the late popular elections in certain sections of the Union
threaten yet more seriously to disturb the repose, which for a brief period has
existed" (*House Journal*, p. 27).

spite of the efforts of societies which had been formed for the purpose of aiding immigrants of free-soil opinions. The first governor of Kansas did not arrive in the territory until October 7. The first election, for territorial delegate, was held on November 29. On that day the proslavery group in the territory, with the superfluous aid of several hundred armed invaders from Missouri, elected their candidate, who was seated by Congress in December with little ado.[9]

South Carolina viewed the events in Kansas with aloofness, not because of overconfidence that the territory would become a slave state, but because of a belief that soil and climate had predetermined it to be a free state.[10] There was no agitation in South Carolina to make Kansas a slave state. Even the activities of the emigrant-aid societies did not, in 1854, excite great protests. The usually captious *Mercury* was restrained and between June and December did not average one editorial a month on the subject.[11] On June 24 the *Mercury* observed

[9] Craven, *The Coming of the Civil War*, pp. 357-360; G. F. Milton, *Douglas*, pp. 187-191; Nichols, *Pierce*, pp. 407-409; Randall, *The Civil War and Reconstruction*, pp. 135-136; Rhodes, *History of the United States*, I, 78-80; James Schouler, *History of the United States of America under the Constitution* (7 vols.; New York, 1894-1913), V, 320-327; Smith, *Parties and Slavery*, pp. 121-125.

[10] The Charleston *Mercury* repeatedly warned that the South had nothing in a material way to gain from the Kansas-Nebraska Act, since slaves would not be taken in large numbers to a region whose soil and climate were not favorable for slavery. The Edgefield *Advertiser* said that the Kansas-Nebraska Bill would "not benefit the slaveholding portion of the Confederacy one iota. It is not expected by any of them that our institutions will ever be introduced upon any part of the broad expanse of territory now under legislation. On the contrary, it is admitted to be next to impossible" (March 8, 1854). William Porcher Miles wrote to James Henry Hammond, Nov. 10, 1858: "When the Kansas-Nebraska bill was under discussion Southern man after Southern man declared in his seat in Congress that all the South wanted was a practical, legislative acknowledgment of her equality—that slavery by the laws of climate could never take foot-hold in Kansas—but that a just deference to the sensitive honour of the Southern people demanded that there should be at least a *distinct theoretical* recognition of her constitutional rights &c. This was a bad way certainly of preparing the Southern mind for a war to the knife on the question of making Kansas a slave state." A. G. Magrath wrote to Hammond, Feb. 18, 1858: "The great doubt also of the adaptation of that territory for slave labor did tend beyond question to chide the fever with which under different circumstances the right would have been maintained."

[11] Charleston *Mercury*, Sept. 8, 27, Dec. 16, 1854.

that the people of Missouri had been willing that settlement of Kansas should follow its natural course but that they refused to become the victims of the abolitionist associations in the North. "It is now beyond hope that emigration will be allowed to take its natural course, and determine calmly, in the progress of time, what shall be the institutions of Kansas. It is to be a struggle of fanaticism and political rancor on one side, and plain self-defence on the other." Six months later, commenting upon the territorial election, the *Mercury* asserted that it had "always said that if the settlement of Kansas had gone on in a quiet natural way, it would have probably been a free state."[12]

While the slavery question was serving to keep South Carolina at arm's length from the North, the proceedings in Congress on other matters did nothing to make it less dissatisfied with developments in national politics. The delegation parted company with their Democratic friends from the Northwest and Southwest, who desired to use the federal government in their promotional schemes. Again, in this Thirty-third Congress, only James L. Orr would join the Westerners in granting alternate sections of public land to states to aid in railroad construction. Whether it happened to be a bill to grant land to the Northern state of Michigan or the Southern state of Louisiana, Senator Butler insisted that it was unconstitutional. The South Carolinians were equally opposed to another measure desired by many of their Northwestern friends, that is, the giving of public land to homesteaders. Constitutional-minded Butler was not even moved by appeals to benevolence. On May 16 he made a prepared speech against a bill to grant ten million acres of public land for the purpose of aiding the states to care for their insane. Likewise, the South Carolina members evinced no eagerness to grant public lands to aid in the construction of a transcontinental railroad and telegraph.[13]

[12] Dec. 16, 1854.
[13] *Congressional Globe*, 33 Cong., 1 Sess., pp. 357, 358, 360-361, 504, 506, 519, 526, 532, 535, 536, 547, 549, 568, 711-714, 1127, 1392, 1603, 1659-1660, 1698, 1703-1705, 1708-1709, 1717, 1796, 1812, Appendix, pp. 120, 648-653, 923-926, 1092, 1100, 1115, 1116, 1166, 1167, 1173, 1191, 1195.

Was there any question which South Carolina thought worth consideration by Congress? The tariff perhaps, if the *Evening News* and *Mercury* were representative. These papers complained that the entire first session of the Thirty-third Congress was devoted to problems of no material consequence to the state, and they accused the administration and the Democratic party of sidetracking tariff revision. They both applauded W. W. Boyce's speech on the tariff, in which he raised numerous objections to the recommendations submitted to Congress by Secretary of the Treasury James Guthrie. Although Guthrie had proposed downward revision of the tariff of 1846, which was only mildly protective, Congressman Boyce and the Charleston newspapers were not satisfied. Essentially they desired free trade.[14]

For the intransigents of the state there was little or nothing about the North or the federal government worthy of commendation. Even the Pierce foreign policy, clearly framed to propitiate the South, provoked no gratification. Two notable diplomatic achievements this year, the Perry treaty with Japan and a commercial treaty with Canada, were too remote from South Carolina's interests to excite attention. More pertinent was a treaty with Mexico negotiated by James Gadsden of South Carolina. Although this treaty settled several disputed issues and enabled the United States to purchase a strip of land south of the Gila River that was valuable as a railroad route to the Pacific, it also failed to bring much credit to the administration. Forceful measures employed in Nicaragua to protect the interests of an American transit company were not praised. The efforts of the administration to acquire Cuba through peaceful means had the good wishes of the state, but there were no demands to sustain the aggressive minister to Spain, Pierre Soulé, who was known to favor war if other methods of obtaining Cuba failed.[15]

[14] *Congressional Globe*, 33 Cong., 1 Sess., Appendix, pp. 209-212; Charleston *Evening News*, June 23, Nov. 25, 1854; Charleston *Mercury*, Feb. 22, 25, 28, June 19, 27, 1854. W. W. Boyce, in a public letter dated June 26, 1857, referred to the tariff as "the most important of all subjects after slavery" (quoted by Washington [D. C.] *States*, July 3, 1857).

[15] Nichols, *Pierce*, pp. 325-329; Rhodes, *History of the United States*, II,

In his message to the legislature in November, the governor expressed South Carolina's dislike for imperialism. Manning said that the nation should

carefully avoid both the reality and appearance of attempting, directly or indirectly, to grasp any portion of foreign dominion. Whatever can be effected that is desirable for the country to achieve, by open treaty with a distinct and separate power, is a question of policy alone, to which there can be no objection; but beyond this the government has no right to go, whether through the agency of unlawful enterprises at home; or indiscreet and anomalous ministerial interference abroad.[16]

A party revolution occurred in the North during the summer months.[17] The old parties fell back before two upstarts—the Republicans and Know-Nothings. The Republican party had its origins in the public reaction to the repeal of the Missouri Compromise; the common denominator of many degrees of antislavery sentiment among its leaders was opposition to further extension of slavery. In 1854 it acquired no interstate organization; rather it consisted merely of coalitions in several states of Free-Soilers, Whigs, anti-Nebraska Democrats, enemies of the South, advocates of promotional legislation, and disgruntled politicians of various opinions. These coalitions were most successful in the Northwest: in Michigan, Indiana, Ohio, and Wisconsin.

In the East in 1854, the American or Know-Nothing party threatened the established parties. It gained converts because of its successful appeal to strong feelings against foreigners and Catholics. Similar to local native-American parties that had appeared in local elections in the forties, it grew from a secret

1-44; Smith, *Parties*, pp. 78-93; *Congressional Globe*, 33 Cong., 1 Sess., pp. 128, 129, 1025, 1540-1541, 1543-1545, 2118, 2119; speech of Lawrence Keitt, Jan. 19, 1854, *ibid.*, pp. 130-131; Charleston *Mercury*, Jan. 9, 21, April 13, May 10, June 16, July 31, Aug. 7, 16, Sept. 25, Nov. 18, Dec. 4, 1854; Charleston *Evening News*, June 3, 28, Sept. 27, 1854.

[16] Message of November 28, in *Journal of the House* (1854), p. 26.

[17] For party history and the national elections in the year 1854, the following authorities were consulted: Rhodes, *History of the United States*, I, 490, 494, II, 45-71; Smith, *Parties*, pp. 109-120; Milton, *Douglas*, pp. 173-174, 184-185.

patriotic society known as the Order of the Star Spangled Banner, which had been founded in New York City in 1848. The aim of the party was to "preserve America for Americans." The Know-Nothings baited Catholics, pledged themselves to vote for native Americans, and advocated rigorous requirements for naturalization. Profiting from the chaotic state of parties following the passage of the Kansas-Nebraska Act, they became a strong force in politics for the first time.

These two parties, together with the antislavery wing of the Whig party, decimated the ranks of the Northern Democracy. The Republicans carried Michigan and Wisconsin. The Know-Nothings won in Massachusetts by a landslide, carried Delaware, elected forty members to the New York legislature, and in Pennsylvania elected some members to the legislature and helped the Whigs to elect the governor. In Iowa an antislavery Whig took the governorship from the Democrats. Fusion groups and anti-Nebraska tickets were successful in Ohio, Indiana, Maine, and Vermont. In Illinois the Democrats elected only four of the nine Representatives to Congress.

Douglas and the administration spokesmen naturally emphasized the role of the Know-Nothings in the election; Republican and other antislavery leaders, contrariwise, asserted that opposition to repeal of the Missouri Compromise caused the upheaval. The South Carolina irreconcilables agreed with the interpretation of the antislavery leaders: the election was proof of the great antislavery sentiment in the North. The movement against slavery was now more dangerous than ever before, they said, for it had been given effective political organization by the Northern wing of the Whig party and by local "anti-Nebraska" parties. Ignoring the Know-Nothings and Republicans and assuming that the Whig party would be in the future the great antislavery party, they argued that Southern Whigs must now join the discredited Democratic party or establish a new Southern party.[18]

[18] Boucher, "South Carolina and the South on the Eve of Secession," p. 106; Charleston *Evening News*, March 23, April 5, July 8, Aug. 23, 31, Sept. 18, 1854; Charleston *Mercury*, May 18, June 8, 26, July 22, Aug. 22,

The irreconcilables were now convinced, more than ever before, that the national Democratic party was incapable of protecting Southern rights and interests. They argued that the Southern wing of the party, alone, had the support of its constituents. The Northern Democrats faced a dilemma: they must choose between friendliness to the South or support from their constituents; they could not have both, because of Northern hostility to slavery. Whatever the choice by Northern Democratic leaders, the South could not place its hopes in the national party. Neither party leaders without followers nor leaders with followers who opposed slavery could aid the South. And the only escape from the dilemma, the suppression of the Northern agitation against slavery, was impossible.[19]

Thus the argument of the irreconcilables always came back to the fundamental assumption that the antislavery movement was the most powerful political force in the North. The elections of 1854 they viewed as conclusive proof. Over and over they pointed to the election returns as a measure of antislavery opinion in the North. "As a test of the true state of things in the free-States, and as an omen of what is to be expected from all their parties (inclusive of the Democracy), look at the late political demonstrations in Maine, New Hampshire, New York and Iowa, which were lately Democratic—now Whig and Abolition," said the *Evening News*.[20] "Thus far the elections have gone against Democracy and the Constitution throughout the Northern States," said the Edgefield *Advertiser* on November 22. "The anti-slavery star is largely in the ascendant." And the "we-told-you-so" argument, always an effective propaganda appeal, was an underlying theme:

When in the midst of the congratulations at the passage of the Nebraska bill, the *Mercury* predicted that so far from giving peace

---

Oct. 2, 3, 9, 13, 17, 25, Nov. 1, 3, 22, 27, 1854; Edgefield *Advertiser*, Oct. 26, Nov. 22, 1854; Sumter *Black River Watchman*, Dec. 1, 1854.

[19] Boucher, "South Carolina and the South on the Eve of Secession," p. 105; Charleston *Evening News*, March 23, April 5, July 8, Aug. 23, 31, Sept. 18, 1854; Charleston *Mercury*, Oct. 9, 13, Nov. 1, 3, 27, 1854; Edgefield *Advertiser*, Nov. 2, 22, 1854.

[20] Sept. 18, 1854.

to the country, or staying anti-slavery aggression, that measure would enkindle the war anew, it was rebuked as an evil prophet, whose predictions would be surely falsified. So, too, when we foresaw the downfall of the Democratic party in the Free States in the recent elections, before one passion—hostility to the South, we were met with the same language and spirit on the part of those whose blindness or party infatuation made them both unwilling and unable to look the truth full in the face. And when the elections had resulted in Wisconsin, Ohio, Indiana, New Hampshire and Maine, in the utter prostration of the Democratic party, and the triumph of Freesoil, and we pointed the South to the plain necessity of rallying herself for the defence of her rights and institutions, the mad-dog cry of "disunion" was raised against us by the Washington *Union*, and in South Carolina even, we were sneered at as "ultraists"—bent on agitation and anarchy.

The *Mercury*, all this time, the editorial continued, had been content to await the outcome. Then, in the fall elections, the Democratic party was routed, and its prophecies were fulfilled.[21]

The irreconcilables, having agreed that the South could not protect its interests through national parties, were in a position to advocate one of three courses: (1) immediate disunion, (2) a Southern party, or (3) isolation. Assuming the continuation of the Union for the time being, they did not discuss the first course. The Charleston *Evening News* asked for the formation of a Southern party. Sooner or later, according to the argument used to justify this proposal, the Southern people would have to organize a sectional party in self-defense against the Northern antislavery party. Then, ignoring its own contention that the North was becoming united into one great sectional party, it advanced the hope that a united South could hold the balance of power between the Northern parties and "dictate her own terms of safety, rights and prosperity." If a united South proved too weak to hold the balance of power, it could leave the Union.[22] Unless the writer for the *Evening News* was

[21] Nov. 27, 1854.
[22] Boucher, "South Carolina and the South on the Eve of Secession," p. 105; Charleston *Evening News*, March 23, Aug. 23, 31, Sept. 18, 1854; Edgefield *Advertiser*, July 13, Sept. 28, Oct. 19, Nov. 22, 1854.

insincere in his contention that the North was united behind a
sectional party hostile to the South or unless he was stupidly
unaware of the error in his own logic, one can only conclude
that he expected a Southern party to prepare the way for
disunion.

The *Mercury* counseled isolation from national party politics. Its distrust of Southern party politicians was too firmly
rooted for it to advocate the course proposed by its competitor.
Its recommendations were general: steer clear of party politics
and maintain a firm resistance to the antislavery movement.[23]

Despite the ominous fall elections, conciliatory leaders such
as Orr and Brooks did not withdraw their support from the
administration and the Democratic party in favor of the courses
proposed by the irreconcilables. They did not deny that the
renewal of the antislavery agitation was a threat, but they were
still willing to go along with the administration. They sympathized with Pierce's attempts to follow broad policies of nationalism and democracy.[24] That South Carolinians could give
support to either was due to the fact that Pierce's interpretation
of both was in harmony with their preconceptions. His nationalism was a combination of patriotic pride in the nation's past
and an assertion of the rights of the states; it did not seek to
merge the individual states into a unitary popular government;
its essence was nonsectionalism. The core of Pierce's conception
of democracy was representative government, not the doctrine
of equality which abolitionists stressed in their propaganda.

Pierce's belief in nonsectional, Constitutional, State-Rights
nationalism was nearer to the traditions of South Carolina than
sectionalism; and it had support in the delegation. A. P. Butler

[23] Charleston *Mercury*, Oct. 9, Nov. 1, 3, 27, 1854.

[24] The Edgefield *Advertiser*, in an editorial of Sept. 28, 1854, entitled
"Should we be Sectional or not?" said: "Those who maintain the negative of
this proposition would perhaps style themselves *National* Democrats; while
those who uphold the affirmative prefer the appellation of *Southern Rights*
Democrats. The former believe that the conservative element of Southern
safety is the friendly disposition of the bulk of our Northern brethren. The
latter feel confident that our surest, and in fact our only real protection, is
to rally the Southern people, in defence of Southern interests and Southern
institutions, under a Southern banner; and this is what we mean by sectionalism."

always made his appeals on the grounds of strict construction rather than sectionalism. Preston Brooks, on June 14, 1854, said: "The time has been when I was sectional, and it has passed. I came here sectional; but the noble trio from New England [MacDonald, Hibbard and Ingersoll] have taught me to tear the word from my political vocabulary, and insert in its place another which is more elevated and patriotic, the word *constitutional*."[25]

The conflict between nationalism and sectionalism was not merely between consciously selected policies. Patriotism for the South as a section had already become an emotional feeling to which appeals could be made without any support from logic or reason. Thus it was sometimes difficult for a leader to be outspoken against sectionalism, however strongly he may have professed a strict interpretation of the Constitution. For his repudiation of sectionalism, Brooks was criticized by several newspapers of his own state.[26]

National politics played no significant part in the canvass which preceded the October election for members of the legislature. The candidates uniformly confined their statements of opinion to subjects that were of import within South Carolina, such as the electoral system, state internal improvements, the state banks, public education, the state judiciary, and the penitentiary. Only in Charleston, where candidates stated their opposition to the Know-Nothing party, was there frequent mention of national party issues.[27]

In the year 1854 there were many sources of discontent in South Carolina. Economic and health troubles alone were sufficient to create an atmosphere of gloom. Business was poor in the cities, money was scarce everywhere, the yield of short-staple cotton was below that of 1853, and crops along the coast

---

[25] *Congressional Globe*, 33 Cong., 1 Sess., Appendix, p. 926.

[26] Edgefield *Advertiser*, July 6, 13, Sept. 21, 28, Oct. 19, 1854; Sumter *Banner*, July 19, Aug. 2, 1854.

[27] Charleston *Courier*, July 22; Oct. 5, 6, 7, 30, 1854; Pickens *Keowee Courier* (n.d.), quoted by the Lancaster *Ledger*, June 28, 1854; Camden *Journal*, Feb. 7, 1854; Sumter *Banner*, May 3, 31, June 7, 28, 1854; Sumter *Black River Watchman*, June 23, 30, July 14, 1854; Lancaster *Ledger*, June 14, 28, 1854.

were destroyed by storms.   Many persons in Charleston and some of the smaller towns were victims of yellow fever.[28] "But few families," said Governor Manning in November, "are without some sorrowful event to call to their recollection the past summer as a period of severe trial and mourning."[29]

Thus it was a South Carolina afflicted with adversities that witnessed the great political changes of 1854.   It is hardly surprising that the pessimists of 1853 should have viewed the events of 1854 with distemper.   Nor would it have been surprising had the irreconcilables made converts during the year. Yet there is no measurable evidence to indicate that there was any great shift in opinion or factional alignments in the state.   Probably the most significant consequence of the political developments of the year was the resurgence of the spirit of resistance among those who had never ceased to believe that the Compromise of 1850 was anything but a truce.   Surely critics of South Carolina's position in the Union at the close of 1853 were no more satisfied a year later.   Even repeal of the Missouri Compromise, which antislavery leaders assailed as a Southern triumph, did not appease apprehensive observers of the antislavery agitation provoked by it.

In 1852 and 1853 the great obstacle to South Carolina's reconciliation with the North had been the belief of some in the inevitability of the revival of the slavery and sectional agitation. In 1854 the great obstacle to reconciliation was the realization by many that the slavery and sectional agitation had already been renewed.

[28] Charleston *Mercury*, Sept. 14, Nov. 29, 1854; message of Governor Manning, Nov. 28, in *House Journal* (1854), pp. 12-13; speech of James Simons, Nov. 27, 1854, in *House Journal*, p. 5.
[29] *House Journal*, p. 12.

CHAPTER V

NATIVISM OR SLAVERY, 1855

LEGISLATIVE ISSUES were unimportant in national politics in 1855. The politicians and their constituents were little interested in the proceedings of the second session of the Thirty-third Congress which lasted from December 4, 1854, to March 5, 1855. It was a Congress which could hardly claim to represent public opinion; too many of its members had been repudiated in the recent elections. So the party leaders made no attempts to initiate important legislation.

The question of slavery in the territories did not come up for debate in the expiring Congress.[1] People who felt keenly on this subject turned their attention from Washington to Kansas, where events began to show the explosive qualities of a mixture of popular sovereignty and the slavery issue. Before this year had ended two autonomous communities were on the verge of civil war. In a rough sort of way one of these communities was composed of the friends of slavery, while the other was composed of the enemies of slavery. Both sides, however, were reinforced by an assortment of mundane politicians, land speculators, feudists, topers, adventurers, and outlaws.

The proslavery group, partly through fraud and force, managed to obtain and keep control of the legitimate territorial legislature, and on October 1, in an election shunned by the antislavery group, elected a territorial delegate to Congress. The free-state group refused to recognize the authority of the legitimate legislature. Instead, they held their own election for

---

[1] For the story of Kansas in 1855, the following authorities were consulted: Craven, *The Coming of the Civil War*, pp. 358-365; Milton, *Douglas*, pp. 191-198; Nichols, *Pierce*, pp. 409-418; Randall, *Civil War*, pp. 136-137; Rhodes, *History of the United States*, II, 78-87, 98-107; Schouler, *History of the United States*, V, 328-333; Smith, *Parties*, pp. 126-134.

congressional delegate and in late October, at Topeka, drafted a new state constitution that was submitted to popular referendum on December 15.

Andrew H. Reeder, who was governor until August, was unable to exert his authority over either of the two antagonistic parties. As he became more friendly to the free-state faction, the proslavery people became more hostile to him and demanded his dismissal. After quarreling with the legislature over a capital site and engaging in questionable land speculation, he was removed by President Pierce. Reeder's successor, Wilson Shannon, who arrived in Kansas in September, upheld the territorial legislature and condemned the moves of the free-state people to hold their own elections and establish their own government.

South Carolina was no longer indifferent about Kansas in 1855, but it was still calm. The press of the state, without great ado, declared its sympathy for the proslavery party and blamed the antislavery faction for all the troubles in the territory. The forceful measures used to get control of the legislature were justified, while the attempts of the free-staters to set up their own government were viewed as revolutionary. Little was said about the territorial governors or the administration policy toward Kansas. Before the year was over, some of the papers began to stress the theme that the cause of Kansas was the cause of the South; yet there was no organized emigrant movement this year, and only a few citizens responded to the appeals of the proslavery leaders to come to the territory. The *Mercury*, in several prescient editorials, asserted that the great conflict over Kansas would arise later—when it became a subject for debate in the next Congress.[2]

Foreign affairs, especially during the first five months of 1855, attracted more attention in South Carolina than the Kansas situation. Despite the failure to secure Cuba the previous year, Pierce still hoped to strengthen the party through some outstanding diplomatic achievement. Relations with Spain con-

[2] Charleston *Mercury*, Jan. 24, April 3, 4, 18, 23, Oct. 27, Nov. 3, 1855; Charleston *Evening News*, Nov. 7, 29, Dec. 5, 18, 1855; Edgefield *Advertiser*, Jan. 31, 1855; Sumter *Banner*, Feb. 7, 1855.

tinued to furnish the main diplomatic problem for the administration. In March a crisis developed between the two countries when a Spanish frigate fired upon the *El Dorado*, a ship flying the American flag. Expansionists urged revenge, and for a while it appeared that there might be war. In April, Pierce sent a squadron of six ships to Cuban waters with the instructions to protect American ships, but those who hoped that this move would lead to war were disappointed. The truth was that Pierce knew that he could not obtain sufficient public or congressional support to risk war; he had made up his mind that Cuba could be acquired only in a peaceful way, as his instructions to the new minister to Spain indicated.[3]

Basically there was no change in the South Carolina attitude toward Cuba. There were no demands for acquisition through war, although it was generally agreed that the United States should intervene if Spain abolished slavery in Cuba or transferred it to another European power. W. W. Boyce, in a speech in the House on January 15, not only argued that the acquisition of Cuba was undesirable but lashed out at the whole idea of "manifest destiny." Even the Charleston *Evening News*, which thought that Spain should not govern Cuba, did not think annexation important enough to justify either war, suspension of the neutrality laws, efforts by the South to take it independently of the federal government, or disunion if the federal government failed to acquire it.[4]

By mid-1855 it was clear that the Pierce policy of expansion was doomed to failure. Intended to propitiate the South, it in no way served to bring South Carolina closer to the North or the Democratic party. Just as in the case of the Kansas-Nebraska Act, the irreconcilables complained against Northern hostility to the policy instead of praising the administration for its good

[3] Nichols, *Pierce*, pp. 376, 392-396.
[4] Speech of W. W. Boyce, Jan. 15, 1855, in *Congressional Globe*, 33 Cong., 2 Sess., Appendix, pp. 91-94; Charleston *Courier*, Nov. 17, 1855; Charleston *Evening News*, April 26, 1855; Charleston *Mercury*, Jan. 18, 20, March 12, 27, 28, 29, 30, 31, April 2, 6, 10, 11, 12, 13, 23, 25, 26, Nov. 13, 17, Dec. 18, 22, 1855; Edgefield *Advertiser*, Jan. 31, 1855; Sumter *Banner*, Jan. 24, 31, April 18, 1855.

intentions. To newspapers such as the *Mercury, Evening News,* and Sumter *Banner* it appeared that Northern antislavery opinion had forced Pierce to abandon his Cuban policy and would in the future paralyze the administration in all foreign fields.[5]

More important to South Carolina this year than the fugitive-slave law, the territories, foreign affairs, or any other specific issue were the political parties.[6] The irreconcilables in 1854 had been convinced that the antislavery party would supplant all others in the North. Yet, as the year opened, it was by no means clear whether the question of slavery or "Americanism" would determine party success in the future. The strength of the Republicans this year was hardly great enough to frighten either the administration or alarmist South Carolinians; only in Ohio, where Salmon P. Chase was elected governor, did they score an outstanding victory.

The April elections this year seemed to indicate that the Know-Nothings would sweep ahead of the field; they carried Connecticut, Rhode Island, and even New Hampshire, Pierce's state and traditionally Democratic. In later state and local elections their vote fell off, but they carried New York and Massachusetts. In the South, where many Whigs had joined the party, the Know-Nothings were less successful. They carried Maryland and Kentucky but failed in Virginia. In spite of continued strength, there were signs that the American party might fail to become a great national party. In June the national convention at Philadelphia divided along sectional lines when the Southern delegates secured the adoption of a proslavery platform. The American party, like the other national parties, at last found that it could not escape the plague of slavery and sectionalism.

The losses of the Know-Nothings and Republicans were gains for the Democrats. The elections of 1854 and early

[5] Charleston *Evening News*, April 26, 1855; Charleston *Mercury*, March 31, 1855; Sumter *Banner*, April 18, 1855.

[6] For the story of the political parties and the elections of 1855, the following authorities were consulted: Milton, *Douglas*, pp. 206-210; Nichols, *Pierce*, pp. 388-392, 426-427; Schouler, *History of the United States*, V, 317-318, 333-335; Smith, *Parties*, pp. 136-145.

1855 persuaded party and administration leaders that the Know-Nothings had been responsible for their defeat; so they concentrated their arguments and patronage against that party. Their success in Virginia, where Henry A. Wise defeated the Know-Nothing candidate after an intense campaign, was the first significant victory for the Democrats since the debacle of 1854, and they were encouraged to hope for a turn in their fortunes. The result was perhaps more agreeable than they anticipated: they carried Maine, New Jersey, Pennsylvania, Indiana, Illinois, Wisconsin, and five Southern states.

In South Carolina the Know-Nothings never became a threat to the supremacy of the Democrats.[7] In Charleston an exiguous combination of obscure politicians organized a party which took part in local elections. Their mouthpiece was the *Evening News*. John Cunningham, editor of this newspaper and leading spirit in the movement, had altered his views but little since 1851, when he had favored secession; a correspondent for the Charleston *Courier* who saw him speak at the Philadelphia convention in June described him as a "perfect fire-eater and secessionist."[8] F. D. Richardson, the Know-Nothing candidate for mayor, was also known to resent the place of South Carolina in the Union. Indeed, the leaders of the American party in South Carolina were among the most extreme partisans of the South-

[7] The following account of the Know-Nothings in South Carolina is based upon these sources: Boucher, "South Carolina and the South on the Eve of Secession," pp. 107-109; Lancaster *Ledger*, Jan. 25, April 14, July 18, Aug. 8, 22, 29, Sept. 5, 26, 1855; Charleston *Courier*, Aug. 16, Nov. 8, 17, 1855; correspondence of the *Courier*, June 12, 1855, in Charleston *Courier*, June 16, 1855; Charleston *Evening News*, Feb. 17, 20, March 2, May 30, June 30, July 6, 7, 9, 11, 12, 28, Aug. 3, 6, 13, 15, 16, 17, 19, 20, Sept. 1, 3, 4, 27, Oct. 6, 8, 10, 15, 19, 20, 27, Nov. 8, 10, 17, 1855; Charleston *Mercury*, July 7, 13, 17, 19, 23, 26, Aug. 15, 29, Oct. 3, 8, Nov. 9, 1855; Edgefield *Advertiser*, July 18, Aug. 1, 12, Oct. 21, 1855; Camden *Journal*, March 13, July 17, Aug. 21, 1855; Sumter *Watchman*, Oct. 17, 1855; speech of Lawrence Keitt in the U. S. House of Representatives, Jan. 3, 1855, in *Congressional Globe*, 33 Cong., 2 Sess., Appendix, pp. 66-70; Lawrence Keitt to Sue Sparks, May 30, Sept. 19, Oct. 13, 1855; W. R. Taber to John Cunningham, July 20; John Cunningham to W. R. Taber, July 20, 1855 (in Rhett papers possessed by Mrs. Joseph Ransom of Memphis, Tennessee); W. H. Trescot to W. P. Miles, April 16, Sept. 6, 1855.

[8] Correspondence of the *Courier*, June 12, 1855, in Charleston *Courier*, June 16, 1855.

ern cause. The *Evening News* proclaimed: "The American Party in South Carolina is the very essence of our State Rights Democracy."[9] The editor of the *Mercury* was pained to attack the party in South Carolina, because it included many "true men" who were some of his "warmest personal and political friends."[10]

The editorials of the *Evening News* advanced the usual Know-Nothing arguments against the influence of foreigners and Catholics in American politics. They urged a modification of the naturalization and election laws so as to limit the influence of foreigners, raise the standards for naturalization, prevent fraud and perjury in obtaining naturalization papers, require citizenship as a voting qualification, and provide punishment for bribery and rioting in elections. The policy of the American party toward the Catholic Church, according to Cunningham, was to check its "political and property pretensions in this country."[11] The ultimate goal of all reforms proposed by the party was "an America ruled by Americans."

In South Carolina these arguments on the immigrant and Catholic questions had to share space with others not generally advanced by orthodox Know-Nothings. John Cunningham obviously intended to make the American party in his state something quite different from what it was in the North. In his first confession of sympathy for the principles of the movement he said that the Southern people could not support the American party of the North, but that they could support parties organized independently in the Southern states. That these state parties should be quite different from existing American parties in the South was also made clear. Cunningham was not trying to organize a new Union-saving party, and he had no good wishes for Southern Know-Nothings if they failed to measure up to his standard of loyalty to Southern rights and interests. Thus it was that he rejoiced in the defeat of the Know-Nothings in Virginia in May.

[9] Charleston *Evening News*, July 23, 1855.
[10] W. R. Taber to John Cunningham, July 20, 1855; Charleston *Mercury*, July 26, Nov. 9, 1855.
[11] Charleston *Evening News*, Oct. 15, 1855.

The South Carolina leaders never expected that an American party of their design would become a national party capable of fulfilling its avowed objectives. None of them ever tried to co-operate with the national organization. Apparently the Know-Nothing party in South Carolina was a subterfuge for a small group of leaders who wanted to organize a Southern party. Cunningham's approval of the proposal to form a Southern party is perhaps the best proof of his intentions:

> The American party entirely concurs in this Southern sentiment, and it is their purpose, when aggression by Congress makes it requisite, to act at once for the union and safety of the South. It cordially shakes hands with all other Southerners on this determination. It has repudiated and holds no connection with the Northern Know-Nothings, who have so universally rejected the slavery portion of the Philadelphia Platform. Their association is strictly a Southern one. They are perfectly disposed and free to affiliate with all those intent upon preserving Southern and State Rights.[12]

In short, Cunningham's American party of 1855 was merely his proposed Southern party of 1854 mixed with Native Americanism.

The hybrid was not popular. The *Evening News* lost subscribers because it championed Native Americanism, while the Know-Nothing candidates for mayor and city council were defeated in the October election. Soon after this election the party disbanded.

The movement in opposition to the Know-Nothings tended to bring together leaders who were usually uncongenial. Supporters of the national Democratic party, such as Orr and Brooks, joined with advocates of isolation from the party organization, such as Keitt, McQueen, and Boyce, in a campaign against the Know-Nothings. The Southern Rights party that was organized in Charleston to oppose the American party included both moderates and extremists.

The arguments of the opponents of the Know-Nothings had two purposes: (1) to prevent an American party of any one of

[12] *Ibid.*, Sept. 27, 1855.

the types which had been organized in other states from taking root in South Carolina, and (2) to destroy the party that had been organized in Charleston. Most of the speeches and public letters publicized outside of Charleston were designed for the first purpose. In general, the same arguments that were used for the first purpose were also used for the second, in spite of the protests from Charleston Know-Nothings that their party differed from all others of the same name. Because association with a party that included Northern antislavery members and Southern Unionists would serve to discredit any party before the voters of the state, the critics of the Know-Nothings were inclined, perhaps with some guile, to overlook the distinctive features of the American party in South Carolina.

Since South Carolinians resented the influx of foreigners who were contributing to the population, wealth, and antislavery movement of the North, the opponents of the Know-Nothings did not argue against limiting immigration into the United States. They agreed that the number of immigrants admitted should be reduced, but they opposed proscription of aliens, naturalized citizens, and Catholics. The spirit of Native Americanism, they asserted, was hostile to the traditional civil and political liberties of the Republic. They also objected to the secrecy of the party, to its interference in the private affairs of individuals, to the ambition of its leaders, to its tendency to break down the rights of the states, and to the support that it received from abolitionists in the North and Unionists in the South.

The menace of the Know-Nothings to Southern unity was stressed in the South Carolina argument against nativism. Why should the South allow itself to be divided on a question of secondary importance when the supreme issue was slavery? "We of the South have no politics but the negro," declared Preston Brooks.[13] "Slavery is the absorbing question," said W. W. Boyce, who was "amazed and saddened" by party divisions in the South. "We are like the Greeks of the lower empire, who exhausted themselves in insane discussions, while the Barbarians were thundering at their gates. We are upon the

[13] Lancaster *Ledger*, Aug. 22, 1855.

eve of revolution, and occupying ourselves with foreigners and Catholics, as though we had nothing at stake ourselves."[14]

Among the extremists who supported the coalition formed to counteract Know-Nothingism, a few were faintly inclined to discuss the question of converting the American party into a strongly pro-Southern and proslavery party. Most of the extremists, however, distrusted national parties, and they were not disposed to change their minds about one that obviously contained many antislavery supporters. Nor did the plan of converting the American party into a Southern sectional party seem plausible. Aside from the fact that the party raised secondary issues, they pointed out that the Southern branch of the American party was strongly opposed to sectionalism.

While Know-Nothingism was still a question for public debate in the early part of the autumn, several editors and obscure politicians began talking about the need for a Southern party.[15] They were mostly men who were unwilling to make any move toward supporting the Pierce administration, and some of them probably had toyed with the idea of using the Know-Nothing movement as a means of asserting their independence of the national Democratic party. Insurgent newspapers such as the *Mercury*, *Evening News*, Sumter *Watchman*, and Columbia *Carolina Times* were sympathetic to the cause.

An abortive attempt to organize a Southern party in the state was made in Fairfield district, where a meeting was held on October 1. Speeches and resolutions at this meeting stated that the growing antislavery opinion in the North, attested by recent elections and the Northern press, required that the South unite behind a Southern party. This party should have as its motto equality in the Union or independence out of it. Its immediate objective should be the nomination of a Southern

[14] *Ibid.*; Camden *Journal*, Aug. 21, 1855.
[15] The following account of the movement for a Southern party is based upon these sources: Boucher, "South Carolina and the South on the Eve of Secession," p. 106; Charleston *Evening News*, Sept. 27, Oct. 4, 1855; Charleston *Mercury*, March 14, 16, 26, July 3, 7, 15, 16, 18, 25, Sept. 27, 1855; Columbia *South Carolinian* (n.d.), quoted by Sumter *Watchman*, Oct. 3, 1855; Camden *Journal*, Aug. 21, 1855; Sumter *Watchman*, Sept. 12, Oct. 3, Nov. 7, 1855.

man with Southern principles for the Presidency. The resolutions asked for the participation of other state districts in the movement and called for the organization of similar parties in the other Southern states.

The idea of a Southern party never became an actuality in South Carolina. Leaders who favored it most had the least abilities for organization. Men such as Rhett, Keitt, McQueen, Boyce, Gregg, Means, Allston, Gist, Adams, and their political friends were sympathetic; but they seemed innately incapable of anything more than words. Fundamentally, they distrusted parties. If most of their objections were aimed at national parties, at least one important one applied to a sectional party: the leaders of a Southern party, too, might become more interested in electing a president or securing federal offices than in taking a firm stand for Southern rights and interests.

Talk of a Southern party may have been fostered by some irreconcilables to forestall an anticipated move to associate South Carolina more closely with the national Democratic party. In the fall of 1855 James L. Orr and his friends made the novel proposal that the state send delegates to the next presidential convention.[16] The state had always occupied a relatively independent position in regard to national parties. After the nullification crisis, the state was left without ties to either national party. During the period from 1832 to 1856 the state was never more than an independent ally of any national party. Its independence was strikingly asserted when it voted twice for presidential candidates who were not nominated by a national

[16] The following account of the convention movement in 1855 is based upon these authorities and sources: Kibler, *Perry*, p. 281; Laura A. White, "The National Democrats in South Carolina, 1852-1860," *South Atlantic Quarterly*, XXVIII (Oct., 1929), 370-389; White, *Rhett*, pp. 135-137; Charleston *Evening News*, Oct. 19, 1855; Charleston *Mercury*, Aug. 7, 25, Sept. 7, 27, Oct. 30, Dec. 4, 20, 1855; Edgefield *Advertiser*, Aug. 1, Sept. 12, 19, Oct. 24, Nov. 7, 28, 1855; Camden *Journal*, Nov. 13, 1855; Columbia *Carolina Times*, Jan. 7, 1856; Sumter *Watchman*, Nov. 14, 1855; Lancaster *Ledger*, Aug. 29, Nov. 7, 1855; *The Cincinnati Convention. Letter from James L. Orr, of South Carolina, to Hon. C. W. Dudley, On the propriety of having the State of South Carolina represented in the Democratic National Convention, to be held in Cincinnati* ([dated Anderson, S. C., Nov. 23, 1855] Washington, 1855).

party. Even when the state cast its electoral vote for a party candidate, it had no part in nominating him; from the first Democratic nominating convention in 1832 to the convention of 1852, it was never officially and properly represented by a delegation. An attempt was made during Van Buren's administration to organize a Whig party, but it made little headway. It sent delegations to the national conventions, but it was never a power in the state. South Carolina during the Calhoun era was a state of independent Democrats.[17]

Orr's convention movement developed slowly. In October and November a few newspapers suggested that it would be a good idea to be represented at the next convention, while the *Mercury* and its kin protested vigorously. Congressmen John McQueen, Lawrence Keitt, and W. W. Boyce spoke against the proposal. But all the while James L. Orr was working behind the scenes. Four days before the legislature met, he publicized a letter stating his reasons for wanting to send delegates. Then, while the legislature was in session, he discussed the question with the politicians. The result of Orr's visit to Columbia was a manifesto signed by forty-eight members of the legislature who favored the convention.

As the year 1855 closed it was apparent that there had been little shifting of factional alignments. The Know-Nothing scare had tended to unite the conciliationists and most of the irreconcilables, but this alignment was temporary and soon broke down when the convention issue was raised.

The irreconcilables were still convinced that the antislavery movement in the North was a great danger to the South. They appealed—in vain, they thought—for Southern unity, Southern organization, and Southern resistance to what they called Northern aggression. A few tried to take positive steps by founding a sectional party, but they soon lapsed into inactivity. Discour-

[17] F. W. Pickens wrote to J. C. Calhoun, Dec. 28, 1844: "There are but very few (and none from the Low Country) who can understand or appreciate our relations to any general parties out of the State. They are no more a part of the general Democratic party than if they were out of the Union" (in Jameson [ed.], "The Correspondence of John C. Calhoun," II, 1016-1017).

aged that so many South Carolinians and other Southerners ignored their warnings, they unwillingly stuck to their course of passive resistance. They would keep their faith and await events.[18] Governor James Hopkins Adams, in his November message, spoke the mind of the irreconcilable:

The agitation in relation to slavery continues to increase, and is rapidly tending to its bloody termination. Measures which it was hoped by some would give quiet to the country, and dignity to its deliberations, have served but to redouble the efforts and augment the power of abolition. Civil war is a direful calamity, but its scourges are to be endured in preference to degradation and ruin. The people of South Carolina are alive to the issue, and are mindful of their obligations. They are calm because they are prepared and self-reliant. They have not forgotten their history, and they will not fail to vindicate their teachings. The right "to provide new guards for their future security" has been sealed by the blood of their ancestors, and "they will do their duty and leave the consequences to God."[19]

[18] The Charleston *Mercury*, Aug. 7, 1855, said: "This State has declared that she belongs to no national party; that her duty is sectional; that she waits upon the South to move onward for the common interest. . . . She will bide her time. Until that time comes, she is content to stand apart from all political strife—a silent but busy witness of the truth of Southern rights— the strength of Southern policy—watching, with undimmed eye, and hopeful heart, for the rising into glorious immortality of a Southern Confederacy."

[19] Message of the governor, Nov. 27, 1855, in *House Journal* (1855), p. 30.

It is interesting to note that Governor Adams, while gloomy about the antislavery agitation, was cheerful about economic and health conditions in South Carolina: "Commerce continues to prosper and widen her domain; Agriculture rejoices over full harvests; Labor of every description feels the stimulus of remunerating prices. The year has been one of unexampled health, and our people, in quiet and security, have successfully devoted themselves to their various vocations" (*ibid.*, p. 18).

CHAPTER VI

ISOLATION OR AFFILIATION, 1856

IN THE FIRST QUARTER of 1856 factional alignments
in South Carolina became clearly drawn. Most of the moderates became organized into a well-defined group behind the
movement to send delegates to the national convention. James
L. Orr was generally recognized as the leader of this faction,
although he never claimed any such position. Of the South
Carolina Congressmen, only Preston Brooks, of the Fourth District, actively co-operated with Orr. The two Senators, Andrew
Pickens Butler and Josiah J. Evans, reluctantly gave their endorsement in March, after it became probable that the state
would be represented at the convention. By the end of January
about two thirds of the newspapers in the state were favorable
to the convention.[1]

The main argument of the advocates of the convention was
designed to show that South Carolina should become more
closely associated with the national organization of the Democratic party.[2] The most persuasive appeal was made on the

[1] Darlington *Flag*, Jan. 2, 1856, quoted by the Charleston *Courier*, Jan.
9, 1856, and by the Sumter *Watchman*, Jan. 23, 1856; Cheraw *Gazette*, Feb. 6,
1856; Orangeburg *Southron* (n.d.), quoted by Charleston *Mercury*, April 4,
1856; Edgefield *Advertiser* (n.d.), quoted by Lancaster *Ledger*, March 26,
1856; Spartanburg *Carolina Spartan*, March 20, 1856; pseudonymous writer
["Paul Pry"] in Columbia *Carolina Times*, May 14, 1856. The Lancaster
Ledger, Jan. 30, 1856, published a list of newspapers that favored or opposed
representation in the convention. A list published by the Winnsboro *Register*
(n.d.) and quoted by the Edgefield *Advertiser*, Jan. 23, 1856, differed slightly
from the list published in the *Ledger*.

[2] The summary of the argument in favor of the party convention given
here is based upon: Boucher, "South Carolina and the South on the Eve of
Secession," p. 109; Kibler, *Perry*, pp. 283-284; White, "National Democrats,"
pp. 373-377; Cheraw *Gazette*, Feb. 6, 1856; Darlington *Flag*, Jan. 2, quoted
by Charleston *Courier*, Jan. 9, and Sumter *Watchman*, Jan. 23, 1856; Lancaster *Ledger*, Nov. 21, 1855, Jan. 30, Feb. 6, 13, 1856; Edgefield *Advertiser*, March 12, 19, April 23, 1856; Newberry *Rising Sun* (n.d.), quoted by

ground that the state should sustain Northern friends of the South. In the opinion of South Carolinians, their greatest friend in the North was Franklin Pierce. Hardly a person in the state voiced anything but warm approval for Pierce, and even opponents of affiliation with the party agreed that his policies were more suitable to South Carolina than they had ever expected. The Columbia *Carolina Times,* "against everything and everybody," frequently made disparaging remarks about his administration, but it was alone in its sarcasm. With such universal approval of the President the advocates of the convention were able to call upon the voters' sense of fair play and justice in their efforts to mobilize opinion behind the movement. South Carolinians should do their part in prolonging an administration that they all endorsed. They should join with the rest of the Lower South and bring about the renomination of Pierce. This appeal was sufficiently effective to prompt opponents of the national party to make the counterproposal that a nonpartisan state convention meet and endorse Pierce.

Since many men who agreed that the President deserved the approbation of South Carolina drew a distinction between his administration and the Democratic party, the proponents of the national party had to advance arguments to prove that the party as well as the administration deserved the active and loyal support of the state. First of all, it was necessary to show that

Carolina Times, March 6, 1856; Spartanburg *Carolina Spartan,* March 20, May 22, 1856; Chester *Standard* (n.d.), quoted by Columbia *Carolina Times,* March, 1856; Winnsboro *Register* (n.d.), quoted by Lancaster *Ledger,* Jan. 16, 1856; Columbia *Carolina Times,* Feb. 18, 1856; *The Cincinnati Convention. Letter from James L. Orr, of South Carolina;* P. S. Brooks to W. R. Farley, March 4, 1856, in Lancaster *Ledger,* April 2, 1856; letter by John W. Cooke in Lancaster *Ledger,* Feb. 6, 1856; letter by P. T. Hammond in *Ledger,* Feb. 6, 1856; letter by Wade Hampton, Jr., quoted by Charleston *Mercury,* Feb. 5, 1856; letter by John C. Hope, Jan. 9, in Columbia *Carolina Times,* Jan. 18, 1856; letters by pseudonymous writer ["Malachi"] on "South Carolina Policy" in Charleston *Courier,* Dec. 25, 1855, Jan. 4, 7, 15, 1856; speeches of Francis W. Pickens and James L. Orr, May 5 and 6, at the Democratic state convention, in *Proceedings of the Democratic State Convention of South Carolina, held at Columbia, 5th and 6th of May, 1856, for the purpose of electing delegates to the Democratic National Convention, to meet in Cincinnati in June* (Columbia, 1856), pp. 5-18, 20-26; Augusta [Ga.] *Daily Constitutionalist,* March 8, April 6, 1856.

there were many Northern Democrats and other opponents of the antislavery agitation in the North. James L. Orr assured the people that the entire population had not become abolitionists:

I once thought so myself, but have seen reason to change my views. I recently visited the states of New Hampshire and Connecticut, prior to the election, and I spoke to the people there as I would here. I discussed our rights before them, and I hesitate not to say that nowhere have Southern sentiments met with a heartier response than from the Democracy of those Northern States.[3]

This map shows the proportion of slaves to total population in the three groups of state districts presented in Table I.

Horizontal lines indicate districts with the highest proportion of slaves (from 63 to 85 per cent), perpendicular lines indicate districts with the lowest proportion of slaves (from 21 to 47 per cent), and the unlined districts belong to the intermediate group (from 48 to 60 per cent). The heavy irregular lines define congressional districts; dotted lines separate state districts within congressional districts.

Secondly, these Northern friends were led by Democratic politicians who would stand with the South. So long as men like

[3] *Proceedings of the Democratic State Convention* (1856), p. 24.

FIG. 1.   This graph shows how members of the legislature from three groups of state districts, ranked according to slave population, gave support to the proposal to have South Carolina represented in the national Democratic convention in 1856.

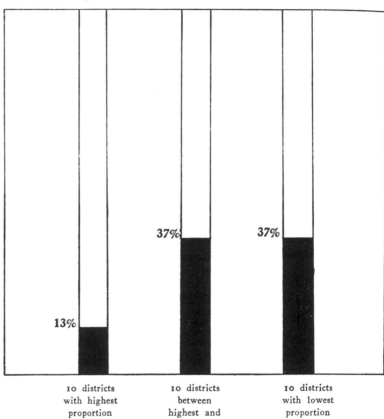

| 10 districts with highest proportion of slaves to population | 10 districts between highest and lowest groups | 10 districts with lowest proportion of slaves to population |

Proportion of members who signed a public pronouncement in favor of representation to the total number of representatives and senators apportioned to the districts comprised in each group.

Cass, Douglas, Shields, Buchanan, Dodge, Richardson, Petit, and Bright fought for the Southern cause, there was a chance of protecting Southern interests in the Union. These men had proved that they were "sound" on the slavery question by repealing the Missouri Compromise line.

TABLE I. DISTRICTS RANKED ACCORDING TO SLAVE POPULATION IN 1860

DISTRICTS WITH HIGHEST PROPORTION OF SLAVES TO POPULATION	Proportion of Slaves to Population	DISTRICTS BETWEEN TWO GROUPS WITH HIGHEST AND LOWEST PROPORTION OF SLAVES TO POPULATION	Proportion of Slaves to Population	DISTRICTS WITH LOWEST PROPORTION OF SLAVES TO POPULATION	Proportion of Slaves to Population
Districts		Districts		Districts	
Georgetown	85	Edgefield	60	Marion	47
Beaufort	81	Richland	60	York	46
Charleston (rural)*	79	Chester	60	Lexington	40
Colleton	77	Kershaw	60	Anderson	37
Fairfield	70	Darlington	58	Chesterfield	37
Sumter†	68	Barnwell	57	Charleston (city)‡	34
Orangeburg	67	Marlborough	55	Greenville	32
Williamsburg	66	Laurens	55	Spartanburg	31
Newberry	66	Union	55	Horry	30
Abbeville	63	Lancaster	48	Pickens	21

*Does not include the two parishes of St. Philip's and St. Michael's.   †Comprises Claremont and Clarendon.   ‡Parishes of St. Philip's and St. Michael's.

SOURCE: Percentages were calculated from data in *Population of the United States in 1860; Compiled from the Original Returns of the Eighth Census, under the Direction of the Secretary of the Interior, by Joseph C. G. Kennedy, Superintendent of the Census* (Washington, 1864), pp. 448-452.

NOTE: The three groups of state districts referred to in the graphs that appear subsequently are those presented in the table above.

Since 1852, when both the secessionists and co-operationists agreed that South Carolina should strive for the unification of the South, one of the chief arguments used by the adherents of the national party was that the state could best become closely associated with the other Southern states through the Democratic party. When there had been a marked opposition to organized ratification of Pierce's nomination, Christopher G. Memminger had defended participation in national party politics on that ground. "Isolation will give neither security nor concert," said James L. Orr. "When we meet Virginia and Georgia, Alabama and Mississippi, in consultation, as at Cincinnati, it is the supremacy of Pharisaism to flippantly denounce such association as either dangerous or degrading."[4] This was, no doubt, an appeal that would be most effective with one-time co-operation secessionists, those men who had felt so keenly the state's isolation from the other slaveholding states. The Edgefield *Advertiser*, which had advocated independent secession in 1851 but which was in a district evenly divided between co-operationists and secessionists, declared that the convention was the best means for South Carolina to secure the good will of the South and to use its influence to promote sectional unity. "For one," said the editor, "we have based our position in this matter, from first to last, mainly upon Southern grounds."[5]

The fact that most of the opponents of the convention were still passive supporters of the Democratic party was helpful to the pro-convention argument. Everyone agreed that the state's electoral votes would go to the Democratic candidate. Why, then, should South Carolina give up the privilege of trying to nominate the man it would vote for? The assailants of the convention retorted: South Carolina is too small; its handful of votes would count for nothing in the convention. Yes, said the conventionists, the delegation would be small, but its votes might be decisive; they might make the difference between victory and defeat for the man they wanted most.

[4] *The Cincinnati Convention, Orr to Dudley, Nov. 23, 1855,* p. 3.
[5] Edgefield *Advertiser*, March 19, 1856.

A minor argument for the convention justified the nominating convention as a political institution. In general, no attempt was made to prove that the party convention was the best method of nominating candidates. Whatever the case for or against this method, said the conventionists, the other states had accepted it long ago, and it was inconceivable that the desires of South Carolina for a different way could prevail in the nation. James L. Orr, in his typical manner, posed the question: "May we not hesitate long before we shall, with self-complacency, say they are all wrong, and we are right?"[6]

South Carolina had remained aloof from the national conventions for so many years that the practice was commonly accepted as a traditional policy. And in South Carolina "a time-honored policy" was something not to be put aside without cautious deliberation. The people of the state prided themselves on their conservatism in adopting political innovations. The other states in the Union had changed their constitutions to make them more popular, but not South Carolina. Other states elected the presidential electors by popular vote, but not South Carolina. And all the other states had taken up the convention method of nominating candidates, but not South Carolina. The affection of the leaders for the old forms was deeply ingrained, and the feeling that the state had maintained a distinctive and characteristic political life superior to that of the other states was widespread. Senators Evans and Butler were hesitant about supporting the convention, because they felt that the movement might lead to a subversion of the old state traditions. Butler would have preferred that South Carolina maintain its "old position," but doubted its ability to stand alone. "The tide of events and the current of popular opinion," he said, "emanating in the North and running to the South, has [*sic*] brought to bear upon us a force which our people cannot, I suppose, resist." Giving his reluctant consent to the convention movement, he ended with a plea: "But in anything that is likely to be done, do not let us de-Carolinaize ourselves."[7]

[6] *The Cincinnati Convention*, p. 4.
[7] Quoted by Columbia *Carolina Times*, March 7, 1856, Sumter *Watchman*, March 12, 1856.

A few leaders associated with the convention movement did not share Senator Butler's exalted feelings of loyalty for the old South Carolina traditions and would have put some of them aside without misgivings. Benjamin F. Perry was perhaps the most outstanding of these men who urged "progressive" changes.[8] Only a few leaders of the convention movement, however, made their appeals in the name of progress. Some, like Francis Pickens, attempted to show that the absence of South Carolina from national conventions had been fortuitous, not calculated. James L. Orr took a simple but practical view: traditions should be kept only if they proved their worth.

Convention leaders made their best bid for support from those people in the state who preferred the Federal Union to a Southern confederacy. Orr and his friends were not Unionists in the Northern sense of the word; they did not feel that their allegiance to the American nation was greater than to their state or section. But they were willing to work with Northerners who opposed the slavery agitation in a last attempt to preserve the Union. The crux of the whole question of disunion to them was the power of the Northern antislavery movement. If the antislavery movement ever became sufficiently popular to place the antislavery party in power, they would join all Southerners in forming a Southern confederacy.

There was one glaring risk implied in this flexible course proposed by the National Democrats. If a triumph for the antislavery party was to bring disunion, the unconditional secessionists might secretly work for the success of that party. And there was an obvious way that the unconditional secessionists could help the antislavery party: they could try to split the national Democratic party. Thus, if the Orr policy was to have a fair trial, it was imperative to strengthen the bond between Northern and Southern Democrats. Since the policy of isolation from national parties tended to weaken that bond, there was all the more reason for everyone who upheld the national Democratic party as a means of preserving the Union to back the convention

[8] For Perry as a "Progressive Reformer," see Lillian Kibler, *Benjamin F. Perry*, pp. 302-313.

movement. The Winnsboro *Register*, in an editorial supporting the convention, said that if all Southern states followed
South Carolina practice, the Democratic party would break up,
the Republicans would win, and dissolution of the Union would
be necessary.[9] In a public letter calling for a meeting in Lancaster to elect delegates to the state convention, John W. Cooke
said that preservation of the Union depended upon the continuation of the national Democratic party: "Have no such
party and array one section against another, and the Union is
already gone, without the formality of a dissolution."[10]

Not all the men who used these impersonal arguments were
unconcerned about the effect of the convention movement upon
their own pursuits. For James L. Orr, who had been in line
for the Speakership for some time, or the local politician who
wanted a postmastership or a clerkship in a government office,
a more hearty participation in the party would surely gain the
preference of the administration. But whatever their motives—
altruistic or selfish—the men who argued for the convention
were constantly accused of being scheming, office-seeking politicians who would sacrifice the interests of the South and the
state for the sake of party success.

The Orr Democrats were perhaps fortunate that the old
secessionists of 1851 were vulnerable to similar attacks. Benjamin F. Perry with delight turned his sarcastic pen against the
convention critics:

We had thought that the game of bluster and brag had been played
often enough in South Carolina. We were under the impression,
too, that so many of the leading disunionists had been put into federal office by President Pierce, that we should have a truce during
the remainder of his Administration. We thought, too, that South

[9] Quoted by the Lancaster *Ledger*, Jan. 16, 1856.
[10] Quoted by Lancaster *Ledger*, Feb. 6, 1856.

James L. Orr wrote in a public letter, July 23, 1860: "My hope, as you
know, for years past for the preservation of the rights of the South in the
Union, has been upon the Democratic party. . . . Its disruption extinguishes
my ardently cherished hope of preserving not only our rights, but the Union
itself" (in Lancaster *Ledger*, Aug. 8, Spartanburg *Carolina Spartan*, Aug. 9,
and Augusta [Ga.] *Daily Constitutionalist*, Aug. 7, 1860).

Carolina would be an administration state out of gratitude for the loaves and fishes bestowed on her fire-eating sons.[11]

Most of the irreconcilables publicly opposed the Orr program. Of the delegation in Congress, John McQueen, Lawrence Keitt, and W. W. Boyce spoke against it. Numerous other prominent leaders, including four men who held the governorship during the fifties, opposed participation in national party politics. The leaders of this faction, with only a few exceptions, had favored separate secession in 1851.[12]

Opponents of the convention could see no advantages from close association with the organization of the national Democratic party. Efforts to sustain Northern friends they looked upon as futile. Pierce was blameless, but they could see little use in trying to get him nominated. First of all, his administration had proved that the South was foolish to try to save itself through the Presidency. Secondly, because he had been friendly to the South and strictly constitutional, he had lost support in the North and all chances for a second term. The other Democratic leaders, while hardly as praiseworthy as Pierce,

[11] Greenville *Southern Patriot* (n.d.), quoted by the Camden *Journal*, Sept. 11, 1855.

[12] The following account of the opposition to the convention movement is based upon these authorities and sources: Boucher, "South Carolina and the South on the Eve of Secession," pp. 109-112; White, *Rhett*, pp. 137-141; Lancaster *Ledger*, Nov. 7, 1855, Jan. 30, 1856; Georgetown *Pee Dee Times*, May 14, quoted by the Columbia *Carolina Times*, May 16, 1856; Georgetown *Pee Dee Times* (n.d.), quoted by the Orangeburg *Southron*, May 21, 1856; Charleston *Evening News*, Oct. 19, 1855, Feb. 16, April 24, 1856; Charleston *Mercury*, Sept. 7, Oct. 30, Nov. 7, Dec. 4, 20, 1855, Jan. 15, 30, Feb. 5, 12, 15, March 4, 5, 11, May 5, 6, 10, 13, 20, June 16, 25, Sept. 27, 1856; Laurensville *Herald* (n.d.), quoted by Charleston *Mercury*, April 1, 1856; Newberry *Mirror* (n.d.), quoted by the Columbia *Carolina Times*, March 3, 1856; Columbia *Carolina Times*, Jan. 2, 8, 12, 16, 18, 19, 23, 30, Feb. 2, 12, 14, 15, 18, 25, 26, 29, March 1, April 11, 15, 16, 29, May 3, 8, 10, 12, 17, 22, 1856; Columbia *South Carolinian* (n.d.), quoted by Charleston *Mercury*, Feb. 5, 1856; Sumter *Watchman*, Nov. 14, 1855, Jan. 30, Feb. 20, March 12, 1856; public letter of John McQueen, Sept. 3, 1855, in Lancaster *Ledger*, Sept. 26, 1855; letter of Dixon Barnes in Lancaster *Ledger*, Feb. 13, 1856; letter of W. C. Cauthen in Lancaster *Ledger*, Feb. 13, 1856; W. W. Boyce to W. S. Lyles, April 7, 1856, in Sumter *Watchman*, April 16, 1856; speech of W. W. Boyce, Nov. 7, 1855, reported in Sumter *Watchman*, Nov. 14, 1855; letter of W. S. Lyles, March 21, 1856, in Charleston *Mercury*, April 2, 1856; pseudonymous writer ["Newberry"] in Columbia *Carolina Times*, Jan. 16, 1856.

were no more capable than the President of protecting Southern interests and rights.

The main argument against the Democratic party was the same that had been current since 1854: it was undependable because it could not withstand the onslaught of the antislavery party. The doctrine of the party was acceptable, but it was ignored in the North. The national party could not command support in the North without betrayal of the South.

The one belief held in common by all the irreconcilables was that the antislavery movement must ultimately triumph in the North. Whereas the National Democrats thought that there was still a chance of defeating the antislavery forces, the irreconcilables saw no hope. The results of the recent elections, the trend of opinion in the press, the crusade against slavery in Northern pulpits, the turmoil in Kansas, and the defeat of the Northern Democrats who voted for the Kansas-Nebraska Act were viewed as unmistakable proof of enduring hostility to slavery and the South.

While denying that there were any advantages to be gained from affiliation with the national party organization, they affirmed that there were grave disadvantages. The state would lose the benefits which had been derived from the traditional policy of isolation from party machinery. By adhering to an independent policy, which gave it great freedom of action, South Carolina had been able to exert an influence in national politics out of proportion to its wealth and resources. A small state, it possessed more influence as an ally than it would have as an integral part of the organization. The unity of the state, which also added to the power of the state in national politics, was attributed to the absence of party contests. In the other Southern states division had arisen because supporters of two parties had organized themselves to obtain federal offices and emoluments. Once South Carolina discarded its traditional policy, it too would be divided like the other states. Furthermore, the traditional aloofness from parties explained why South Carolina leaders had always been more sensitive to the wrongs of the

South and less willing to submit to "Northern aggression." Over and over again, the irreconcilables warned of the corrupting influence of federal patronage. If the state admitted "the Federal Government on the stage, with her tons of gold and her national distinctions," declared W. W. Boyce, "the exclusive devotion to South Carolina" would "be weakened, the star of the State" would "pale before the gorgeous sun of the central system."[13]

Our great object [said a pseudonymous writer in a Columbia newspaper] should be to unite the Southern States in opposition to Northern aggression and this will be impossible so long as our leaders at the South shall engage in the strife for Federal offices and honors. It is this strife for the "spoils" that has, heretofore, rendered the South impotent for self-protection. It has paralyzed the action of every other Southern State except South Carolina. Ours has been the only State that has been prepared to resist encroachments upon our rights. Why has this been so? Because we have kept out of these conventions, whose object is the spoils. We have refused to engage in the corrupting scramble for the Federal patronage. The other Southern States have pursued a different course. Their politicians have been more concerned for the success of national parties than for Southern honor and rights. The result has been, that every effort, heretofore, to unite the South in concerted action has been in vain.[14]

Among the irreconcilables were some of the proudest defenders of the peculiarities of South Carolina. To them the opinions of the outside world counted for little if they subverted the traditional beliefs of the state. The argument that South Carolina should adopt the convention system because other states had done so was regarded as proof of the disloyalty of the conventionists. What was there to justify these conventions? Did they actually express the popular will? And were they authorized by the Constitution? No, the irreconcilables answered, for they were invariably controlled by wirepulling politicians and

---

[13] Speech of W. W. Boyce, Nov. 7, 1855, reported in the Sumter *Watchman*, Nov. 14, 1855.

[14] Letter by pseudonymous writer ["Newberry"] in Columbia *Carolina Times*, Jan. 16, 1856.

were "unlike anything dreamed of by the framers of the Constitution."[15]

Some of the leaders who opposed the convention, like their opponents, were perhaps motivated by something other than patriotism and altruism. If they had no aspirations for federal offices, they were nevertheless eager to preserve an advantage in political power which the state constitution conferred upon them. It so happened that the system of apportioning members of the legislature to the various state districts, which was based upon taxation as well as the white population and which gave a minimum of one state representative and one state senator to the low-country parishes, tended to favor districts where the irreconcilables were particularly strong.[16] The irreconcilables in the favored districts were naturally loath to make certain electoral reforms which had been demanded for several years.[17] Related to these demands for electoral reforms, they became convinced, was the convention movement. Such party conventions seemed to be another trend toward popular government. More important, there was a directly personal connection between the convention and electoral-reform issues. The very same men who wanted to give the upper part of the state representation in the legislature commensurate with its populalation and who wanted to elect the governor and presidential electors by popular vote were taking a prominent part in this movement to associate closely with the national party.[18] These

[15] Charleston *Mercury*, Dec. 29, 1855.

[16] The constitution of the state of South Carolina, amendment ratified Dec. 17, 1808, printed in *The Rules of the House of Representatives and of the Senate of the State of South Carolina; Various Acts and Resolutions, containing Standing Orders of the House; The Constitution of the State of South Carolina, and the Constitution of the United States* (Columbia, 1857), pp. 246-247.

[17] The story of the agitation for electoral reforms in South Carolina is told in monographs by Chauncey Samuel Boucher: "Representation and the Electoral Question in Ante-Bellum South Carolina," *Proceedings of the Mississippi Valley Historical Association for 1915-1916*, IX, 110-125; "Sectionalism, Representation, and the Electoral Question in Ante-Bellum South Carolina," *Washington University Studies*, IV, Part 2, No. 1 (1916), 3-62.

[18] The Charleston *Mercury*, May 10, 1856, said: "The leaders of the Convention movement are the chief agitators for change in our Electoral system. They object to the present mode, that by making the Legislature

"National Democrats" were actually proposing to change the great constitutional compromise of 1808. These men would alter the South Carolina constitution which their leaders had long boasted was a model for all truly representative governments. The living example of Calhoun's famous theory of the concurrent majority was to be discarded in favor of the democratic rule of the numerical majority. South Carolina was to follow the way of all the states—and end like all of them with a government of irresponsible despotic numbers.

The Orr program was not judged upon the single issue of the nominating convention. It was judged on the general question of national political parties. And it was judged on the local question of electoral reform that so many of Orr's lieutenants advocated. Orr's party represented what the irreconcilables despised most. It was a force for nationalizing the state, and it was a force for democratizing the state. The very name "National Democrat," which the irreconcilables used as a term of opprobrium, stood for two aspects of the party which they feared most.

All prominent leaders who believed in the inevitability or desirability of disunion opposed the Orr Democrats. To the unconditional secessionists the national Democratic party was an obstacle to the success of their plans. "It is evident [wrote the editor of the *Carolina Times*] that one of the strongest obstacles in the way of the dissolution of the Union are [*sic*] the bonds of the Democratic party. Disrupt these, and disruption of the Union may follow."[19] Most editors and politicians, however, refrained from making open attempts to break up the Democratic party.

---

appoint the Electors, the voice of the people is silenced in the Presidential election. They clamor loudly for popular elections—they vex the ears of Heaven with maledictions upon all other elections." The Columbia *Carolina Times*, May 10, 1856, said that the convention was supported by those men who had fought against the compromises of the constitution; by those who wanted popular election of presidential electors; by those who wanted to terminate the parish system; by those who wanted to transfer power from the lower and middle country to the mountain section; by those who would elect the governor and other high state officers by popular vote; "by those, in short, who would subvert the present admirable State policy and transform it from a republican representative government to a purely democratic government."

[19] Columbia *Carolina Times*, Feb. 25, 1856.

They merely proposed to sever or minimize the political ties between South Carolina and the federal government and wait for changes in the other Southern states. They were still aware of the difficulty of South Carolina's openly taking the initiative in "resistance" to the North.

We of Carolina [said Congressman John McQueen] have been twice accused of dictating to, and attempting to lead our sister Southern states, in imprudent resistance to Northern aggressions. Others seem now awakened to the impending danger, and it seems to me as clear as mid-day sun that it is our duty to ourselves as well as to the South, that we should eschew everything calculated to disturb our harmony among ourselves, and stand perfectly still, until some of our sisters at least, are ready earnestly, to assume some common ground to secure our rights, in the Confederacy or out of it—as we may be compelled to choose during a contest that is now not far off.[20]

In January the convention question was not much more than a subject for debate. But already Benjamin F. Perry was calling for definite plans for district meetings to select delegates for the state Democratic convention. In February notices of meetings to be held in several districts appeared in the newspapers. On March 3 delegates were appointed by meetings in twelve of the twenty-nine state districts. From the partisan reports of these meetings it is almost impossible to know just what went on. In some of the districts the turnout was so strong that even the opponents conceded success for the convention movement. In several districts rival meetings were held to denounce the self-appointed men who would presume to speak for the state. To a newspaper like the *Carolina Times* these were always attended by large crowds that completely overshadowed the convention meetings.[21]

[20] Public letter of John McQueen, Sept. 3, 1855, in Lancaster *Ledger*, Sept. 26, 1855.
[21] Boucher, "South Carolina and the South on the Eve of Secession," p. 111; Kibler, *Perry*, pp. 283-285; White, "National Democrats," p. 377; Charleston *Mercury*, March 11, April 4, 1856; Newberry *Mirror* (n.d.), quoted by Charleston *Mercury*, April 5, 1856; Greenville *Patriot and Mountaineer* (n.d.), quoted by Columbia *Carolina Times*, Jan. 7, 1856; Columbia *Carolina Times*, Feb. 9, March 5, 6, 8, 10, 11, 24, 1856; Sumter *Watchman*,

Seventeen state districts had failed to appoint delegates to the Columbia convention. Opponents of the convention exulted. What a miserable fiasco! Now perhaps the question would be dropped. But it was not dropped. On March 4, the day after the first elections, Preston Brooks wrote from Washington his regrets that the convention had been defeated in Laurens, one of the state districts in his constituency. A few days later Senator Andrew Pickens Butler came out for the convention; enough had already been done to commit the state to representation, he said. Almost at the same time Senator Josiah Evans took a stand almost identical with Butler's. The pro-convention newspapers did not drop the question, and meetings held in April added district delegations for the Columbia convention.[22]

The state convention met in Columbia May 5 and 6. Delegates from twenty-three of the twenty-nine state districts attended. None of the low-country parishes, outside of Charleston, were represented, but there were men from every congressional district. Francis W. Pickens, wealthy Edgefield planter who had held no public position since his difference with Calhoun in 1846, was chairman of the convention. His address traced the relationship of the state to the national parties since the beginning of the federal government. Of the state policy during Calhoun's regime, he could tell a great deal from his own experiences, for he had served in Congress during most of that era. He denied that the aloofness of the state had been the result of a deliberate policy and claimed that there was no past action of the state which bound it to isolation. So long as South Carolina was in the Union, he favored fulfilling its duties and obligations and protecting its interests. For the future policy of the state he advocated co-operation with a solid South and conservative Northern Democrats to control the federal govern-

March 5, 12, 1856; Augusta [Ga.] *Daily Constitutionalist*, Feb. 24, March 8, 1856; pseudonymous writer ["A"] in Columbia *Carolina Times*, March 27, 1856.

[22] Lancaster *Ledger*, April 16, 1856; Charleston *Mercury*, March 11, 1856; Columbia *Carolina Times*, March 3, 10, April 3, 9, 11, 1856.

ment.   The only alternative to such a policy, he said, was
secession.

James L. Orr spoke on the second day. In his usual matter-
of-fact, plain, common-sense way of arguing, he replied to critics
of the convention, and without any flourishes of an oratorical
trumpet he quietly announced that this meeting would mark a
new era in the politics of South Carolina. Of the possible candidates for the party nomination, Orr said that Pierce and Douglas
were most deserving of South Carolina's support, but Buchanan
would be satisfactory.

Each of the congressional districts nominated two delegates,
and the convention as a whole selected four delegates at large
to attend the Cincinnati convention. The four delegates at large
were Francis W. Pickens, John L. Manning, Andrew G.
Magrath, and J. M. Gadberry. The resolutions adopted by the
convention reaffirmed their belief in State Rights and strict construction of the Constitution, praised the aid of the Democratic
party in removing the Missouri restriction on slavery in the
territories, and promised South Carolina's co-operation in the
convention upon three conditions. These conditions were that
the party platform recognize the Kansas-Nebraska Act, oppose
any future prohibition of slavery in the territories, and support
an enforced fugitive-slave law. Pierce was declared the first
choice for the nomination.[23]

How representative of the state was this convention? There
is no way to measure accurately popular support for the convention. Perhaps the most reliable index of opinion was the stand
of the members of the legislature on the issue. As early as
December, 1855, before the movement was fully under way,
almost 30 per cent of the members of the legislature publicly

[23] Boucher, "South Carolina and the South on the Eve of Secession," pp.
111-112; Kibler, *Perry*, p. 285; Wallace, *History of South Carolina*, III, 141;
White, "National Democrats," pp. 377-378; Edgefield *Advertiser*, May 24,
1856; Spartanburg *Carolina Spartan*, May 22, June 5, 1856; Columbia *Carolina Times*, May 6, 7, 31, 1856; Columbia *South Carolinian* (n.d.), quoted
by the Augusta [Ga.] *Daily Constitutionalist*, May 7, 1856; *Proceedings of
the Democratic State Convention of South Carolina, Held at Columbia, 5th
and 6th of May, 1856, for the Purpose of Electing Delegates to the Democratic National Convention, to Meet in Cincinnati in June* (Columbia, 1856).

signified their support of the convention. Almost a year later, when the legislature met in November to select presidential electors, the vote on a resolution introduced by an anti-convention member, Edward B. Bryan, indicated that the outspoken opponents of the convention were not in the majority in the legislature. A statement to the effect that South Carolina continued "to regard with unchanged disapprobation the system of National Conventions" was approved by only 44 out of 105 members of the House of Representatives.[24]

This map shows the vote on E. B. Bryan's resolution which declared that South Carolina continued to regard with unchanged disapprobation the system of national conventions.

Opposition to the national convention was strongest in the rural districts of the southern division of the state.

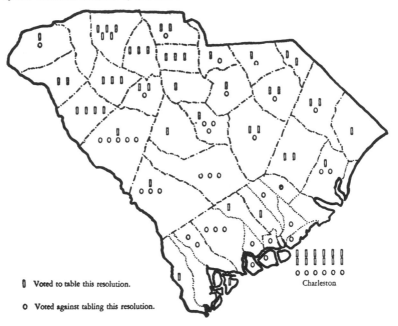

❚ Voted to table this resolution.

O Voted against tabling this resolution.

The convention movement had been organized under unfavorable circumstances. Throughout the first five months of 1856, advocates of the convention had been distracted by the question of Kansas. During that period the same newspapers

[24] *House Journal, Extra Session* (1856), pp. 11-13.

FIG. 2. This graph shows how members of the legislature from three groups of state districts, ranked according to slave population, voted on E. B. Bryan's resolution which declared that South Carolina continued to regard with unchanged disapprobation the system of national conventions.

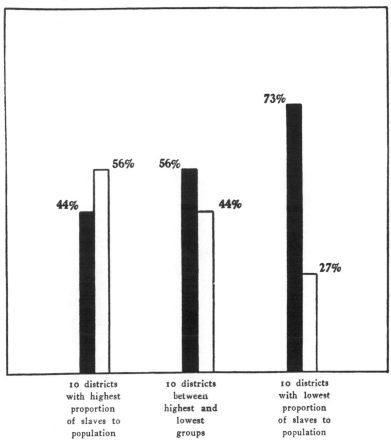

| 10 districts with highest proportion of slaves to population | 10 districts between highest and lowest groups | 10 districts with lowest proportion of slaves to population |

■ Proportion of votes for tabling to total cast by representatives from the districts comprised in each group.

☐ Proportion of votes against tabling to total cast by representatives from the districts comprised in each group.

which discussed the convention question in one column published appeals for emigration to Kansas in another. The same public speakers who argued the question of national parties on one day turned to the Kansas situation the next. Because it divided the attention of the voters and provided more evidence of Northern hostility to slavery and the South, the Kansas agitation tended to create an atmosphere unfavorable to the arguments of the convention leaders.

For the first time, in 1856, emigrant-aid associations were organized for the purpose of sending South Carolinians to Kansas. On this question there was virtually no division of opinion expressed in the state, and politicians and editors representing both factions urged the organization of local Kansas associations. A few self-willed irreconcilables, however, tried to make it appear that the convention Democrats were either indifferent or hypocritical about Kansas. "Simultaneously with appeals for Kansas," said the *Mercury,* "have gone forth appeals for National parties and the Union. With what earnestness could they credit him, who, in one breath, summoned them to a sectional war in Kansas, and a National Caucus at Cincinnati? Kansas and the National Democracy—Sectionalism and Nationalism—Slavery and Abolitionism—how could there be a common sympathy in such opposing extremes?"[25] Edward Britton's *Carolina Times* accused Orr of serving the national party in Northern states when he should be in South Carolina encouraging emigration to Kansas.[26] At a meeting of the Columbia Kansas association, James D. Tradewell, an irreconcilable of the same brand as Britton, mercilessly attacked Orr and his followers in a speech on Kansas.[27]

Kansas became bloody in 1856.[28] In the winter of 1855-1856 it was too cold to do much fighting, but in the spring hostilities were renewed. The proslavery people were determined to put a stop to the unauthorized government of the free-state

[25] Charleston *Mercury,* Feb. 22, 1856.

[26] Columbia *Carolina Times,* Feb. 14, 26, April 19, 1856.

[27] Speech of James D. Tradewell, March 22, 1856, reported in the Columbia *Carolina Times,* March 27, 1856; letter by James D. Tradewell in Columbia *Carolina Times,* April 24, 1856; pseudonymous writer ["Brutus"] in *ibid.,* May 6, 1856.

[28] The story of Kansas in 1856 given here is based upon these authorities: Craven, *Coming of Civil War,* pp. 361-367; Milton, *Douglas,* pp. 198-200, 220; Nichols, *Pierce,* pp. 441-445, 464-465, 473-483; Randall, *Civil War,* pp. 137-138; Rhodes, *History of the United States,* II, 150-167, 216-217, 229-230; Schouler, *History of the United States,* V, 342-346, 357-359; Smith, *Parties and Slavery,* pp. 149-151, 154-156, 160, 164-166, 173.

settlers. The framers of the Topeka constitution, equally determined to carry on their government, elected a state legislature,
governor, two United State Senators, and applied for admission
into the Union. The proslavery forces retaliated through the
judiciary: the leaders of the free-state government were indicted
by the United States District Court for treason. Coercive measures soon followed this indictment. On May 21 the local sheriff
and the federal marshal led a posse of some eight hundred
men into the city of Lawrence, where the rank and file of the
invaders, not so scrupulous about the rights of private property
as some of their leaders, burned down the Free State Hotel,
destroyed the printing presses, terrorized the citizens, and
burned the home of the free-state leader Charles Robinson.
Although little blood was actually shed, this "sack of Lawrence"
was to lead to a real massacre. On the night of May 24 mad
John Brown and a small band of his followers took revenge by
cold-bloodedly murdering five men who sympathized with the
proslavery party. From this time until September, Kansas was
in a state of constant turmoil; bands of partisans carried on
incessant guerilla warfare, and peaceful pursuits came to a
standstill.

Indifferent in 1854, calmly concerned in 1855, South Carolina in 1856 at last became excited about the fate of Kansas.[29]

[29] The account of the emigrant-aid movement in 1856 given here is based
upon the following authorities and sources: Boucher, "South Carolina and the
South on the Eve of Secession," p. 99; Walter F. Fleming, "The Buford
Expedition to Kansas," *American Historical Review*, VI (Oct., 1900), 38-48;
Lancaster *Ledger*, Feb. 27, April 2, 23, May 28, June 18, 25, July 9, 16, 23,
1856; Marion *Star* (n.d.), quoted by Columbia *Carolina Times*, Feb. 28,
1856; Georgetown *Pee Dee Times* (n.d.), quoted by *Carolina Times*, March
15, 1856; Charleston *Courier*, Jan. 23, 30, Feb. 25, 26, March 28, April 2,
11, May 24, 1856; Charleston *Mercury*, Feb. 14, 16, 22, 27, March 13-15,
31, June 13, Nov. 4, 1856; Edgefield *Advertiser*, March 26, Aug. 13, Sept.
17, 1856; Winnsboro *Register* (n.d.), quoted by the Columbia *Carolina Times*,
April 4, 1856; *Carolina Times*, Jan. 24, 28, 29, Feb. 1, 9, 14, 22, 26, 28,
March 4, 6, 8, 18-20, 24-29, April 11, 12, 18, 19, 28, May 6, 13, June
12-14, 27, 1857; Sumter *Watchman*, Jan. 30, Feb. 6, 27, April 23, May 7,
June 9, 11, July 30, Aug. 6, 13, 20, 1856; J. W. Whitfield to James Chesnut,
March 18, 1856, in *Carolina Times*, April 3, 1856; Joseph P. Carr to Wil-
liam Whaley, March 25, 1856, in Charleston *Courier*, April 13, 1856; D. R.
Atchison to D. F. Jamison, April 25, 1856, in Orangeburg *Southron*, May 21,
1856; A. J. Frederick to D. F. Jamison, May 29, 1856, in Orangeburg

The first phase of a movement to send South Carolinians to Kansas was a campaign of appeals in the newspapers. Soon afterwards Congressmen McQueen, Keitt, Brooks, and Boyce in public letters called attention to the critical importance of Kansas to the South. Then prominent citizens or political leaders offered gifts of money to aid emigrants from the state. Here and there, in several districts, unknown but adventuresome young men advertised their desire to lead bands of knights-errant to the Kansas battleground. From February to August meetings were held in most districts to organize local Kansas associations with the purpose of promoting emigration. The enlistment of volunteers was easy; the collection of money, difficult. No great exodus took place, but groups of from ten to thirty men trickled out of the state in the months of March, April, and May. Two weeks before the sack of Lawrence, more than fifty South Carolinians were encamped at Atchison, awaiting their marching orders. Young, brave, confident, they pledged their lives to a Southern victory in the impending battle.[30] The day before the invasion of Lawrence they knew well the objectives of their mission. "In a day or two [wrote E. B. Bell, leader of the South Carolina contingent] we will visit Lawrence and demand certain arms and men. The fortifications and stone hotel (built as a fort) are to be demolished, and the printing offices destroyed; private property will be protected."[31]

In late June and early July, when letters from the emigrants appeared in the newspapers, South Carolina came to know of the heroic deeds of its fighters.[32] One of them wrote:

Southron, June 18, 1856; W. F. Beard to E. H. Britton and Company, May 2, 1856, in Columbia *Carolina Times*, May 19, 1856; pseudonymous writer ["Hampden"] in Charleston *Courier*, June 30, 1856; *Congressional Globe*, 34 Cong., 1 Sess., Appendix, p. 370.

[30] Correspondence from Atchison, Kansas Territory, May 7, 1856, in Charleston *Courier*, May 26, 1856.

[31] Letter from E. B. Bell, May 20, 1856, in Charleston *Courier*, June 4, 1856.

[32] *Ibid.*; A. J. Frederick to D. F. Jamison, May 29, 1856, in Orangeburg *Southron*, June 18, 1856; letter from F. G. P., June 4, 1856, in Charleston *Courier*, June 21, 1856; D. G. Fleming to W. F. De Saussure, June 9, 1856, in *Courier*, June 25, 1856; letter from pseudonymous writer ["D"], June

South Carolina has just cause to feel proud of her sons out here, as they are playing havoc with the abolitionists, and are a terror wherever they go. They are termed by Parson Butler, a rabid abolitionist, in a communication to the "Herald of Freedom," shortly after being tarred and feathered by them, "South Carolina-blood hounds." The Palmetto flag was the first that waved triumphantly on the Hotel and Printing offices in Lawrence, during the late siege—it was planted there by order of Capt. De Treville.[33]

But all was not glory in Kansas. Life and property were in constant danger, and the men who had come from Charleston, many of whom had been clerks, were helpless on this rowdy frontier. A group of fifty laid plans to settle in Marshall County and to found a town to be called Palmetto City, but they had no farming equipment, and many of the men had already spent all their money. On May 29 they decided to send Warren D. Wilkes back to the state to seek help. In his home state in June, Wilkes, a young man and comparatively unknown, knew that he could expect to accomplish nothing "unless aided by gentlemen of prominence and influence." These gentlemen, whom he addressed in a number of meetings all over the state, applauded the bravery of the South Carolinians in the "battle of Lawrence," cursed the vile abolitionist murderers, agreed that Kansas was a vital outpost in the defense of slavery, but they offered little in the way of financial assistance.[34]

The Kansas-aid movement, in spite of continuous propaganda, received even less support in the summer months than

9, 1856, quoted from *Carolina Times* by *Courier*, June 25, 1856; letter from Frank F., May 8, 1856, in *Courier*, May 30, 1856; letter by a Charlestonian, May 13, 1856, condensed in *Courier*, May 30, 1856.

[33] Pseudonymous writer ["Wanderer"] in Lancaster *Ledger*, July 2, 1856.

[34] Charleston *Courier*, June 17, 19, 1856; Charleston *Mercury*, June 21, 1856; Columbia *Carolina Times*, June 26, 1856; Sumter *Watchman*, June 25, 1856; D. G. Fleming to W. F. De Saussure, June 9, 1856, in Charleston *Courier*, June 25, 1856; F. G. P., June 4, 1856, in *Courier*, June 21, 1856; J. W. Harrison to John Cunningham, June 14, 1856, quoted from the Charleston *Evening News* (n.d.), by *Courier*, June 19, 1856; Warren D. Wilkes to John Cunningham, June 13, 1856, quoted from *Evening News* (n.d.), by *Courier*, June 19, 1856; letter by James Simons, June 23, 1856, in *Courier*, June 25, 1856; Warren D. Wilkes to James Simons, June 22, 1856, in *Courier*, June 25, 1856.

in the spring. Atrocity stories, which became sensational after May, made little difference. The Sumter *Watchman,* in June, told how antislavery settlers were guilty of "brutal and savage murdering," of "disgraceful and inhuman treatment of the families of the pro-slavery settlers, and destruction of their homes and property."[35]   But it also told a revealing story of a recent Kansas meeting in the district: "The last meeting, comparatively, was sparse, many, very many of our most wealthy and patriotic planters being absent, doubtless from the business of the season."[36]   The Spartanburg *Carolina Spartan* reported on July 19: "Efforts have and are still being made to send forward emigrants, but there is little heart in the movement. They have been more the result of local excitement than the convictions of a political necessity, and hence the means have only been adequate to the bare defrayal of needful expense of travel. Men give grudgingly—only as charity."

The conduct of the movement to send aid to Kansas was typical of South Carolina in the 1850's. The leadership was more apt at eloquent and direful exhortations than the irksome details of administration. The organization was informal, irregular, and decentralized. The need for a co-ordination of the separate district associations was recognized, but nothing was ever done to create a central agency through a state convention, as was proposed several times.

Over and over the citizens of the state had been told by politicians, publicists, and even preachers that a victory in Kansas was of critical importance to all the slaveholding states.[37]

[35] Sumter *Watchman,* June 18, 1856.

[36] *Ibid.,* June 11, 1856.

[37] Lancaster *Ledger,* Feb. 27, May 28, July 2, Aug. 27, Sept. 24, 1856; Darlington *Flag* (n.d.), quoted by Lancaster *Ledger,* April 23, 1856; Charleston *Courier,* Jan. 23, 1856; Charleston *Mercury,* Feb. 14, 16, 22, June 3, 1856; Orangeburg *Southron* (n.d.), quoted by Columbia *Carolina Times,* March 4, 1856; Edgefield *Advertiser* (n.d.), quoted by *Carolina Times,* Feb. 22, 1856; Winnsboro *Register* (n.d.), quoted by *Carolina Times,* April 4, 1856; Columbia *Carolina Times,* Jan. 24, 29, Feb. 9, 14, 26, 1856; Sumter *Watchman,* Feb. 27, 1856; T. J. Withers to James Chesnut, Feb. 29, 1856, in Lancaster *Ledger,* April 2, 1856; resolutions adopted at a public meeting at Sumter Court House, in Sumter *Watchman,* May 7, 1856.

Their "social as well as political existence" depended upon preventing antislavery control of Kansas. The outcome of the Kansas struggle would settle the question of the union or disunion for years to come. The "issue about to be made in Kansas and forced" upon them by "an unholy crusade and northern agrarianism" portended "imminent peril" to their institutions. If they did not win this battle, more "overt acts of wanton aggression" would follow and "should be instantly met by open, bold and unflinching resistance." If this antislavery aggression were permitted to continue, slave property would become worthless. Kansas was merely the first step in a campaign to abolish slavery in all the states. After Kansas would come Missouri, then Kentucky, and one by one all the other Southern states. "If abolitionism be successful in Kansas," declared the *Carolina Spartan*, "we believe the battlefield of Southern rights will be brought to our own doors in less years than the life of man."[38] The loss of Kansas to the South would be "a defeat more disastrous and humiliating than any that she has ever yet sustained," declared the Lancaster *Ledger*; it would give an "incentive to Northern fanaticism and aggression, that the South, dispirited and groaning under a sense of ignoble defeat, may never be enabled to check."[39]

The men who spoke these words gave no clear exposition of what could be accomplished by emigration. Their talk about planting slavery in Kansas was mostly gasconade. For two years they had expressed the belief that slavery could not thrive in that territory. But if few of them expected to establish permanent slavery in the territory, many of them sincerely believed that they could make Kansas a slave state. A grasp of the distinction between introducing slaveholders with slaves and slaveholders and their friends without slaves is essential to an understanding of the objectives of the South Carolinians. They realized that few owners would take their valuable slaves from the stability and security of the Southern states to a less desirable territory populated by avowed enemies of their property.

[38] Spartanburg *Carolina Spartan*, June 19, 1856.
[39] Lancaster *Ledger*, July 16, 1856.

They thought, however, that ambitious and adventuring young men in the South who owned no slaves would gladly go to the territory and stay at least long enough to bring it into the Union without any prohibition against slavery. They were right in their calculations to the extent that the enlistment of volunteers proved easy enough. But they failed to see that the South could not finance through charity alone an army of occupation in a distant land.

What did South Carolina hope to gain from making Kansas a slave state? Most of the leaders wanted to prevent another "victory" of the antislavery movement. Their frame of mind was one of defense against an aggressor.

Every new slave state [John Cunningham said] is at once a political and moral addition either to the relative strength or separate power of the South, and whether the end be union or disunion, such addition is of vital consideration to her. In a political view, extension on its outer limits is to slavery what strategic lines and posts are to an army in a campaign.[40]

It was as a barrier that Kansas was important.

It saves [said the *Mercury*] Missouri from becoming the prey of Abolition; and, therefore, in contending for its settlement by the South, we are not contending merely for the extension of slavery to a new country, which is a matter of trifling importance in itself, but for its protection where it already exists, which is a matter of vital importance.[41]

The Kansas question was the major topic for discussion in Congress this year. The excited debate that took place was essentially a part of the presidential campaign, for hardly a move was made by the politicians without first considering what the effects would be on their parties. Before May 20 South Carolina did not play a prominent part in the debates. On March 5 A. P. Butler, in the Senate, delivered an address on Kansas, and W. W. Boyce, in the House, the next day, spoke on the contested seat of the territorial delegate. In early April

[40] Quoted in Charleston *Courier*, March 15, 1856.
[41] Charleston *Mercury*, Feb. 5, 1856.

Butler made some brief remarks against receiving the petition of the so-called territorial legislature for admission into the Union under the Topeka constitution.[42]

After May 20 no member of the South Carolina delegation could remain inconspicuous. On that day Charles Sumner, Republican Senator from Massachusetts, finished a speech on the Kansas situation. Unfortunately for those who desired peace and good will between the sections, his declamation included some provocative aspersions upon the character of South Carolina and one of its Senators. The honor of South Carolina was a precious thing; it was always dangerous for any man to attack it.

Forty-five years old, six feet four in height, scholarly, urbane, Charles Sumner was in 1856 the most eloquent orator for the antislavery cause.[43] He had been one of the leaders of the Free-Soil party when it was first organized in Massachusetts in 1848. Since December, 1851, he had been in the Senate, where he had early attracted the attention of Southern Senators by his opposition to the fugitive-slave law. In 1854, at the time of the debate on the Kansas-Nebraska Bill, he had gained a reputation in the South as the most obnoxious representative of the antislavery party in Congress. In June, 1854, Sumner had been incensed by—and apparently did not forget—some spirited and caustic remarks addressed to him by A. P. Butler.[44]

Sumner had already assumed a leading role in organizing the Republican party when he made his speech on Kansas. He spoke at a time when passions were at a boiling point; the day after he concluded his speech, the proslavery forces stormed the headquarters of the free-state men in Lawrence. The composition and delivery of the speech were perfected before he walked into the Senate on May 19. Sumner knew that he had concocted an explosive oration. He was going, he promised, to pronounce

[42] *Congressional Globe,* 34 Cong., 1 Sess., pp. 584-587, 826, 847-848, Appendix, pp. 118-122, 382.

[43] Biographical sketch of Sumner by George H. Haynes in *Dictionary of American Biography,* XVIII, 208-214.

[44] *Congressional Globe,* 34 Cong., 1 Sess., p. 1404.

"the most thorough philippic ever uttered in a legislative body."[45]

In speaking on "The Crime Against Kansas," Sumner displayed his great knowledge of literature and ancient history.[46] Figures of speech drawn from great writers of all the ages were used to describe the horrors of the proslavery party and the noble virtues of the free-soil settlers. Hour after hour he poured out an unending stream of epithets, allusions, and metaphors in condemnation of the "Slave Power" which had raped "a virgin territory." Over and over again Sumner made his attacks, always embellished with the tinsel of learning and erudition, against the indecencies, sinfulness, wickedness, and degeneracy of the leaders of the Southern "slavocracy." Had his speech contained no specific accusations against personalities in the Senate, it would have been sufficiently provocative to stir the wrath of Southerners and Democrats; but Sumner took as illustrations of the perfidious and iniquitous influence of the "slave power" Stephen A. Douglas, David R. Atchison, and Andrew P. Butler.

After charging that Douglas and Butler had "raised themselves to eminence, on this floor in championship of human wrongs," Sumner turned upon the latter with a suggestive metaphor:

The Senator from South Carolina has read many books of chivalry, and believes himself a chivalrous knight, with sentiments of honor and courage. Of course he has chosen a mistress to whom he has made his vows, and who, though ugly to others, is always lovely to him; though polluted in the sight of the world, is chaste in his sight—I mean the harlot, slavery. For her, his tongue is always profuse in words. Let her be impeached in character, or any proposition be made to shut her out from the extension of her wantonness, and no extravagance of manner or hardihood of assertion is then too great for this Senator. The frenzy of Don Quixote, in behalf of his wench Dulcinea del Toboso, is all surpassed.[47]

[45] Edward L. Pierce, *Memoir and Letters of Charles Sumner* (3 vols.; London, 1878-1893), III, 439.

[46] The text of Sumner's speech is in the *Congressional Globe*, 34 Cong., 1 Sess., Appendix, pp. 529-544.

[47] *Ibid.*, p. 530.

Butler, who consistently refrained from making public appeals to Southern sectional feelings, was branded "the uncompromising, unblushing representative of a flagrant *sectionalism*," one of the "maddest zealots" of "tyrannical sectionalism."[48] On the second day, the subject of Sumner's malice was a vocal affliction of Butler:

> With regret I come upon the Senator from South Carolina, who omnipresent in this debate, overflowed with rage at the simple suggestion that Kansas had applied for admission as a State; and with incoherent phrases, discharged the loose expectoration of his speech, now upon her representative, and then upon her people. There was no extravagance of the ancient parliamentary debate which he did not repeat; nor was there any possible deviation from truth which he did not make, with so much passion, I am glad to add, as to save him from the suspicion of intentional aberration. But the Senator touches nothing which he does not disfigure—with error, sometimes of principle, sometimes of fact.[49]

To most Southerners and Democrats and many observers in Washington, Sumner's speech was reprehensible and unnecessarily provocative. To South Carolinians, traditionally sensitive to criticism of their state, such a speech required some form of reply. Sumner had not only slurred their Revolutionary history, which someone in the delegation had always jumped to the floor to defend; he had also attacked their senior Senator, who was then absent from the capital and unable to come to his own defense.

Summoned to the Senate while Sumner was speaking was a man who was destined to assume responsibility for replying to this wanton assault upon the South Carolina Senator.[50] That man was Preston Brooks, nephew of Butler and Congressman from the same district in which his uncle resided. Brooks, an ordinary politician of the South Carolina of his generation, was related to prominent families in his district, had gone to the

[48] *Ibid.*

[49] *Ibid.*, p. 543.

[50] Speech of A. P. Butler, June 14, 1856, in *Congressional Globe*, 34 Cong., 1 Sess., Appendix, p. 632.

South Carolina College, and had served in the Mexican War. In his early youth he had fought a duel in which he had suffered a severe wound.[51]

No firebrand, Brooks cordially supported the Pierce administration and was closely associated with James L. Orr in the movement to affiliate the state with the national organization of the Democratic party. During his first session in Congress, in 1854, he had been criticized in South Carolina for repudiating sectionalism, and his connection with the Orr group had evoked further adverse criticism of his conduct. He had come to Congress, in December, 1855, feeling that he had been "taunted" in his home state for being "a little too national."[52]

Brooks was also troubled by "excessively bad" health. On May 19, the day Sumner began his speech, a Columbia newspaper reported that he had a liver disorder and that travel had been recommended for him by his doctor.[53]

Brooks left the Senate on May 20 conscious of his duty to vindicate the honor of himself, his kinsman, and his constituents. For the next two days, wherever he went in Washington, on the streets, in the drawing rooms, at the dinner table, his friends and colleagues asked:

"Has the chivalry of South Carolina escaped, and is this to be tame submission?" When this question was asked, Brooks felt that if something was not done he could not face his constituents without losing his usefulness and without there being a taunt on his honor and courage.[54]

[51] Biographical sketch of Preston Smith Brooks by James Elliott Walmsley, in *Dictionary of American Biography*, III, 88; account of Brooks's life by Ben Lane in the Montgomery [Ala.] *Mail*, quoted by Lancaster *Ledger*, June 25 and by Augusta [Ga.] *Daily Constitutionalist*, June 12, 1856; Charleston *Courier*, Jan. 29, Feb. 6, 1857; obituary of Brooks in Charleston *Evening News*, Jan. 30, 1857, quoted by Augusta [Ga.] *Daily Constitutionalist*, Feb. 4, 1857; speech of Lawrence Keitt, Jan. 29, 1857, in *Congressional Globe*, 34 Cong., 1 Sess., p. 501; speech of Josiah J. Evans, Jan. 29, 1857, *ibid.*, pp. 499-500.

[52] *Congressional Globe*, 34 Cong., 1 Sess., p. 77.

[53] Columbia *Carolina Times*, May 19, 1856. The Augusta [Ga.] *Daily Constitutionalist*, May 27, 1856, quoted a comment on Brooks's health from Newberry *Mirror* (n.d).

[54] Speech of A. P. Butler, June 13, 1856, in *Congressional Globe*, 34 Cong., 1 Sess., Appendix, pp. 630-631.

That he must do something, Brooks did not question. But what? A challenge? Such a course would be a cheap form of bravery, since there was little likelihood that Sumner would accept, and would subject him "to legal penalties more severe than would be imposed for a simple assault and battery."[55] Sumner must be chastised. But how and where? Brooks deliberated as to whether he should employ a horsewhip or a cowhide, but at length decided to use a gutta percha cane.[56] After failing to meet Sumner on the Capitol grounds, he went to the Senate, where, at the close of a short session on the morning of May 22, he found Sumner at his desk absorbed in his correspondence. He walked to Sumner's seat and said: "Mr. Sumner, I have read your speech with care and as much impartiality as was possible and I feel it my duty to tell you that you have libeled my State and slandered a relative who is aged and absent and I am come to punish you for it."[57] With these words concluded, he struck Sumner repeatedly with his cane. "Every lick went where I intended it," Brooks wrote to his brother. "For about the first five or six licks he offered to make fight but I plied him so rapidly that he did not touch me. Towards the last he bellowed like a calf. I wore my cane out completely but saved the Head which is gold."[58]

The news of this assault created a sensation in Washington. Republicans, already aroused by the sack of Lawrence, were enraged. Southerners idolized Brooks as a conquering hero. The fragments of his broken cane were "begged for as *sacred* relics."[59] A week after the event Lawrence Keitt wrote: "The feeling is pretty much sectional. If the northern men had

[55] *Ibid.*, p. 632; speech of Preston Brooks, July 14, 1856, *ibid.*, pp. 831-833.

[56] Speech of Brooks, *ibid.*, Appendix, p. 832.

[57] Preston S. Brooks to J. H. Brooks, May 23, 1856, quoted by C. S. Boucher, "South Carolina and the South on the Eve of Secession," pp. 114-115.

[58] *Ibid.*

[59] *Ibid.*; Washington correspondence, May 23, 1856, in Charleston *Courier*, May 26, 1856; Washington correspondence of New York *Herald*, May 22, 1856, quoted by Memphis [Tenn.] *Daily Appeal*, May 31, 1856; New York correspondence, May 24, 1856, in Charleston *Courier*, May 27, 1856.

stood up, the city would now float with blood. The fact is the feeling is wild and fierce. The Kansas fight has just occurred and the times are stirring. Everybody here feels as if we are upon a volcano."[60]

As the date for the two national conventions approached, the Brooks-Sumner incident was a constant source of controversy in Congress. Speech after speech was made in both houses. Opinon was drawn on sectional and party lines. Democrats and Southerners stressed the provocation of the act and said that Sumner had wantonly abused his senatorial privilege by saying in the Senate what he dared not to say elsewhere for fear of retribution. Republicans, ignoring Sumner's aspersions, said that "Bully Brooks" had brutally attacked a Senator because he dared to speak out for liberty and freedom in Kansas.[61]

The antislavery feeling received a new stimulus. Brooks's cold-blooded manner overshadowed the attending circumstances which had provoked the act. The Congressman who beat Sumner, in the opinion of many Northerners, was a brutish bully, who exemplified the leaders of the Southern "slave power." Republican politicians, with success, appealed to Northern voters not to support the presidential candidate of the party of Southern bullies.[62]

In South Carolina kinsfolk, neighborhood, electorate, officialdom, and press with unbroken solidarity stood behind Brooks. His wife was glad that he had chastised the abolitionist and told him that she would willingly accept any penalty which the act might incur.[63] A matronly lady of his district wrote to him that the ladies of the South would be pleased to send him hickory sticks with which to chastise abolitionists and Republicans.[64] From every part of the state he received token gifts, such as

---

[60] Lawrence Keitt to Sue Sparks, May 29, 1856 (Duke University Library).

[61] Craven, *Coming of Civil War*, pp. 368-370; Milton, *Douglas*, pp. 235-237; Randall, *Civil War*, p. 140; Rhodes, *History of the United States*, II, 143-148; Joseph Carlyle Sitterson, *The Secession Movement in North Carolina* (Chapel Hill, 1939), pp. 121-122; Smith, *Parties*, pp. 158-160.

[62] Milton, *Douglas*, p. 231.

[63] Lawrence Keitt to Sue Sparks, June 8, 1856 (Duke University Library).

[64] Columbia *South Carolinian* (n.d.), quoted by the Memphis [Tenn.] *Daily Appeal*, June 6, 1856.

canes, sticks, pitchers, and goblets.[65]   His constituents in Newberry held the first meeting in the state to demonstrate approval
of their Representative.   The people at this meeting told the
state and the nation why they approved the action of Brooks:

> Our Senators and Representatives in Congress have for a series
> of years patiently submitted to these tirades of calumny and vitupera-
> tion, and they have in vain attempted to meet insults by argument
> and reason.   We were not surprised, therefore, that the spirit of
> resentment should break forth into acts of violence.   Ordinarily we
> might not be ready to justify such measures of redress, but the
> aggravated insults given by the Senator from Massachusetts on the
> occasion referred to, in keeping with his uniform conduct, furnish
> an ample justification of our Representative.[66]

Later similar gatherings met in many districts of the state.[67]
By July 12 every member of the delegation in Congress had
spoken in his defense.   Newspapers, without regard to their
political leanings, congratulated him.[68]   When he came back to

[65] Charleston *Courier*, May 30, June 17, 1856; Columbia *Carolina Times*,
June 15, 1856; Columbia *South Carolinian* (n.d.), quoted by Spartanburg
Carolina Spartan, Oct. 9, 1856; P. S. Brooks to W. W. Boyce, July 15, 1856,
in Sumter *Watchman*, Aug. 13, 1856.

[66] Newberry *Mirror* (n.d.), quoted by Memphis [Tenn.] *Daily Appeal*,
June 3, 1856.

The meeting was held Saturday evening, May 24.   Proceedings of this
meeting were also reported in Columbia *Carolina Times*, May 27, 1856, and
the Lancaster *Ledger*, June 4, 1856.

[67] Lancaster *Ledger* (n.d.), quoted by Columbia *Carolina Times*, June 7,
1856; Lancaster *Ledger*, June 4, 1856; Darlington *Flag* (n.d.), quoted by
Carolina Times, June 6, 1856; Charleston *Courier*, May 30, June 4, 1856;
Charleston *Evening News*, May 28, 1856; Abbeville *Banner* (n.d.), quoted
by *Carolina Times*, June 6, 1856; Winnsboro *Register* (n.d.), quoted by
Carolina Times, May 30, 1856; Chester *Standard* (n.d.), quoted by *Carolina
Times*, June 13, 1856; Columbia *South Carolinian*, May 23, 1856, quoted by
Charleston *Courier*, May 28, 1856; Columbia *Carolina Times*, May 28-31,
June 5, 14, 1856; pseudonymous writer ["M"] in Orangeburg *Southron*,
July 2, 1856.

[68] Lancaster *Ledger*, May 28, 1856; Charleston *Evening News*, May 28,
June 6, 13, 1856; Charleston *Mercury*, July 25, Oct. 7, 1856; Orangeburg
Southron, May 28, June 4, 18, 1856; Edgefield *Advertiser*, May 28, July 23,
Aug. 13, 1856; Spartanburg *Carolina Spartan*, May 29, June 5, July 17, 24,
Aug. 7, 1856; Greenville *Patriot and Mountaineer* (n.d.), quoted by *Carolina
Times*, June 2, 1856; Columbia *Carolina Times*, May 24, 26, June 6, 1856;
Columbia *South Carolinian* (n.d.), quoted by Memphis [Tenn.] *Daily Appeal*,
June 6, 1856; Sumter *Watchman*, July 30, Oct. 1, 1856; Augusta [Ga.]
Daily Constitutionalist, June 5, 1856.

South Carolina after the adjournment of Congress, he was feted with numerous banquets and dinners.[69]

The Brooks-Sumner episode increased the hostility of South Carolinians toward those people whom they had begun this year to call Black Republicans. The irreconcilables, however, were most rabid in their declarations of the significance of the affair. Was this not the last word in the argument that South Carolina could no longer expect peace, security, and honor in the Union? Did it not disprove the basic argument of the National Democrats and other compromisers?

We have heard [said the Sumter *Watchman*, August 6, 1856] a great deal from certain quarters about the conservatism still existing in the North, and about the decline and want of respectability of Abolitionism among the thinking people of that region—but if the Representatives of a people are any index of their feelings and opinions, then the North is rotten to the core, and our only hope of peace, quiet and prosperity is to dissolve the partnership and set up for ourselves.

If Brooks provided the opponents of national parties with an argument, he nevertheless enabled the convention Democrats to present the state with a hero. Brooks was the most publicized man in South Carolina in the summer of 1856, and so long as he remained loyal to the national party, it was not likely that the irreconcilables would reap immediate advantage from the episode. Indeed, it is possible that the National Democrats derived more immediate benefit than their opponents from Brooks's act. At least Brooks did not have to be "taunted" with the charge that he was "a little too national." Yet, in the long run, the effect of the caning was probably harmful to the primary aim of the convention Democrats. In so far as the Brooks-Sumner episode contributed to the growth of the Republican party, it moved them closer to the condition that they had

[69] Charleston *Mercury*, Oct. 7, 1856; Edgefield *Advertiser*, Aug. 27, Sept. 17, 1856; Spartanburg *Carolina Spartan*, Sept. 25, 1856; Columbia correspondence, Oct. 7, in *Carolina Spartan*, Oct. 9, 1856; Columbia *South Carolinian*, Oct. 4, quoted by Spartanburg *Carolina Spartan*, Oct. 9, 1856; Sumter *Watchman*, Oct. 1, 1856.

declared would cause them to abandon co-operation with Northern friends and seek security in a Southern confederacy.

Eleven days after Brooks caned Sumner, the Democratic convention met in Cincinnati. The South Carolina delegates, with little expectation of success, voted on the first fourteen ballots for Franklin Pierce, undoubtedly the first choice of their constituents. Douglas was perhaps the second choice for most voters in the state, and he had especially strong support from certain leaders of the convention movement. On the fifteenth and sixteenth ballots South Carolina followed the last of the Pierce supporters in a switch to Douglas. After the sixteenth ballot Douglas's name was withdrawn, and South Carolina joined all the other states to elect James Buchanan. South Carolina voted for all provisions of the platform dealing with slavery, which included an endorsement of the Compromise of 1850 and the principle of popular sovereignty in the territories as stated in the Kansas-Nebraska Act. The delegation opposed several resolutions on the Caribbean area which the convention adopted, and thus indicated once more that South Carolina had no desire for an aggressive foreign policy.[70]

In South Carolina during the summer the convention leaders were unanimous in their support of the Democratic candidate, and they took the initiative in organizing ratification meetings and issuing public statements in his favor. They admitted that they would have preferred Pierce or Douglas but declared that Buchanan, because of his soundness on the slavery question and his experience as a political leader and diplomat, was acceptable and worthy of support. They not only praised the Democratic candidate and platform but they also continued to use the argument that the South had friends in the North who deserved

[70] *Official Proceedings of the National Democratic Convention held in Cincinnati, June 2-6, 1856* (Cincinnati, 1856), pp. 29, 31, 39-43, 45, 51; Cincinnati [Ohio] *Times* (n.d.), quoted by Spartanburg *Carolina Spartan*, June 12, 1856; Yorkville *Enquirer* (n.d.), quoted by Columbia *Carolina Times*, May 19, 1856; Washington correspondence of New York *Herald*, May 18, 1856, quoted by Memphis [Tenn.] *Daily Appeal*, May 27, 1856; Charleston *Mercury*, June 7, 1856; J. H. Hammond to George Douglas, June 21, 1856; Lawrence Keitt to Sue Sparks, May 10, June 8, 1856.

South Carolina's active support.[71]   Preston Brooks, less than a month after his attack on Sumner, declared in a public letter: "We have friends throughout the entire North who are true to us.   Good and true men are confined to no region, and not only the political fortunes of such are embarked in this contest, but in many instances their social position and pecuniary interests will be affected by the result."[72]   James Farrow came back from the Cincinnati convention with assurances for his constituents in the Fifth Congressional District: "I may say also, that being necessarily thrown much in the way of Democrats of the North in the railroad cars, in reading rooms, and in hotels, and under circumstances to be obliged to hear much of their conversation among themselves, I testify with pleasure to the invariable nationality that characterized their conversation, and the uncompromising hostility they evinced towards Black Republicanism in all its phases."[73]

Opponents of the convention Democrats were divided on the question of supporting Buchanan.   Congressmen Keitt, Boyce, and McQueen declared their approval of Buchanan.   Of the anti-convention newspapers, the *Mercury, Evening News*, Camden *Journal*, and Yorkville *Citizen* endorsed the Democratic candidate.   The *Mercury*, the most influential and probably the first of these papers to declare its unequivocal support for Buchanan, carefully maintained its independence from the convention faction. It argued that the nomination of Buchanan was a signal disappointment for those who had started the convention

[71] Kibler, *Perry*, p. 286; Lancaster *Ledger*, June 11, 18, July 9, 30, 1856; Charleston *Courier*, June 27, 1856; Edgefield *Advertiser*, June 25, July 16, Sept. 10, 24, Oct. 29, Nov. 5, 1856; Spartanburg *Carolina Spartan*, June 12, 19, 26, Oct. 9, 1856; Sumter *Watchman*, Sept. 3, 1856; S. A. Douglas to a Charleston Democratic committee [composed of J. Johnston Pettigrew, T. Y. Simons, Jr., B. H. Rutledge, James Connor, Samuel Lord], June 20, 1856, in Charleston *Courier*, June 27, 1856; James L. Orr to Charleston Democratic committee [composed of J. Johnston Pettigrew, etc.], June 16, 1856, in Charleston *Courier*, June 26, 1856.

[72] P. S. Brooks to Charleston Democratic committee [composed of J. Johnston Pettigrew, etc.], June 16, 1856, in Charleston *Courier*, June 26, 1856.

[73] Speech of James Farrow, June 30, in Spartanburg *Carolina Spartan*, July 3, 1856.

movement and that only those who had remained aloof from the convention could consistently support him. It attacked the leaders of the convention movement for trying to capitalize upon South Carolina's attitude toward Buchanan in order to attach it to the national party organization.[74]

The thought that the convention leaders might profit from a state campaign for Buchanan was too great in the minds of a considerable number of editors for them to follow the course of the *Mercury*. The Orangeburg *Southron*, the Newberry *Mirror*, the Abbeville *Banner*, the Columbia *Carolina Times*, and a few others refused to give editorial commendation to the Democratic nominee.[75]

Far more significant than this division of opinion about the Democratic candidate was the unity of opinion about the Republican candidate. The leaders of all factions, regardless of their attitude toward Buchanan, stood as a unit in their hostility to Frémont. As early as January 3, W. W. Boyce had declared that the success of the Republican party in a presidential election would bring disunion. Lawrence Keitt, four months later, made the same prophecy. In the summer and fall, during the presidential campaign, the promise that the South would secede in case of Frémont's election became a virtual ultimatum of all the leaders. The threat of disunion did not come from the fire-eaters alone. Moderates such as James L. Orr and Preston Brooks, in several speeches and letters, told their constituents that Frémont's election would mean disunion.[76]

[74] Charleston *Evening News*, June 14, 1856; Charleston *Mercury*, June 7, 9, 11, 12, 19, 23, 24, 25, 27, 30, July 2, 10, 12, 18, 23, 1856; John McQueen to Brooks Dinner Committee [Arthur Simkins, E. R. Calhoun, James Gillam, Robert Cunningham], Sept. 29, 1856, in Lancaster *Ledger*, Oct. 22, 1856; report of speech by Lawrence Keitt at Lynchburg, Va., in Spartanburg *Carolina Spartan*, Sept. 25, 1856. A list of newspapers favorable or unfavorable to the Democratic nomination was published by the Newberry *Rising Sun* (n.d.) and copied by the Lancaster *Ledger*, July 9, 1856.

[75] Orangeburg *Southron*, June 11, 1856; Columbia *Carolina Times*, June 7, 9-15, 18, 19, 23, 24, 26, 28, 1856; Sumter *Watchman*, July 9, 1856; Newberry *Rising Sun* (n.d.), quoted by Lancaster *Ledger*, July 9, 1856.

[76] Lancaster *Ledger*, Oct. 22, 29, Nov. 5, 1856; Charleston *Evening News*, Sept. 14, 1856; Charleston *Mercury*, Oct. 21, 1856; Edgefield *Advertiser*, Oct. 15, 1856; Columbia *South Carolinian* (n.d.), quoted by Spartanburg *Carolina Spartan*, Aug. 28, 1856; Charleston correspondence, July 5, in *Car-*

Few of the leaders thought that they would have to carry out their promises. They were fairly confident that Buchanan would be victorious. Indeed, the strength of Frémont came as a surprise to most South Carolina politicians. He received only sixty fewer electoral votes and 10 per cent less of the popular vote than Buchanan. This phenomenal success of the Republican party in its first presidential election, with its support confined to the North alone, was a blow to moderates in South Carolina. Some began to waver in their belief that a solid South together with Northern Democrats could continue to control the federal government. Few were able to rejoice at the result. The irreconcilables, on the other hand, felt that their predictions had been vindicated.[77] Governor Adams, in his message to the legislature in late November, said of the election:

Considered in reference to the vital issue between the North and South, I fear that it will be a barren triumph—that it will prove to be, at best, but a brief respite of feverish, exhausting excitement, destined to end in embittered feeling and distracted counsel among

olina Spartan, July 17, 1856; speech of W. W. Boyce, Jan. 3, 1856, in *Congressional Globe,* 34 Cong., 1 Sess., pp. 143-144; speech of Lawrence Keitt, April 7, 1856, in *Congressional Globe,* 34 Cong., 1 Sess., Appendix, pp. 442-446; resolution adopted at public meeting at Barnwell Court House, Oct. 20, 1856, quoted by Sumter *Watchman,* Nov. 5, 1856; "Views of Hon. John McQueen," in Lancaster *Ledger,* Oct. 29, 1856; letter from J. I. M. [John Izard Middleton?] to Charleston *Mercury,* Sept. 8, 1856, quoted by Sumter *Watchman,* Sept. 24, 1856. James L. Orr wrote in his letter to the Charleston Democratic Ratification Committee, June 16, 1856: "If the Black Republican candidate is successful, then we will have reached the last chapter in the history of the Republic. It is impossible that the Union can survive such an administration." Preston Brooks wrote to the Charleston committee: "The issue in the pending election of a President is the issue of Union or Disunion." The Newberry *Mirror,* Oct. 13, 1856, reported that Orr said in a speech at Newberry that if the government fell into the hands of Republicans, he was prepared to give up the Union (quoted by Lancaster *Ledger,* Oct. 22, 1856).

[77] Boucher, "South Carolina and the South on the Eve of Secession," p. 113; Lancaster *Ledger,* Sept. 17, 1856; Charleston *Mercury,* Nov. 7, 10, 11, 14, 17-20, Dec. 20, 1856; Edgefield *Advertiser,* Oct. 29, Nov. 5, 1856; Spartanburg *Carolina Spartan,* Oct. 9, Nov. 13, 1856; inaugural address of Governor R. F. W. Allston, as reported by Columbia *South Carolinian,* Dec. 12, quoted by Spartanburg *Carolina Spartan,* Dec. 18, 1856; J. H. Hammond to W. G. Simms, Oct. 2, 1856. Benjamin F. Perry took an optimistic view of the political situation following the presidential election (Kibler, *Perry,* pp. 286-287).

ourselves.   Slavery and Freesoilism can never be reconciled.   Our enemies have been defeated—not vanquished.   A majority of the free states have declared against the South, upon a purely sectional issue, and in the remainder of them, formidable minorities fiercely contended for victory under the same banner.   The triumph of this geographical party must dissolve the confederacy, unless we are prepared to sink down into a state of acknowledged inferiority.   We will act wisely to employ the interval of repose afforded by the late election, in earnest preparation for the inevitable conflict.[78]

The irreconcilables in 1856 became outspoken in voicing their preference for a Southern confederacy over the Federal Union. For four years they had complained about their position in the Union; but only a few unbridled leaders, such as Edward Britton of the *Carolina Times*, boldly professed to be unconditional disunionists.   This year, when prominent politicians in South Carolina and the Gulf States began to talk of disunion in case of a Republican triumph, the irreconcilables stated explicitly what they had been implying since 1852.   "We believed then that secession was the rightful and the only remedy," said the Orangeburg *Southron*, "and the entire train of events from that day to this has but confirmed us in that faith."[79]   The Sumter *Watchman*, October 29, asserted that dissolution of the Union was inevitable.   The *Mercury*, June 19, said:

We have an abiding conviction that it is impossible for the Union to last.   As soon as the element of slavery entered into the politics of the Union, its doom was sealed.   The South has the simple alternative of separating herself from the Union or being destroyed by it. We have faith to believe that the South will not be destroyed, but will yet live, an honored member in the great family of nations.

The rise of the Republican party did not make disunionists of the men who uttered these words.   They had been disunionists before that party was organized.   But the menace of the Republican party confirmed their faith and provided them with more evidence to show the moderates that reconciliation with the North was impossible and that disunion was inevitable.   Most

[78] Message of Nov. 24, 1856, in *House Journal* (1856), p. 28.
[79] Orangeburg *Southron*, May 28, 1856.

important from the point of view of the secessionists, the Republican party had furnished an issue upon which not only South Carolina but most of the Southern states were willing to unite. In September and October, outstanding leaders in Virginia, Georgia, Alabama, and Mississippi had declared that the Southern states should secede if the Republican candidate became President.[80]

This map shows the vote on J. I. Middleton's resolution which stated that a resumption of all the powers delegated by the states to the general government was indispensable to "the tranquility, the prosperity, the security, the very existence of the Southern States, as free political communities, unless such amendments be made to the federal Constitution as will serve as barriers against aggression."

The movement for Southern independence was strongest in the rural districts of the southern division of the state.

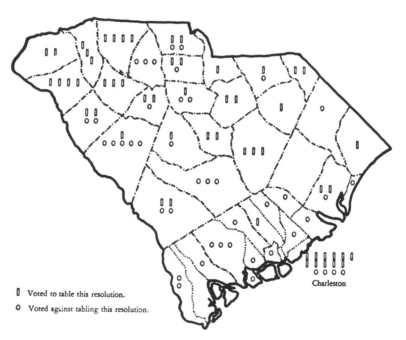

Ⅱ Voted to table this resolution.

O Voted against tabling this resolution.

Charleston

[80] Henry T. Shanks, *The Secession Movement in Virginia, 1847-1861* (Richmond, Va., 1934), pp. 52-54; Rainwater, *Mississippi: Storm Center of Secession*, pp. 35-38; Irons, "Secession Movement in Georgia," pp. 165-169; Milton, *Douglas*, p. 240; Craven, *Coming of the Civil War*, pp. 377-380.

Although there was unity in regard to the course to be taken if a Republican were elected President, there still remained after November a division of opinion on the question of whether such an event must inevitably occur. Many National Democrats still hoped that they could prevent the Republicans from controlling

FIG. 3. This graph illustrates how three groups of state districts, ranked according to slave population, voted on J. I. Middleton's resolution which called for disunion "unless such amendments be made to the federal Constitution as will serve as barriers against aggression."

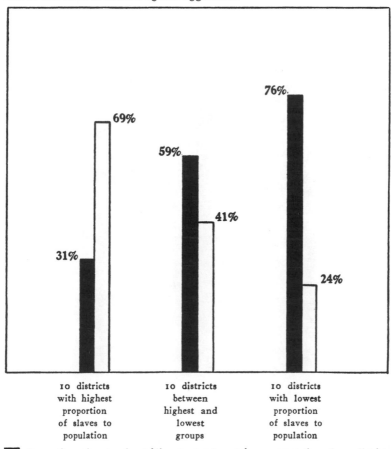

| | 10 districts with highest proportion of slaves to population | 10 districts between highest and lowest groups | 10 districts with lowest proportion of slaves to population |

■ Proportion of votes for tabling to total cast by representatives from districts comprised in each group.

☐ Proportion of votes against tabling to total cast by representatives from districts comprised in each group.

the federal government, and they refused to co-operate with the secessionists in any move toward immediate disunion. In the legislature that was in session in December, less than half of the membership was willing to take steps to establish a Southern confederacy.

FIG. 4. This graph shows how senators from three groups of state districts, ranked according to slave population, voted in 1856 on a motion to table Alexander Mazyck's resolution which called for the formation of a Southern confederacy.

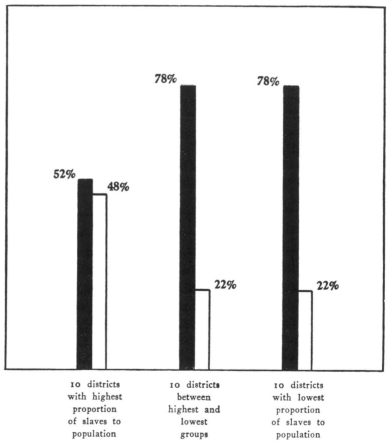

10 districts	10 districts	10 districts
with highest	between	with lowest
proportion	highest and	proportion
of slaves to	lowest	of slaves to
population	groups	population

■ Proportion of votes for tabling to total cast by senators from districts comprised in each group.

□ Proportion of votes against tabling to total cast by senators from districts comprised in each group.

John Izard Middleton, a wealthy rice planter of Georgetown district, presented a resolution to the state House of Representatives that provided a crude measurement of disunion opinion in that body. His resolution included a lengthy preamble that stated that none of the objectives of the Constitution, from the Southern point of view, had been fulfilled and that it was dangerous for Southerners to commit their rights, interests, and social and industrial organization to their enemies. It concluded with a statement to the effect that a resumption of all the powers delegated by the states to the general government was indispensable to "the tranquility, the prosperity, the security, the very existence of the Southern States, as free political communities, unless such amendments be made to the federal Constitution as will serve as barriers against aggression." Upon the motion of B. H. Wilson, who had been a delegate to the Cincinnati convention, this resolution was tabled by a vote of 56 to 44.[81]

In the state Senate a similar resolution, introduced by Alexander Mazyck, of Saint James, Santee, was tabled by a vote of 26 to 15. This resolution differed from Middleton's in that it did not mention amendments to the Constitution and asked for the formation of a Southern confederacy.[82]

Since the votes on the Middleton and Mazyck resolutions were on motions to table, they were not necessarily precise tests of disunion opinion, but an analysis of the names indicates that well-known disunionists voted against tabling. From the vote on these two resolutions, it seems safe to conclude that between 35 and 50 per cent of the members of the legislature favored taking steps toward secession, while between 50 and 65 per cent opposed action at that time.

Political factions in the state were not publicly organized on the issue of disunion, but opinion on this issue was related to the convention and anti-convention groups. By comparing the vote on E. B. Bryan's resolution declaring disapproval of the system of national conventions with the vote on Middleton's secession

[81] *House Journal* (1856), pp. 104, 241-243; Charleston *Courier*, Dec. 17, 1856.
[82] *Senate Journal* (1856), pp. 30, 94; Charleston *Courier*, Nov. 29, 1856.

resolution, the relationship between the convention and disunion groups may be shown. Eighty-four men voted on both resolutions. Of forty-five who voted to table Middleton's disunion resolution, forty had also voted to table Bryan's anti-convention resolution. Of thirty-nine who opposed tabling Middleton's resolution, twenty-eight had opposed tabling Bryan's resolution. Further evidence of the Unionist sympathies of the convention Democrats can be seen in the vote of the members of the House who had served as delegates to the state convention held in Columbia in May. Of seventeen members of the House who had been delegates, two did not vote on Middleton's resolution, one voted against tabling it, and fourteen voted for tabling it.

The success of the course marked out by the leaders of the faction that favored the national Democratic party and opposed immediate disunion depended not only upon reducing the power of the Republican party but also upon keeping their party national and friendly to the South. Before the year 1856 closed, two issues had been raised that boded evil for those who were anxious to keep intact the bond between Northern and Southern Democrats. One of these issues was the foreign slave trade; the other was the doctrine of popular sovereignty.

Toward the end of 1853 L. W. Spratt, on the editorial staff of the Charleston *Standard*, proposed that the foreign slave trade be reopened.[83] For the next three years Spratt, who had encouragement from the *Mercury* and several kindred spirits during a period of about six months in 1854, continued to agitate his proposal. Outside South Carolina his proposal attracted little attention, although it was discussed in the commercial conventions at New Orleans in 1855 and at Savannah in December, 1856. In his message to the legislature in Novem-

[83] The following account of the slave-trade agitation, 1853-1856, is based upon these authorities and sources: W. J. Carnathan, "The Proposal to Reopen the African Slave Trade in the South, 1854-1860," *South Atlantic Quarterly*, XXV (Oct., 1926), 410-420; Harold Schultz, "Movement to Revive the Foreign Slave Trade, 1853-1861" (master's thesis, Duke University, 1940), pp. 1-10; Lancaster *Ledger*, July 19, Nov. 19, Dec. 3, 1856; Charleston *Mercury*, July 7, 17, Oct. 24, 27, 31, Nov. 4, 8, 21, Dec. 7, 1854, Nov. 8, 26, 1856; Camden *Journal*, Oct. 10, 1856; Robert N. Gourdin to W. P. Miles, Nov. 28, 1856.

ber, Governor Adams created a mild sensation by recommending a revival of the foreign trade in slaves. He said that repeal of the federal law prohibiting importation of slaves would remove the last stigma of immorality on the institution of slavery and that an influx of cheap Negroes from Africa would enable the South to produce cotton more cheaply and, by increasing the population, would give the South a greater representation in Congress.[84] In both the state House and Senate this proposal was referred to special committees that were permitted to present reports to the legislature of 1857.[85]

The proposal had not yet been widely debated in South Carolina, but it was already clear that the National Democrats were anxious to avoid discussion of the slave-trade question. The federal prohibition of slave importations had possibilities of developing into another Southern grievance—one that could never be removed while the Union lasted, since Northern public opinion would never permit a revival of the foreign slave trade. In the North this new demand from the South might be used to drive Northern Democrats from the party.

In December, in the short session of Congress, opponents of the national Democratic party seized the issue as a means of influencing opinion against slavery and the Democratic party. Emerson Ethridge, a Whig from Tennessee, proposed that Congress resolve that all suggestions for a revival of the African slave trade were "shocking to the moral sentiment of the enlightened portion of mankind." The Democrats, who preferred to avoid discussion of the question, failed in a move to table the resolution. One hundred and fifty-two members of the House voted for the resolution while fifty-seven voted against it. Of these fifty-seven votes against the resolution, all except two came from the slaveholding states.[86] Thus the resolution evoked an expression of opinion that divided the Democratic party along Northern and Southern lines.

[84] Message of Nov. 24, 1856, in *House Journal* (1856), pp. 34-37, and *Senate Journal* (1856), pp. 10-13.
[85] *House Journal* (1856), p. 165; *Senate Journal* (1856), p. 79.
[86] *Congressional Globe*, 34 Cong., 3 Sess., pp. 123-125

James L. Orr followed this move with a resolution on the slave trade designed to gain the approval of the entire House. Orr presented a resolution which declared that it was "inexpedient, unwise, and contrary to the settled policy of the United States, to repeal the laws prohibiting the African slave trade." His resolution did not quite succeed in uniting all the House, for 8 out of 191 opposed the resolution. Two of the opposition votes were cast by Keitt and Brooks of South Carolina, while four were from Mississippi and two from Alabama.[87]

There was no popular demand in the South for revival of the slave trade as the year closed, but the possible consequences to the national Democratic party of the agitation of this issue were already apparent. It could only alienate Northerners and divide Southern Democrats.

The debate on popular sovereignty in December also portended troubles for the national Democratic party. From the time when the Kansas-Nebraska Bill was first proposed, there had been two interpretations of the meaning of popular sovereignty in the territories. Some Northern Democrats held that the inhabitants through their territorial legislatures could prohibit slavery. Most Southern Democrats, on the other hand, thought that the people of a territory were free to choose to enter the Union as a free or slave state, but that neither Congress nor the territorial legislature could exclude slavery before application for admission. All the South Carolina Congressmen subscribed to the Southern version of popular sovereignty. James L. Orr, however, suggested that the question of the power of a territorial legislature to enact legislation prohibiting slavery was immaterial; since slavery could not exist without local police regulation, the majority of the people of a territory could effectively exclude slavery by declining to pass laws for its protection. Characteristically, Orr had proposed a practical solution for the dilemma of his party. The Southern Democrats could still hold to their constitutional theory that neither Congress nor a territorial legislature could prohibit slavery,

[87] *Ibid.*, p. 125.

while Northern Democrats were assured that the will of the people in a territory to exclude slavery would not be thwarted. Orr's point of view, however, was not accepted by other members of the South Carolina delegation.[88]

In South Carolina the tendency of the argument over popular sovereignty and the slave trade was to weaken the National Democrats. Already Preston Brooks was showing a disposition to desert the Orr program. He voted against Orr's resolution on the slave trade, spoke against Orr's view of the territorial problem, and took a position similar to that of McQueen, Keitt, and Boyce when he defined his relationship to the national Democratic party. He said that he was "not much of a national Democrat" and warned the Northern party leaders: "If the advocates of squatter sovereignty persist in their construction of the Kansas-Nebraska Act, they will inevitably drive off many of us from the South, who desire to act in concert with them."[89]

[88] *Congressional Globe*, 34 Cong., 3 Sess., pp. 77-78, 103.

Senator James Henry Hammond, in a speech in the Senate, May 21, 1860, traced the history of South Carolina's interpretation of the doctrine of popular sovereignty (*Congressional Globe*, 36 Cong., 1 Sess., p. 2213).

[89] *Congressional Globe*, 34 Cong., 3 Sess., pp. 109-110.

CHAPTER VII

EXTREMISM OR MODERATION, 1857

THE FIRST two months of 1857 were a period of lull in national politics. The elections over, the new President yet to come in, there were few events or issues to stir party controversies. Both the slave-trade and the territorial problem dropped out of sight in the closing days of the Thirty-fourth Congress. The most important legislation passed in this session, an act that lowered the tariff of 1846, was the work of no single party or section. A compromise, it was supported by representatives of both manufacturing and agricultural interests. Although all the members of the South Carolina delegation voted for the bill, they thought it faulty. The remarks of Keitt, Boyce, and Butler showed that the South Carolina goal was free trade. Butler said that he was willing to have no customhouses at all. The *Mercury* denounced the act as "far more unequal and unjust" than the tariff it superseded.[1]

In spite of the lull in January and February, the insurgent press found subjects for editorial complaint. The *Mercury* repeatedly said that the recent presidential election "should be rather regarded by the South as a warning, than a triumph."[2] The prospective entrance of Minnesota and Oregon into the Union as free states it saw as "The Handwriting on the Wall."[3] The Sumter *Watchman* reprinted what a Boston newspaper said about the death of Preston Brooks with the following prefatory comment: "It is but the hissings of a vile serpent, the inhabitant of a loathsome Abolition den, whose infectious disgorgings are

---

[1] Lancaster *Ledger*, Jan. 14, 1857; Charleston *Mercury*, March 9, 1857, Jan. 18, 1858; *Congressional Globe*, 34 Cong., 3 Sess., p. 343, Appendix, pp. 215-218, 350.

[2] Charleston *Mercury*, Jan. 12, 1857.

[3] *Ibid.*, Feb. 7, 1857.

frequent, and are stench to the nostrils and violence to the sensations of all honorable hearts, and we only publish the following in order that our people may know what sort of beings they are dwelling in Union with!"[4] Lobbying, particularly evident in Washington this winter, and the exposure of the corrupt practices of three Representatives also provided editorial topics. "It is a striking fact," said the *Watchman,* "but certainly in keeping with the deeds, history and principles of that party, that *all* these *money seekers* should hail from the ranks of the Black Republicans."[5] Even an act of courtesy by a South Carolina Congressman to a "Black Republican" was considered treacherous by several newspapers; when William Aiken introduced a resolution complimenting Nathaniel P. Banks for the manner in which he had fulfilled his duties as Speaker of the House, the *Carolina Times,* the Camden *Journal,* and the Sumter *Watchman* censured him.[6]

Two days after Buchanan's inauguration, the Supreme Court rendered a decision in the famous Dred Scott case that administration leaders hoped would put an end to the slavery question in the territories. The opinion of the Court that slavery could not be prohibited in the territories, although commonly considered pro-Southern by Republicans, was not greeted with enthusiasm by South Carolinians. Because, from their point of view, it was the only correct decision that could have been rendered, they were not moved to regard it as a victory. Perennial insurgents, reacting to the decision in much the same way as they had reacted to repeal of the Missouri Compromise, were most concerned about Northern opinion of the decision. Denunciations of the Supreme Court by Republican leaders they took as more evidence of the impossibility of staying in the Union.[7]

[4] Sumter *Watchman,* Feb. 18, 1857.

[5] *Ibid.,* Jan. 28, 1857.

[6] Sumter *Watchman,* April 1, 1857; Petersburg [Va.] *Intelligencer* (n.d.), quoted by the Charleston *Courier,* March 20, 1857; *Congressional Globe,* 34 Cong., 3 Sess., p. 998.

[7] Charleston *Mercury,* March 17, 1857; Columbia *Carolina Times* (n.d.), quoted by the Sumter *Watchman,* April 8, 1857; Sumter *Watchman,* April 8, 29, 1857; message of Governor R. F. W. Allston, Nov. 23, 1857, in the *House Journal* (1857), pp. 18-31, and the *Senate Journal* (1857), pp. 13-26.

The Supreme Court did not settle the Kansas question.[8] The Buchanan administration still had on its hands the thorny problem of making popular sovereignty work. It was the paramount challenge for the incoming administration; party leaders realized that the fate of the Democratic party, if not the Union, depended upon the outcome of the Kansas controversy. At least one obstacle to a settlement had been removed when Buchanan took office: armed warfare had been permanently suppressed. The task of the new administration was to secure a representative convention that would draw up a state constitution embodying the will of the majority of the voters of the territory. If this were done and Congress admitted Kansas as a state, the great source of sectional tension would be removed, the Democratic party would prosper, and the Union would be preserved. In order to make this plan practicable, the proslavery faction in the territory would have to be persuaded to consent to a fair election, while the antislavery faction would have to be persuaded to take part in the election of convention delegates and the referendum. Without a capable, impartial, and fearless governor in the territory, it was hardly likely that the opposing factions could be led to the ballot boxes as a means of settling their differences. The selection of a man to succeed John White Geary, who had resigned, was therefore of utmost importance.

President Buchanan selected Robert J. Walker, an able man who had had experience in high offices of the federal government. He had been Senator from Mississippi, and as Secretary of the Treasury in Polk's administration had been instrumental in securing the passage of the tariff of 1846. His policy in Kansas was based upon the conviction that the majority of the residents of the territory did not want it to be a slave state. He also believed that a coalition of the pro-Southern group with Northern Democrats in Kansas could prevent it from becoming a

[8] For the story of the territorial problem in 1857 the following authorities were consulted: Craven, *Coming of the Civil War*, pp. 387-389; Milton, *Douglas*, pp. 261-282; Randall, *Civil War*, pp. 157-159; Rhodes, *History of the United States*, II, 271-289; Schouler, *History of the U. S.*, V, 382-386, 391-392; Smith, *Parties*, pp. 210-221.

Republican state.   In his first address to the people he made a
plea for peace and promised fair play to all parties.   His promise
that he would demand submission of the constitution to a popular vote of the people made it clear that he was not to be
merely the tool of the proslavery party.   In vain he urged the
free-state party to participate in the election of convention delegates on June 15.   Before the summer was over, however, he
made headway with his arguments, and the free-state party decided to take part in the territorial election of October 5.   At
this date Walker still hoped that the constitutional convention
would frame a satisfactory document and submit it to a referendum in which people of all parties might voice their approval
or disapproval.   But when the constitutional convention met in
its second session on October 19, it was clear that Walker had
gained the confidence of the antislavery faction only to lose the
confidence of the opposing faction.   The proslavery party was
determined not to submit its constitution in its entirety to a
referendum.   Instead, the Lecompton convention decided to
submit the question of slavery alone to popular vote; on December 21 the voters of the territory were to have an opportunity
to choose the constitution with slavery or the constitution without
slavery.   Regardless of the outcome of the election, Kansas was
to come into the Union under the Lecompton constitution, which
could not be amended for seven years.   Included in this constitution were provisions safeguarding ownership of slaves then
in the territories.   In short, even if the opponents of slavery
should vote for the constitution without slavery, ownership of
slaves would nevertheless continue in Kansas until 1864.

Would the President countenance this pseudo referendum?
Walker, who denounced the convention for not submitting the
constitution to popular ratification, expected the administration
to support him.   As late as October 22 the President had written
that he and the cabinet firmly supported the governor's program and approved submission of the constitution to popular
vote.   But when Walker came to Washington in November, he
found that Buchanan had convinced himself that the December

election would satisfy the requirements of popular sovereignty.[9] In his message to Congress he recommended that all parties in Kansas take part in the election.[10]

Buchanan's decision did not prevent a schism in the ranks of the Democratic party. The power of patronage and party loyalty kept all but three Northern Democratic senators in line, but there were loud protests from Democratic Congressmen, local leaders, and newspaper editors in the nonslaveholding states of the Ohio and upper Mississippi valleys. The gravity of the crisis in the party was dramatized in the Senate on December 9, when Stephen A. Douglas denounced the Lecompton constitution as a travesty upon popular sovereignty. The defection of Douglas, who had never before bolted the party, was an ominous indication of how strongly many Northern Democrats disapproved of the Lecompton constitution.

In South Carolina interest in Kansas was revived in April when another drive to raise money for the benefit of pro-Southern Kansans was started. Public meetings, supervised by leaders representing both major factions, were held in several districts. Alpheus Baker, agent of a committee in Kansas, toured the state soliciting aid, but he had only mild success in arousing the citizenry. The Sumter *Watchman* complained that the people of South Carolina had no realization of the great perils facing them and could not see that a victory of the abolitionists would lead to others, until the whole South was "abolitionized." After July no further efforts to raise funds in the state were

[9] Congressman William P. Miles, in a letter to J. H. Hammond, Nov. 10, 1858, said that the administration was "frightened into repudiating Walker and was bent upon conciliating Alabama, Georgia and Mississippi in particular and the Southern people generally" (Hammond Papers).

[10] The free-state leaders would have nothing to do with the Hobson's choice presented to them by the Lecompton convention. They induced the acting governor, Frederick P. Stanton, to convoke the legitimate territorial legislature, which they now controlled. This legislature then passed an act calling for an election on January 4, 1858, so that the people could vote for or against the Lecompton constitution. On this date, the free-state people cast 10,226 votes against the constitution. In the election of December 21, which had been called by the Lecompton convention, most of the free-state people did not vote. The result of that election was 6,226 for the constitution with slavery; 569 for the constitution without slavery.

made.[11] From no less an authority than David R. Atchison, the Senator from Missouri who was a prominent leader of the proslavery party in Kansas, South Carolina learned that it was useless to raise more money.[12]

Efforts to muster emigrants and raise funds ceased, but the extremists continued to oppose the admission of Kansas as a free state. They knew that the admission of Kansas as a slave state would hardly be supported by Northern Democrats; consequently, it would seem, they denounced Walker's policy, which they thought was to bring Kansas into the Union as a nonslave-holding state. Popular ratification of the constitution, which Walker insisted upon so vigorously, they said was merely a ruse to bring Kansas in as a free state in order to save the Democratic party. Again they appealed to the Southern people not to sacrifice their rights for the sake of the national party.

The extremist press began to attack Walker about a week before the publication of his inaugural address (May 27), and continued to vilify him mercilessly throughout the year. Hesitant to blame the Buchanan administration, the newspapers in the beginning confined their criticisms to the governor alone.

[11] Boucher, "South Carolina and the South on the Eve of Secession," pp. 100-101; Charleston *Courier*, April 3, 7, 22, May 9, 18, 20, 1857; Charleston *Mercury*, March 31, April 1, 9, 1857; Spartanburg *Carolina Spartan*, May 7, 1857; Columbia *Carolina Times* (n.d.), quoted by the Augusta [Ga.] *Daily Constitutionalist*, July 8, 1857; Sumter *Watchman*, April 15, 29, May 6, 27, 1857; Edgefield *Advertiser*, May 20, Aug. 26, 1857; Augusta [Ga.] *Daily Constitutionalist*, Aug. 12, 1857; letter of Alpheus Baker, Jr., to the editors of the *Mercury*, Aug. 8, 1857, in Charleston *Mercury*, Aug. 11, 1857; letters of D. R. Atchison to Alpheus Baker, Jr., July 12 and 20, 1857, in Augusta [Ga.] *Daily Constitutionalist*, Aug. 12, 1857. Atchison said in his letter of July 12 to Baker: "I see that not even thunder and lightning will arouse the South. I doubt whether an earthquake—a moral and political earthquake, shaking the institution of slavery to the earth, and bringing ruin upon the whole South, would arouse her to action."

[12] In a letter to James Tradewell, dated June 12, 1857, Atchison said that Southerners who had once given wholehearted support to the Kansas cause were now in despair, while others had turned their attention to speculation and money making. He suggested that no more money be raised in South Carolina, whose people had been "liberal above all others of the Southern States." This pessimistic letter, although intended as a private communication, was released to the Columbia *Carolina Times*, from which it was copied by other papers in the state (Lancaster *Ledger*, July 8, 1857; D. R. Atchison to Gen. W. C. Moraigne [n.d.], in Charleston *Courier*, Aug. 27, 1857).

Later, when they began to denounce the administration too, they asserted that there was no difference between Walker's and Buchanan's policy. They knew that Walker had accepted the appointment only after persuasion on the part of Buchanan, and they assumed that he would not have taken the place without the promise of full support from the President. If the President did not approve of Walker's course, why did he permit him to stay in office? This question was frequently asked in the fall and early winter. Politicians close to the Washington scene also thought that Walker was carrying out Buchanan's policy. Congressman Keitt wrote privately on June 15 that Buchanan had a finger in the Kansas treachery. In October John McQueen made a speech at Cheraw in which he held the administration responsible for Walker's course in Kansas.[13]

Not until Buchanan gave his sanction to the work of the Lecompton convention, did the press stop its attacks upon the administration. On December 23 the *Mercury* summarized the extremist view:

If the South loses Kansas, it will undoubtedly be from the course of the agents of the Administration in that Territory—Walker and Stanton. Undoubtedly they ought to have been removed as soon as they manifested, by their active and unscrupulous intervention, their determination to make Kansas a Free State. The call of the States of Georgia, Alabama, and Mississippi, for their removal, ought to have been regarded. The cause of this paper and of the other Southern journals in denouncing them, has been fully justified by the results; nor does the course of the Administration now exempt it from the just inculpation and censure it incurred by keeping them in power. But latterly, the course of the Administration has been so fair, in supporting the proceedings of the Lecompton Convention,

[13] Boucher, "South Carolina and the South on the Eve of Secession," p. 101; Charleston *Courier*, Sept. 23, 1857; Charleston *Mercury*, April 16, May 19, 20, 21, June 9, 10, 27, July 5, 15, 16, 17, 25, 28, Sept. 1, Oct. 10, 26, 30, 31, Nov. 1, 3, 9, 13, 21, 23, 24, 1857; Spartanburg *Carolina Spartan* Oct. 22, 1857; Columbia *Carolina Times* (n.d.), quoted by Augusta [Ga.] *Daily Constitutionalist*, July 8, 1857; Sumter *Watchman*, Aug. 19, Sept. 9, 1857; Lawrence Keitt to Richmond [Va.] *Examiner* (n.d.), quoted by the Augusta [Ga.] *Daily Constitutionalist*, July 9, 1857; Lawrence Keitt to William P. Miles, June 15, 1857; William S. Lyles to Columbia *Carolina Times* (n.d.), quoted by the Charleston *Courier*, Aug. 18, 1857.

and in promptly removing Stanton from office, that a disposition to support, rather than to blame, the administration, must be the natural impulse of every generous mind. Through error, or a false confidence in his agents, the President may have done—most probably has done—immense and irreparable injury to the South in Kansas; but he now sees his error. He has discarded his vicious agents, and now strives to fulfill the high duties of his office, and to do justice to the South, by an impartial administration of the affairs of Kansas. For one, we are disposed to forget the past. . . .

Least critical of the administration's Kansas policy were those editors who were most friendly to James L. Orr, such as Perry of the Greenville *Patriot and Mountaineer*, Simkins of the Edgefield *Advertiser*, and Gaillard of the *Fairfield Register*.[14] The *Advertiser*, for example, in an editorial of August 26, stated that it had "reluctantly yielded to the opinion that Kansas never" could "be a Slave State," and had "therefore thought and said that it was well at least to make it a sound Democratic State, with a strong leaven of Southern sympathy in its population." The Spartanburg *Carolina Spartan*, also friendly to Orr, saw nothing wrong with "the intention of the administration and Gov. Walker to evolve a fair and deliberate expression of opinion from the whole people of Kansas" as to the nature of their institutions.[15] The Pickens *Keowee Courier*, a convention paper which reflected the view of the up-country yeomen, declared on July 25: "There is nothing, in submitting the constitution to the people for their ratification or rejection, that should alarm the public mind." The Lancaster *Ledger*, which had also supported the convention in 1856, said on July 22 that the administration should be condemned if it supported Walker but argued that the national Democratic party should not be blamed if Kansas became a free state through the efforts

[14] Lancaster *Ledger*, June 17, July 22, Sept. 9, Nov. 18, 1857; Charleston *Courier*, May 20, June 10, 16, 26, July 8, 18, 22, 25, Aug. 4, 24, 31, Sept. 2, 4, 12, 23, 28, 30, Oct. 5, 29, Nov. 2, 1857; Washington correspondence, Nov. 6, in Charleston *Courier*, Nov. 10, 1857; Charleston *Mercury*, Aug. 31, 1857; Edgefield *Advertiser*, June 17, Aug. 5, 26, Sept. 30, Nov. 11, Dec. 16, 23, 1857.
[15] Spartanburg *Carolina Spartan*, June 11, 1857.

of another party. It was absurd, this paper declared, to charge everything that went wrong to the convention party of the state.

Neither of the major factions seems to have gained decided advantage from the Kansas controversy in 1857. Differences on the question between leaders representing the two factions were slight and, of course, were virtually removed in December by Buchanan's support of the Lecompton convention. The *Mercury* interpreted the result of a special election in August for a member of the legislature as evidence of Charleston's hostility to the administration policy and to the National Democrats in South Carolina, but the differences between the two candidates were insufficient, as even the Sumter *Watchman* admitted, for the election to serve as a significant indicator of opinion.[16] On the other hand, the failure of the legislature to bring to a vote a resolution which denounced Walker and expressed regret that Buchanan had not removed him[17] should not be interpreted to mean that the "Nationals" were stronger than the "Anti-Nationals," since it may be reasonably surmised that the latter would refrain from pressing their resolution after they learned of Buchanan's support of the Lecompton convention.

The proposal to revive the foreign slave trade proved less troublesome in 1857 than some of the leaders of the National Democrats had anticipated. L. W. Spratt, editor of the Charleston *Standard*, and Edward B. Bryan, a planter from St. John's, Colleton, took a prominent part in the debate on the question at the commercial convention at Knoxville, Tennessee, in May. Bryan's resolution recommending a withdrawal of the naval squadron used to suppress the African slave trade and Spratt's resolution proposing a committee to investigate the subject of reopening the trade were both passed.[18]

[16] Charleston *Courier*, Aug. 20, 24, 25, 29, 1857; Charleston *Mercury*, Aug. 27, Sept. 17, 1857; Sumter *Watchman*, Sept. 2, 1857.

[17] This resolution was introduced by F. D. Richardson in the state House of Representatives on December 3 (Columbia correspondence, Dec. 3, in Charleston *Courier*, Dec. 5, 1857; *House Journal* [1857], pp. 105-106, 259, 261, 276, 285).

[18] Schultz, "Movement to Revive the Slave Trade," pp. 25-26; *De Bow's Review*, XXIII (Sept., 1857), 298-336.

Back in South Carolina Spratt and Bryan made less progress. The arguments for and against the slave trade were ably stated in reports submitted to the state House of Representatives. The majority report was signed by six men of strong disunion proclivities, while the minority report was written by J. John-

FIG. 5. This graph shows how state senators from three groups of state districts, ranked according to slave population, voted in 1857 on a motion to postpone indefinitely the report and resolutions on the slave trade.

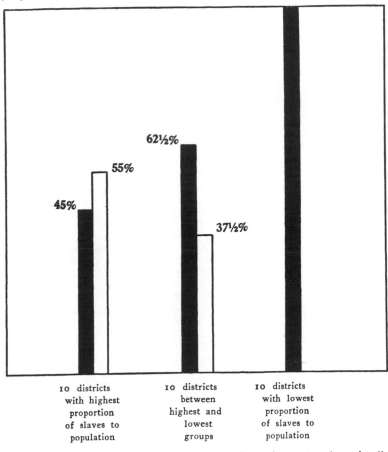

10 districts with highest proportion of slaves to population

10 districts between highest and lowest groups

10 districts with lowest proportion of slaves to population

Proportion of votes for postponement to total cast by senators from the districts comprised in each group.

Proportion of votes against postponement to total cast by senators from the districts comprised in each group.

ston Pettigrew, a young man of twenty-nine who had attended the state Democratic convention in May, 1856. In the House the reports and resolutions on the slave trade were placed on the table, and two thousand copies of both reports were ordered to be printed. In the Senate the reports and resolutions on the slave trade were postponed indefinitely.[19]

Hostility to the Republican party continued this year to be the most cohesive force in South Carolina politics.[20] Leaders of all factions agreed that its aims were antagonistic to the interests of the South. The extremists, however, set the pace in the output of warnings about the menace of Black Republicanism. Congressman Keitt and McQueen and such newspapers as the *Mercury* and *Watchman* were furious in their denunciations of the party that they thought was determined to subvert constitutional, economical, honest, and just government and to overthrow the institutions of the South. Congressman McQueen wrote:

They scruple at no barrier interposed in their march; our Constitution they prostrate, and take "higher law" for theirs; the

[19] *Report of the Special Committee of the House of Representatives, of South Carolina, on so much of the Message of his Excellency Gov. James H. Adams, as Relates to Slavery and the Slave Trade* (Columbia, 1857); *Report of the Minority of the Special Committee of Seven to whom was Referred so much of his Late Excellency's Message No. 1, as Relates to Slavery and the Slave Trade* (Columbia, 1857); *House Journal* (1857), p. 147; *Senate Journal* (1857), p. 89.

[20] The following summary of the extremist view of the Republican and Democratic parties is based upon these sources: Charleston *Mercury*, March 23, 25, 27, April 22, 23, May 4, 12, 19, 21, 28, June 3, July 1, 2, 3, 4, 5, 6, 7, 8, 9, 15, 20, 27, Aug. 15, 17, Oct. 22, Nov. 13, 1857; Charleston *Courier*, July 23, 1857; letter of John McQueen to John S. Bradley, Robert Fraser, H. D. Green, W. K. Dixon, and Charles Spencer, June 30, 1857, in Lancaster *Ledger*, July 22, 1857, and the Charleston *Courier*, July 23, 1857; letter of Lawrence Keitt to a committee of "State Rights Democrats," of Marion district, Aug. 3, 1857, in the Sumter *Watchman*, Aug. 19, 1857; letter of Lawrence Keitt to the Richmond [Va.] *Examiner*, June 30, 1857, quoted by the Charleston *Courier*, July 9, 1857; speech of Lawrence Keitt at Cheraw, May 22, 1857, reported in the Sumter *Watchman*, June 3, 1857, and the Charleston *Courier*, June 1, 1857; speech of D. F. Jamison at Cheraw, May 22, 1857, reported by Charleston *Courier*, June 1, 1857; speech of W. W. Boyce at Yorkville, quoted by Spartanburg *Carolina Spartan*, Oct. 29, 1857, and Pickens *Keowee Courier*, Oct. 31, 1857; speech of Lawrence Keitt, Jan. 15, 1857, in *Congressional Globe*, 34 Cong., 3 Sess., pp. 140-145.

Federal Court, to which they would urge us to resort, when it suits them to rob us, they repudiate, and villify the Judges as corrupt men and "scoundrels"; their Bible is the sword, the rifle and pistol; their pulpits are converted into magazines of powder, while their preachers are more like raving, howling fiends, than gentle ministers of God. They make war on our citizens in the rightful enjoyment of their own land, or lawful pursuit of their property, and cease when they please, and no punishment has been visited upon them.[21]

The extremists were convinced that the Republican party was growing stronger and eventually would get control of the federal government. They had little confidence that the President, Congress, the Supreme Court, the Democratic party, or Northern friends could protect the South from the antislavery menace. Those leaders who told the people to put their trust in a branch of the federal government or a political party were, they thought, lulling the South into a false sense of security. When the Republicans lost ground in local elections this year, the extremists made no retreat from their position. The Republican party might suffer temporary setbacks, they warned Southerners who began to talk of its crumbling, but it would not be put down permanently.

A corollary of the argument that the Republican party was growing stronger was the argument that the Democratic party was growing weaker. The extremists repeated again and again what they had been saying since 1854 about the incompetency of the national Democratic party to protect the South. This year, moreover, they were inclined to distrust the Northern wing of the party not only because of its weakness but also because of its heterodoxy. They had predicted that the Northern Democrats would have to deviate from party doctrine and sacrifice Southern friendship in order to stay in office. Now they thought they saw the beginnings of the fulfilment of their prophecies. The advocacy of "squatter sovereignty" by some Northern Democrats and the initial policy of the administration in Kansas, they said, sprang from the necessity of Northern

[21] Letter by John McQueen, June 30, 1857, in Lancaster *Ledger*, July 22, 1857, and Charleston *Courier*, July 23, 1857.

Democrats to compromise with the antislavery movement. The gains that the Democrats made this year in local elections they attributed to an abandonment of the party doctrine. The victorious Democratic party in Pennsylvania, said the *Mercury*, might be "nothing more than the Black Republican party, so far as slavery in the South, and the questions it may occasion in Congress are concerned."[22]   In effect, the extremists believed that Northern Democrats must be either sound on the slavery question and powerless, or unsound on the slavery question and powerful.

Although the extremists frankly said that the South should not entrust its security to any political party, they made no move to sever all relations with the Democratic party. They did not openly advocate either the disruption of the Democratic party or the organization of a separate Southern party. They said that they would support the Democratic party in so far as it upheld the strict construction of the Constitution and fought against the antislavery movement.

The National Democrats in the state were not inclined to make a rebuttal in detail to these arguments. They feared the Republicans and felt that unless they were vanquished the Union could not last much longer, but they were still, through the Democratic party, trying to prevent the necessity of a break from the federal government. They thought that those leaders in the state who had already made up their minds that disunion was inevitable exaggerated Northern hostility to the South. Most of the editorial criticism of the moderates this year was aimed at the disposition of the irreconcilables to take an extreme stand on every issue. The Edgefield *Advertiser*, the Spartanburg *Carolina Spartan*, and the *Fairfield Register* tried to show that the fire-eaters were injurious to the Southern cause.[23]

[22] Charleston *Mercury*, Oct. 22, 1857.
[23] Charleston *Mercury*, Feb. 7, June 30, July 9, Nov. 13, 1857; Edgefield *Advertiser*, Jan. 21, May 6, June 24, July 1, 8, 15, 22, 29, Aug. 5, Oct. 14, 1857; Pickens *Keowee Courier*, July 4, Sept. 19, 1857; Spartanburg *Carolina Spartan*, Aug. 27, Oct. 1, 1857; Winnsboro *Register* (n.d.), quoted by Pickens *Keowee Courier*, Sept. 19, 1857. A letter from F. W. Pickens to B. F. Perry, June 27, 1857, in Perry, *Reminiscences* (1883), pp. 168-169, is an excellent exposition of the point of view of the National Democrats in South Carolina.

They are always in an alarming mood [said the *Fairfield Register*] and imagine that they are true sentinels, because, forsooth they sound the alarm at every fleeting cloud-shadow, as though it were the solid phalanx of an approaching enemy. Next to the sentinel who sleeps on duty, is he who is constantly attempting to arouse the garrison unnecessarily. They imagine that they are keeping up the appearance of vigilance, but surely the disregard they meet with ought to convince them to the contrary.[24]

The factional alignment that had developed in 1856 in relation to the convention issue continued throughout 1857. The leaders of the National Democratic group kept their lines intact, so that the isolationists were constrained, despite their insistence that the convention issue belonged to the past, to mobilize their own forces into some kind of a working group.

A test of strength between these factions was made in the Senatorial election to fill the unexpired term of A. P. Butler. Of the four men who had the most votes on the first ballot of the legislature, none was an outspoken opponent of the convention system or the national organization of the Democratic party. The only prominent extremist in the contest, R. Barnwell Rhett, received less than 5 per cent of the total votes cast on the first ballot. Francis W. Pickens, leading candidate of the National Democrats, received about 40 per cent of the total votes cast on the third and final ballot. The victor in the election, James Henry Hammond, had the support of the group that urged isolation from the activities of national parties, but he had made commitments to no faction in the state, and his views in regard to current party issues were not known.[25]

---

[24] Quoted by Charleston *Mercury*, July 6, 1857.

[25] F. W. Pickens to Lucy Holcomb, Nov. 6, 1857 (Duke University Library); J. H. Hammond to John Cunningham, June 26, and to George Douglas, July 15, 1857; John Cunningham, June 20, and William M. Lawton, July 15, 1857, to J. H. Hammond; Charleston *Courier*, Oct. 8, Nov. 30, Dec. 2, 1857; Charleston *Mercury*, Nov. 28, Dec. 1, 1857; Spartanburg *Carolina Spartan*, Dec. 10, 1857; Sumter *Watchman*, Nov. 18, 1857; *House Journal* (1857), pp. 60, 67. F. W. Pickens wrote to B. F. Perry, Nov. 21, 1859, that he had been defeated because of his "conservatism and supposed connection with the national Democracy" (Perry, *Reminiscences* [1883], p. 176).

The election of Hammond was greeted with enthusiasm in all parts of the state. Extremists of the low country told the state that his election was a triumph of the anti-national party. National Democrats praised his qualifications and denied that the election was a mandate for isolation from the convention system of the national party. Friends of Hammond said that his election was a recognition by the people of South Carolina of his pre-eminent personal qualifications. Nostalgics said that his election was a return to the good old days when the office sought the man, a rebuke to electioneering which had become so rife in the state in recent years.[26]

Possibly a few National Democrats voted for Hammond, but his election certainly was not a victory for the convention faction. A large part of the support for Hammond came from the isolationists, but because he was under no obligations to them and had made no public statements against the convention system or national parties, his election was hardly a triumph for the policy of the isolationists. Nor was Hammond's election a rebuke to electioneering. Although Hammond himself had no part in his own election, there was plenty of wirepulling by the politicians at Columbia. Nor was the election a result of the spontaneous desire of the people to reward a man who stood head and shoulders above the field. Hammond was indeed among the most able men in the state but not greatly superior to the other candidates.

The decisive factor in bringing about the election of Hammond was his middle-ground position. Because of his undefined relationship to the contending candidates and electors, he was able to gain support not only from most of the isolationists

[26] Merritt, *Hammond*, pp. 115-116; Lancaster *Ledger*, Dec. 9, 1857; Charleston *Courier*, Dec. 2, 4, 1857; Charleston *Mercury*, Dec. 1, 1857; Spartanburg *Carolina Spartan*, Dec. 10, 1857; letters to J. H. Hammond from J. H. Adams, Dec. 3, 1857, A. P. Aldrich, Dec. 1, 18, 1857, James Gadsden, Jan. 31, 1858; Lawrence Keitt, Dec. 18, 1857, William M. Lawton, Dec. 1, 1857, James Legaré, Dec. 4, 1857, William S. Mullins, Dec. 16, 1857, W. D. Porter, Dec. 13, 1857, John Russell, Dec. 28, 1857, J. J. Ryan, Dec. 4, 1857, James D. Tradewell, Dec. 23, 1857, Samuel Y. Tupper, Dec. 1, 1857, and J. L. Whitten, Dec. 4, 1857.

but also from the fluid group of doubtfuls who were confined to neither of the dominant factions. It was this intermediate group that possessed the balance of power in the South Carolina legislature in 1857, for neither the National Democrats nor their enemies could muster a majority behind one of their own leaders.

CHAPTER VIII

PROVOCATION OR NONAGGRESSION, 1858

THE KANSAS ISSUE was finally removed from national politics in 1858. Events in the territory ceased to inspire party controversy either in Kansas itself, Washington, or the nation at large. The governor who succeeded Walker in December, 1857, escaped the difficulties of his predecessors, and he attracted little attention. South Carolina, like the other Southern states, made no efforts this year to send men or money to Kansas. It was in Congress, among the party politicians, that the Kansas problem spent its last year.

In the Thirty-fifth Congress, which convened December 7, 1857, the Democratic party had a majority in both branches. James L. Orr was elected Speaker of the House by a vote of 128 to 84. About Orr's election, which had been expected in the state, the extremist press said little; newspapers which had growled warnings of impending disaster when a Republican had been elected Speaker in 1856 by a plurality vote after a two-month struggle did not contrariwise make optimistic comments upon the election of a native son on the first ballot.[1]

South Carolinians for several years had been critical of Congress, and some intransigents had openly declared that there was no honor attached to serving in it. The first session of this Congress was particularly turbulent, and the inclination to disparage the federal legislative body was more marked than ever.

[1] *Congressional Globe*, 35 Cong., 1 Sess., p. 2; Washington correspondence of the Columbia *Carolina Times* (n.d.), quoted by the Pickens *Keowee Courier*, Sept. 26, 1857; Washington correspondence of the *Carolina Times*, Nov. 26, quoted by the Spartanburg *Carolina Spartan*, Dec. 3, 1857; Spartanburg *Carolina Spartan*, Oct. 1, Dec. 17, 1857; Edgefield *Advertiser*, Dec. 16, 1857; Washington [D. C.] *States*, Dec. 7, 8, 30, 1857; pseudonymous writer ["S"] in the Charleston *Courier*, Oct. 22, 1857.

A. P. Calhoun refused to become a candidate for Congress on the grounds that he could not serve his country there. "A Southern member of Congress has but little to do," he said, "being in a hopeless minority, beyond hearing his section or State abused."[2] A voter in the Fifth Congressional District felt that physical courage was a necessary qualification for a member of Congress. "The House of Representatives in Congress [he wrote] is a most boisterous, stormy sea, for any one to enter, and requires great nerve, stern courage and unconquerable will to maintain one's position in it."[3] Benjamin Evans was sorry that his friend William Porcher Miles could not be "back in dear old Charleston again" rather than in Washington. "What little I have seen of Washington and the House [he wrote] is that it requires a considerable amount of rascality in the first place, some smartness in the second and a prodigious quantity of impudence and noise to make an impression in it, and that an honest man and a gentleman has not a half chance there."[4] An editorial of the Newberry *Rising Sun* expressed indignation at members of Congress who received three thousand dollars a year merely to turn out buncombe and challenge one another: "We think it's high time for them to adjourn. They are doing nothing, will do nothing, and have done nothing, and we further believe it would be a blessing to the Union if they would never meet there again."[5]

The session opened with three new members from South Carolina. James Henry Hammond had the Senate seat which had been held by Butler until the latter's death; Milledge L. Bonham had the seat vacated by the death of Preston Brooks; and William Porcher Miles, rather than William Aiken, who had resigned, was representing the Second Congressional District. In May, Josiah J. Evans died, and Arthur P. Hayne was appointed by the governor to fill his place for the rest of the

[2] A. P. Calhoun to the Anderson *True Carolinian*, Feb. 22, quoted by the Sumter *Watchman*, March 10, 1858.
[3] Letter in the Greenville *Patriot and Mountaineer* (n.d.), quoted by the Pickens *Keowee Courier*, April 24, 1858.
[4] Benjamin Evans to William Porcher Miles, March 4, 1858.
[5] Newberry *Rising Sun*, June 16, 1858.

session. The new delegation was perhaps slightly more inclined to disunion than the preceding one. Miles, who privately expressed the belief that disunion was inevitable,[6] was more extreme than Aiken; and Bonham, like Brooks during the closing months of his career, had little confidence in the national Democratic party. Senator Hammond gave no evidence of being either more or less inclined toward disunion than Butler, while the old members, Evans, McQueen, Keitt, Orr, and Boyce, had made no discernible changes in their positions.

The revolt of the Northwestern Democrats did not cause Buchanan to change his mind about the Lecompton constitution, and in February he asked Congress to approve it.[7] In spite of Democratic majorities in both houses, the administration could not put through its first bill for the admission of Kansas. Southern speakers denounced Douglas, and rebellious Democrats were deprived of the presidential patronage, but only the Senate would fall in line. Subsequently, both houses approved the English Bill, a complicated compromise proposed by a conference committe. When, under the terms of this legislation, a referendum was held in Kansas in August, opponents of the Lecompton constitution were overwhelmingly victorious.

The South Carolina delegation unanimously favored the admission of Kansas under the Lecompton constitution. Hammond, Keitt, Boyce, and Miles spoke for the administration's first bill. They defended the legality of the Lecompton constitution, testified that the South had nothing but its honor at stake, attributed opposition to the bill to Northern determination

[6] Miles wrote to J. H. Hammond, Nov. 15, 1858: "Every man's views on politics at the South must in the last analysis be traced back to one of two roots—must be somewhat shaped and coloured by one of two motives. Either he desires to perpetuate the Union (of course at the same time endeavoring to make it move in the Constitutional orbit in which our fathers meant it to revolve) or he desires to try the experiment of a Confederacy of slaveholding, agricultural, free trade States. I confess I belong to that class which holds this latter view" (in Hammond Papers).

[7] For the story of the Kansas question in Congress in 1858, the following authorities were consulted: Craven, *The Coming of the Civil War*, p. 389; Milton, *Douglas*, pp. 284-293; Randall, *Civil War*, pp. 159-160; Rhodes, *History of the United States*, II, 291-301; Schouler, *History of the United States*, V, 393-400; Smith, *Parties*, pp. 221-226.

to prevent the admission of a slave state, warned that rejection of a new state because its constitution upheld slavery would lead to disunion, and argued that the South had the resources to maintain an independent existence. Except for Bonham, the delegation also supported the conference bill on the grounds that it was not a violation of their previous position and that it alone could unite the South.[8] Miles gave a succinct explanation of why the South Carolina members voted for the English Bill: "We voted for it because the South did. Kansas was already lost. We were sick and tired of the whole matter and felt instinctively that we ought not to vote with Seward, Hale, Wilson, Giddings."[9]

The delegation was representative of opinion in South Carolina. The state was united in favoring admission of Kansas under the Lecompton constitution. Leaders as far apart as R. B. Rhett, Jr., and Benjamin F. Perry stood together on this issue. Only in their inclination to compromise and greater eagerness to settle the Kansas problem was there any discernible difference between the National Democrats and the isolationists.[10]

[8] *Congressional Globe*, 35 Cong., 1 Sess., pp. 959-962, 1009-1013, 1359-1361, Appendix, pp. 285-289, 509-511; J. H. Hammond to W. G. Simms, Dec. 19, 1857; J. H. Hammond to M. C. M. Hammond, March 9, 1858, May 1, 1858; J. H. Hammond to W. G. Simms, May 3, 1858; Lawrence Keitt to J. H. Hammond, Dec. 18, 1857.

[9] W. P. Miles to J. H. Hammond, Nov. 10, 1858 (Hammond Papers).
A Washington correspondent ["Palmetto"] of the Sumter *Watchman*, reported that the members of the South Carolina delegation were very lukewarm on the subject of the conference bill. All were disgusted with the Kansas question, he said, and eager to get it out of Congress "at almost any cost" (Sumter *Watchman*, May 12, 1858).

[10] Kibler, *Perry*, pp. 289-290; Lancaster *Ledger*, Feb. 3, 10, 1858; Charleston *Mercury*, Dec. 11, 23, 1857, Jan. 6, 23, Feb. 2, 5, 22, March 8, 9, 13, 24, 25, 27, 30, 31, April 16, 1858; Edgefield *Advertiser*, Dec. 16, 23, 1857, Feb. 17, April 14, May 19, July 21, 1858; Newberry *Rising Sun*, March 10, 1858; Pickens *Keowee Courier*, Jan. 30, May 8, 1858; Spartanburg *Carolina Spartan*, Feb. 18, 1858; Columbia *South Carolinian* (n.d.), quoted by *Keowee Courier*, May 8, 1858; résumé of undated editorial from Columbia *South Carolinian*, Washington [D. C.] *States*, March 15, 1858; correspondence of the *South Carolinian* (n.d.), quoted by the Washington [D. C.] *States*, March 29, 1858; letters to J. H. Hammond from R. W. Barnwell, Jan. 18, John A. Calhoun, March 26, A. B. Crook, Feb. 5, John

South Carolinians frequently expressed the opinion that Kansas could not remain permanently a slave state. They knew that the South had nothing to gain in a practical way from the admission of Kansas as a slave state, but they thought that the point of honor was important.[11] The very fact that the South

---

Cunningham, Jan. 25, Allan J. Green, June 7, I. W. Hayne, Jan. 24, D. F. Jamison, Feb. 22, Benjamin F. Perry, Jan. 8, March 7, James D. Tradewell, Feb. 11, 1858.

[11] Senator Josiah J. Evans wrote to J. H. Hammond, Dec. 7, 1857: "There is no chance of Kansas remaining a slave state even if admitted with the slave clause in the Lecompton Constitution and I do not care whether she ever is admitted." To B. F. Perry, Evans wrote: "I am heartily sick of the subject, and care not if Kansas were sunk in the bottomless ocean. In fighting for the Lecompton Constitution we are fighting for a shadow, so far as any ultimate good can come to the South; but we are contending for a principle of vital importance. I have long since given up all hopes of Kansas becoming a slave State" (Perry, *Reminiscences*, 1883, p. 122).

William Porcher Miles wrote to J. H. Hammond, Nov. 10, 1858: "The Lecompton Constitution came before us at the last session when the apathy, indifference or sincere conviction of the Southern people (it was I believe a combination of these elements) had allowed the contest to go by default. It was a foregone conclusion that Kansas was to be a free state. . . . But still the point of honor was something" (Hammond Papers).

R. W. Barnwell wrote to Hammond, Jan. 18, 1858: "It is now apparent that Kansas, if rejected, has not the power to organize a separate slaveholding people. On the contrary it seems to me that a majority of the inhabitants are willing to vote against slavery. But whilst I frankly state this is my own opinion I also think that the South is under the highest obligation to support our friends in Kansas and if Missouri can be depended upon South Carolina I am sure will leave the Union upon this issue altho a feeble one."

I. W. Hayne wrote to Hammond, Jan. 24, 1858: "The Kansas issue was, in my opinion, accepted in this state as a 'point of honor' merely. We were disposed to *back our friends & that was all.*"

Allan J. Green wrote to Hammond, March 7, 1858: "I don't think the South is to gain anything more than a very empty victory by the admission of Kansas, but if we could make it the rock upon which to split the Union, I confess it would suit me precisely."

Benjamin F. Perry wrote to Hammond, Jan. 8, March 7, 1858, that he doubted whether slavery could exist in Kansas. "But there is a great principle at stake in the contest which the South never can give up & remain in the Union. This I say as a Union man, and which I said in the state convention of 1851."

W. Gilmore Simms told Hammond in a letter dated May 9, 1858, that he had believed from the first that Kansas could never be made a slave state.

A correspondent of the Columbia *South Carolinian* (n.d.), quoted by the Washington [D. C.] *States*, March 29, 1858, wrote: "The admission of Kansas is no longer a question of any practical interest. Kansas is gone from the South. A constitution recognizing slavery, in opposition to the public opinion, of the majority, is not worth to the South the paper it is written on."

had nothing material to gain from the admission of Kansas perhaps made the moderates more disposed to insist upon its acceptance. It would be "dirt cheap" for the North to concede the point, said W. D. Porter. If it did not admit Kansas, which would soon become free, could the South ever expect the admission of a state which would actually become a permanent slave state?[12]

When the House rejected the Senate bill for admitting Kansas under the Lecompton constitution, none of the leaders raised the cry for immediate disunion. Although they asserted that the opposition to the admission of Kansas was based upon Northern determination not to admit a slave state, they failed to carry out their previous promises to secede in case a state was rejected because of slavery. If the other Southern leaders had issued an ultimatum of "admission of Kansas or disunion," South Carolina no doubt would have followed. But the other Southern leaders were aware that the Lecompton constitution did not present a clear-cut issue. There were two outstanding weaknesses in the Southern case at this time. First, Douglas and his followers said that they were against the Lecompton constitution because it did not represent the will of the people of the territory, not because it contained provisions favorable to slavery. Secondly, the Southern leaders realized that the residents of Kansas themselves, overwhelmingly against slavery, would repudiate the South's making a challenge in its name.[13]

South Carolina acquiesced in the decision of Southern leaders to support the English Bill because in reality there was no alternative. Insurgent newspapers denounced the bill as a compromise and praised Bonham for voting against it, but they made no personal attacks upon the rest of the delegation for

[12] W. D. Porter to J. H. Hammond, Jan. 30, 1858.

[13] Edgefield *Advertiser*, April 14, 1858; Spartanburg *Carolina Spartan*, Feb. 18, 1858; correspondence of the Columbia *South Carolinian* (n.d.), quoted by Washington [D. C.] *States*, March 29, 1858; letters to J. H. Hammond from R. W. Barnwell, Jan. 18, John A. Calhoun, Feb. 10, March 26, A. B. Crook, Feb. 5, John Cunningham, Jan. 25, I. W. Hayne, Jan. 6, 24, Allan J. Green, March 7, Benjamin F. Perry, Jan. 8, W. D. Porter, Jan. 30, Henry Summer, March 10, James D. Tradewell, Feb. 11, 1858; J. H. Hammond to W. G. Simms, Dec. 19, 1857, Jan. 20, Feb. 7, 1858.

supporting the measure. The *Mercury*, after putting on record a prediction that this compromise, like the others that preceded it, would fail to allay agitation and would strengthen the enemies of the South, avoided discussion of the subject.[14] George P. Elliot, of Beaufort, told Hammond that no good could come from making an issue over the English Bill. "It will [he said] only serve to divide and distract the South, and extremist as I am I see very plainly that with distractive councils we shall accomplish nothing."[15]

Throughout the period of almost five years during which the territorial problem had been the most controversial issue in national politics, the irreconcilables had taken the lead in the agitation of the Kansas issue. During the first phase, from 1854 to the close of 1856, they attacked the Republican party for trying to make Kansas a free state and for opposing slavery extension. In the summer and fall of 1857 they attacked the Buchanan administration until it finally consented to accept the Lecompton constitution. In 1858 they attacked Douglas Democrats along with Republicans for refusing to admit Kansas as a slave state. At no time during these five years did they encounter organized opposition in South Carolina to their position. National Democrats and other moderates agreed that men and money should be sent to Kansas, that a territorial legislature could not prohibit slavery, and that Kansas should be admitted into the Union as a slave state under the Lecompton constitution. A great advantage was gained by the extremists in late 1857 when Buchanan's sanction of the Lecompton constitution removed the division in the state which had existed during the summer over the course of Walker and the question of a referendum. With one stroke the state was united on the terms which had been demanded by the irreconcilables. In the first

[14] Charleston *Mercury*, June 28, July 22, 1858; Newberry *Conservatist*, May 11, 25, Aug. 3, 1858; Newberry *Rising Sun*, May 12, 26, 1858; Columbia *Guardian* (n.d.), quoted by Washington [D. C.] *States*, May 8 and Lancaster *Ledger*, May 12, 1858; Sumter *Watchman*, May 12, 1858; J. H. Hammond to W. P. Miles, Nov. 17, 1858 (Miles Papers, University of North Carolina).

[15] George P. Elliot to J. H. Hammond, June 5, 1858.

quarter of 1858 the state was so united on the Kansas question that the alignment of factions which had crystallized in 1856 as a consequence of the convention controversy seemed to have vanished entirely.

While the Kansas question tended to unite moderates and extremists, the slave-trade issue tended to divide the latter.[16] The proposal to reopen the trade had never gained the support of the moderates in the state, and a majority of the extremists were opposed to it. Some editors who had supported the measure earlier ceased demanding repeal of the slave-trade laws because agitation of the subject divided the South. For two years the *Mercury* had not objected to examination of the question with a view to throwing light on the necessities and position of the South, but it was opposed, in 1858, to dividing the Southern people by making it a political issue.

In spite of the fact that the press of the state was overwhelmingly opposed to agitating the question, the slave trade attracted considerable attention this year. Discussion of the subject stemmed from three sources. First, in the early part of the year, the legislative reports made in December, 1857, were

[16] The story of the slave-trade agitation in 1858 presented here is based upon the following authorities and sources: Boucher, "South Carolina and the South on the Eve of Secession," p. 93; Avery Craven, *Edmund Ruffin, A Study of Secession* (New York, 1930), p. 160; John Witherspoon Du Bose, *The Life and Times of William Lowndes Yancey* (Birmingham, 1892), pp. 358-359; Joseph Hodgson, *The Cradle of the Confederacy, or the Times of Troup, Quitman and Yancey* (Mobile, 1876), pp. 375-387; White, *Rhett*, p. 144; Lancaster *Ledger*, Jan. 12, June 9, Sept. 8, 9, 1858; Charleston *Mercury*, Jan. 11, May 20, 22, 24, June 1, 3, 5, 9, 14, 1858; Edgefield *Advertiser*, May 26, Aug. 18, Oct. 6, Dec. 22, 1858; Newberry *Conservatist*, June 1, 1858; Newberry *Rising Sun*, March 10, April 21, May 26, Sept. 8, 1858; Pickens *Keowee Courier*, June 12, 1858; Spartanburg *Carolina Spartan*, Jan. 14, March 11, Sept. 16, 1858; Sumter *Watchman*, March 10, June 2, Sept. 8, 15, 1858; Augusta [Ga.] *Daily Constitutionalist*, May 16, June 8, 9, Aug. 29, 31, Sept. 2, 22, 1858; Washington [D. C.] *States*, Dec. 4, 1858; *De Bow's Review*, XXIV (June, 1858), 574-607; "Occasional Letters to the Southern People," by [according to the editor] "a distinguished gentleman from South Carolina," in Washington [D. C.] *States*, Feb. 24, 27, March 4, 11, 24, April 1, 7, 16, 26, May 4, 14, July 8, 1858; speech of James L. Orr at Craytonville, Aug. 12, report of in Anderson *Gazette*, Aug. 18, quoted by Memphis [Tenn.] *Daily Appeal*, Sept. 1, 1858; message of Governor R. F. W. Allston, Nov. 23, 1858, in *House Journal* (1858), p. 21; Allan J. Green to J. H. Hammond, March 7, 1858.

reviewed in the newspapers. Secondly, in the summer, the debate on the proposal in the Montgomery commercial convention was discussed. Thirdly, in the last half of the year, attempts to bring Negroes into the Southern states illegally stirred up some excitement in the state.

At the Montgomery commercial convention in May, L. W. Spratt made the report authorized by the Knoxville convention the year before, but he and his little-known friends were overshadowed by more publicized personalities, such as William Lowndes Yancey, the Alabama firebrand, and R. Barnwell Rhett, owner of the Charleston *Mercury*. The convention, absorbed with the strategy of Southern insurgency, was divided on the expediency of agitating the question; but after a lengthy debate both the friends and the opponents of the measure decided that the best course would be to lay Spratt's report on the table and have it printed.

For several months before the Montgomery convention met, the press of the South had carried reports of illegal importations of Negroes into the Southern states and of schemes to bring native Africans into the South as immigrants to work on the plantations under a system of apprenticeship. In May, when a firm was denied clearance papers to import Negroes into the Port of Charleston, several South Carolina newspapers spoke out against violations of the slave-trade laws and subterfuges designed to evade them. In the late summer interest in the slave trade was excited by the arrival at Charleston of the *Echo*, a ship which had been captured while transporting Negroes from Africa. On August 27, when the ship appeared in the port, 306 native Africans were on board. Almost a third of the Negroes who had left Africa had already died, and before the ship left on September 20 to carry them back, 38 more died. For D. H. Hamilton, who had charge of the Negroes while they were at Charleston, it was not a pleasant episode:

I am heartily glad to get rid of them. Thirty-five died while in my custody and at one time I supposed that one hundred would have fallen a sacrifice to the cruelties, to which the poor creatures had been subjected on board of the Slaver. I wish that everyone in South Carolina who is in favor of re-opening of the Slave-trade, could have seen what I have been compelled to witness for the three weeks of their stay at Fort Sumter. It seems to me that I can never forget it.[17]

I acknowledge most frankly to have been an advocate for the re-opening of the slave-trade—but a practical, fair evidence of its effects has cured me forever.[18]

None of the slave-trade resolutions which came before the legislature in December asked directly for reopening the slave trade. In the House, Spratt presented resolutions which instructed the South Carolina Senators and Representatives in

This map shows the vote on L. W. Spratt's resolution instructing the South Carolina delegation in Congress to try to procure the repeal of restrictions on the foreign slave trade.

Opposition to agitation of the slave trade question was strongest in Charleston and the upper division.

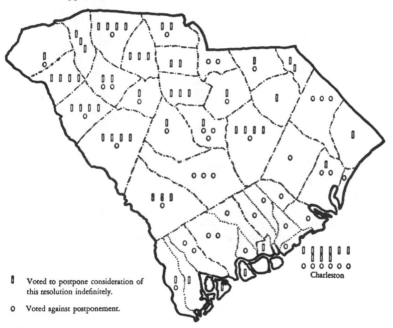

Ⅰ   Voted to postpone consideration of
    this resolution indefinitely.

o   Voted against postponement.

[17] D. H. Hamilton to J. H. Hammond, Sept. 24, 1858.
[18] D. H. Hamilton to J. H. Hammond, Sept. 10, 1858.

FIG. 6.   This graph shows how representatives from three groups of state districts, ranked according to slave population, voted in 1858 on a motion to postpone indefinitely committee reports on the Treaty of Washington.

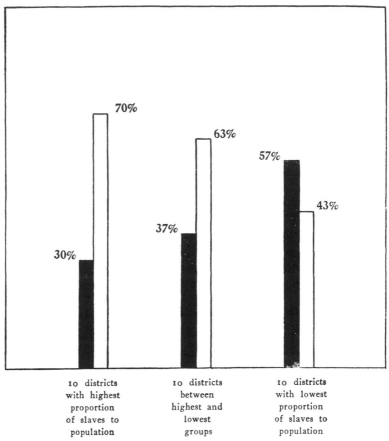

10 districts with highest proportion of slaves to population

10 districts between highest and lowest groups

10 districts with lowest proportion of slaves to population

■ Proportion of votes for postponement to total cast by representatives from the districts comprised in each group.

□ Proportion of votes against postponement to total cast by representatives from the districts comprised in each group.

Congress to try to procure the repeal of restrictions on the foreign slave trade.[19]   In a speech on his resolutions, Spratt carefully pointed out that he was not seeking importation of Negroes from abroad:

[19] *House Journal* (1858), p. 129; Columbia correspondence, Dec. 9, 1858, in Sumter *Watchman*, Dec. 14, 1858.

FIG. 7. This graph shows how representatives from three groups of state districts, ranked according to slave population, voted in 1858 on a motion to postpone indefinitely L. W. Spratt's resolution instructing the South Carolina delegation in Congress to try to procure repeal of restrictions on the foreign slave trade.

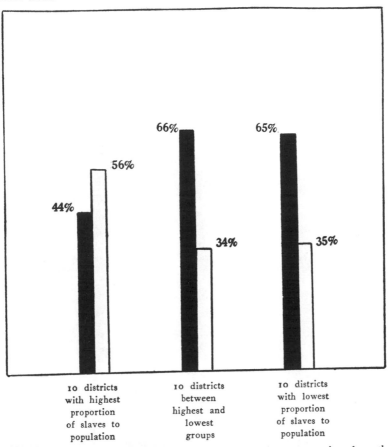

10 districts with highest proportion of slaves to population

10 districts between highest and lowest groups

10 districts with lowest proportion of slaves to population

■ Proportion of votes for postponement to total cast by representatives from the districts comprised in each group.
□ Proportion of votes against postponement to total cast by representatives from the districts comprised in each group.

It will be seen that they do not propose a further importation of foreign slaves. Upon the propriety of that measure there well may be a diversity of opinion, and as it is a measure which will only come in question when the States of the South shall be in a condition to

FIG. 8. This graph shows how state senators from three groups of state districts, ranked according to slave population, voted in 1858 on a motion to table a resolution which declared unconstitutional "Acts of Congress purporting to prohibit or interfere with the slave trade between foreign countries."

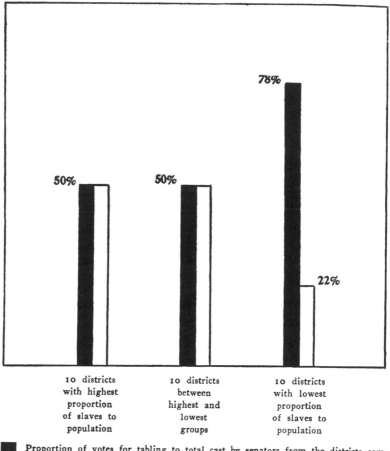

10 districts with highest proportion of slaves to population

10 districts between highest and lowest groups

10 districts with lowest proportion of slaves to population

■ Proportion of votes for tabling to total cast by senators from the districts comprised in each group.

□ Proportion of votes against tabling to total cast by senators from the districts comprised in each group.

act for themselves upon the subject, it is enough for the present to consider the importance of emancipating slavery from the control of Congress, while we leave that question of ulterior policy to that time when it will come in proper order for investigation.

FIG. 9.   This graph shows how senators from three groups of state districts, ranked according to slave population, voted in 1858 on a motion to table a resolution which declared unconstitutional the federal law making the foreign slave trade the equivalent of piracy.

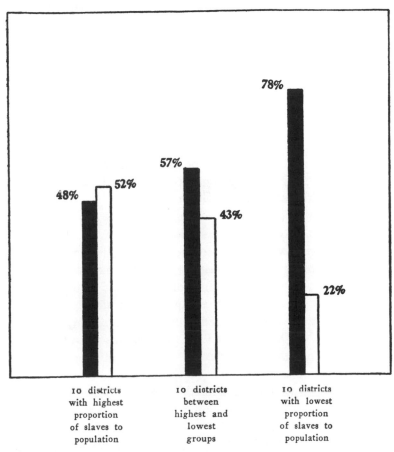

10 districts with highest proportion of slaves to population	10 districts between highest and lowest groups	10 districts with lowest proportion of slaves to population

■ Proportion of votes for tabling to total cast by senators from the districts comprised in each group.

☐ Proportion of votes against tabling to total cast by senators from the districts comprised in each group.

He thought, however, that whenever the foreign slave trade came under state jurisdiction, South Carolina ought not to prohibit importations of slaves from abroad.[20]

[20] Charleston *Courier*, Dec. 22, 1858.

Spratt's resolution, by a vote of 63 to 47, was postponed indefinitely.[21]   In the Senate, Alexander Mazyck's resolution declaring unconstitutional congressional interference in the slave trade between foreign countries was tabled by a vote of 19 to 14.[22] A second resolution by Mazyck which declared unconstitutional the federal law which made the foreign slave trade the equivalent of piracy was also tabled, by a vote of 20 to 15.[23]   The supporters of the slave trade were successful only in putting through a resolution that stated that the eighth article of the Treaty of Washington ought to be abrogated.   This resolution passed the Senate by the overwhelming vote of 38 to 1.   The Senate adopted by a vote of 34 to 5 a companion resolution that declared that the adoption of the preceding resolution did not express the opinion of the legislature as to the expediency or inexpediency of reopening the slave trade.[24]

South Carolina was still, as the year 1858 closed, opposed to reopening the foreign slave trade.   Nevertheless, a small but resolute minority was willing to keep the issue before the public and willing to agitate for placing the trade exclusively under state jurisdiction.   The number of votes cast against tabling the slave-trade resolutions, the eagerness of the opponents of the measure to belittle the strength of the movement, and statements made by *De Bow's Review* suggest that Spratt and his associates were at least attracting more attention as the year ended.[25]

Since 1856, when the National Democrats became organized into a working faction, a pillar of their policy had been the belief

[21] *House Journal* (1858), p. 204.
[22] *Senate Journal* (1858), p. 110.
[23] *Ibid.*, p. 120.
[24] *Ibid.*, pp. 109-110.
[25] In March, 1858, the editor of *De Bow's Review* was not sanguine of success for the movement: "We have often argued the labor question in The Review, in connection with the slave-trade, but the South has seemed to differ with us and we incline to drop the subject."   In October, 1858, he thought that the "general interest regarding the slave-trade" was "far from subsiding."   In Jan., 1859, he suggested that the movement had made some gains: "Certainly no cause has grown with greater rapidity than has that of the advocates of the slave trade, if we may judge from the attitude it is assuming in most of our Southern Legislatures" (*De Bow's Review*, XXIV, 210, XXV, 489, XXVI, 51).

that the Republican party could be weakened in the North sufficiently to prevent it from ever gaining control of the federal government. Neither the presidential election that year nor the local Democratic victories in 1857 were impressive enough to aid the cause of the National Democrats, and they seldom cited these elections as proof that their policy was practicable. In 1858 they still had little or nothing to show the citizenry of South Carolina in the way of achieving a setback for the Republican party. On the contrary the Republicans registered important gains this year. With the aid of the Douglas Democrats they defeated the Lecompton constitution in Congress. The passage of the English Bill eliminated the issue that had given the party great strength from its beginning, but did not result in injury in the fall elections. Outside Illinois and Indiana, where the Douglas Democrats were victorious, the Republicans were quite successful.[26]

The irreconcilables denied that the termination of the Kansas controversy would lead to the decline of the Republicans; the results of the elections that fall were cited as proof that the Republican party was stronger than ever before.[27] Commenting upon Governor Allston's failure to mention the elections in his message to the legislature, the *Mercury* said that they marked "an era in the politics of the country" and were "worthy of the most earnest consideration by the people of the South."[28]

[26] The Edgefield *Advertiser*, which had repeatedly expressed confidence in the Democratic party, the administration, and the strong position of the South (editorials of March 3, 10, July 21, Oct. 27, 1858), stated on Nov. 17, 1858: "Hitherto many of us had hoped that the justice of its [the Democratic Party's] cause would continue its dominance, as a party in the country, to the extent of controlling the legislation of Congress and the administration of the Government. But the recent developments [defeats of Democrats in Northern elections] are of a character to reduce this hopefulness to a narrow and doubtful issue."

[27] Charleston *Mercury*, April 5, May 3, June 14, Aug. 9, Sept. 10, Oct. 25, Nov. 4, 8, 1858; Newberry *Conservatist*, Nov. 23, 1858; Newberry *Rising Sun*, May 5, Nov. 10, 1858; Camden *Journal* (n.d.), quoted by Sumter *Watchman*, May 19, 1858; Sumter *Watchman*, Nov. 9, 1858; correspondence from Cheraw, Nov. 20, 1858, quoted from the Columbia *Southern Guardian* (n.d.), by the Lancaster *Ledger*, Dec. 1, 1858; letters to J. H. Hammond from John Cunningham, Nov. 13 and W. P. Miles, Nov. 15, 1858 (Hammond Papers).

[28] Charleston *Mercury*, Nov. 24, 1858.

The irreconcilables and most of the National Democrats renewed their commitments to support secession in case of a Republican victory in the presidential election of 1860. Mc-Queen, Miles, Keitt, Bonham, and Boyce thought the South should leave the Union if a Republican were elected President, while Orr said substantially the same thing when he predicted that defeat of the Democratic party would mean disunion.[29]

Secession was impending in 1858. If the Republicans won the Presidency in 1860 and if the leaders of the various factions fulfilled their promises to support secession in that eventuality, the goal of the disunionists would probably be reached. This path to success seemed so promising to the disunionists that even the factious *Mercury* urged suppression of minor differences for the sake of keeping South Carolina united behind the one platform of secession in case of Republican victory. In an editorial entitled "Harmony in South Carolina," the *Mercury* explained how the prospect for secession in 1860 was influencing its own policy:

This course [of eschewing division on issues such as the English Bill, the slave trade, and Senator Hammond's speech of October 29] has been pursued, because the tide of events is surely driving us together, and we are satisfied that differences in South Carolina in regard to the General Government and the North will be obliterated by time. They are conjectural rather than real—matters of speculation rather than fact. There are events before us that will unite all the true men of the South; and we desire that South Carolina, by her union and the moral weight she has ever possessed in the

[29] Lancaster *Ledger*, Sept. 22, 1858; Edgefield *Advertiser*, Oct. 27, Nov. 11, 1858; Newberry *Rising Sun*, Sept. 1, 1858; Columbia *South Carolinian* (n.d.), quoted by Washington [D. C.] *States*, March 29, 1858; *Congressional Globe*, 35 Cong., 1 Sess., pp. 1012-1013, Appendix, p. 511; correspondence from Cheraw, Nov. 20, 1858, quoted from the Columbia *Southern Guardian* (n.d.), by the Lancaster *Ledger*, Dec. 1, 1858; speech of Milledge Bonham at Edgefield, Sept. 2, 1858, reported in the Newberry *Rising Sun*, Sept. 22, Pickens *Keowee Courier*, Sept. 18, Sumter *Watchman*, Sept. 21, 1858; statement of D. F. Jamison at Orangeburg, July 4, 1858, quoted by Sumter *Watchman*, July 14, 1858; letters to J. H. Hammond from John Cunningham, Nov. 13, and Lawrence Keitt, July 9, 1858; speech of James L. Orr at Williamston Springs, Aug. 5, reported by Lancaster *Ledger*, Aug. 18, and Pickens *Keowee Courier*, Aug. 14, 1858.

counsels of the South, resulting from her unanimity of opinion and conduct, shall bear her part in the drama of the future, whatever it be. Some of our leading men have confidence in the Democratic party of the North—others have none. Some suppose that Black Republican sectionalism is declining in power—others that it is increasing. Some are confident of the strength of our present position in the Union—others are confident of its weakness. The crisis that will settle these conjectures or deductions is near at hand. What reason is there, then, for pressing these differences of opinion between those who agree in principle and who go together in policy? . . . We deem it almost certain that within less than two years all true men in South Carolina or at Washington will stand together. At all events this is our hope. So strong is our conviction of the steady progress and fatal purposes of the powerful Black Republican faction, that this is our belief.[30]

For the disunionists, the division of the Democratic party was an important strategic gain. If continued, this division would ultimately undermine the second pillar upon which the policy of the moderates rested. In the closing months of the year it appeared that the breach would be permanent. Douglas carefully refrained from attacking the administration, turned his back to Republican wooings, and held to a conciliatory attitude toward the Democratic party leaders; but Buchanan and some important Southern leaders gave no indication of letting bygones be bygones.

The isolationists seized upon the bolt of the Northwestern Democrats to prove that the Northern wing of the party could not be depended upon to stand up for Southern rights. From the opening of Congress they maintained that the contest over the Lecompton constitution would be a test of the reliability of Northern Democrats. The rejection of the Senate bill was advanced as conclusive proof of the futility of trusting in a national party.[31]

[30] Charleston *Mercury*, Nov. 19, 1858.

[31] Charleston *Mercury*, Jan. 6, May 3, June 14, 18, Aug. 20, Sept. 10, 11, Oct. 18, 1858; Sumter *Watchman*, Aug. 18, 1858; letters to J. H. Hammond from John A. Calhoun, Feb. 10, March 26, W. F. De Saussure, Feb. 13, James Gadsden, Jan. 31, 1858; R. B. Rhett, Jr., to W. P. Miles, April 7, 1858.

Have we not [asked the *Mercury*, April 12] been right in our warnings—over and over again repeated—that no party in the North can be relied on by the South to protect her rights in the Union with respect to the institution of slavery? In every sectional contest in Congress, from the tariff of 1828 to this day, the South has been defeated by a sufficient number of Northern Democrats and traitorous Southern men to accomplish her overthrow.

Stephen A. Douglas became the target for severe attacks in the South Carolina press. The extremists set the pace in the publication of diatribes against the Illinois Senator. They started in December, 1857, and continued irregularly throughout 1858. The extremists seemed delighted to tear to pieces the Northern leader whom the moderates had so frequently cited as a true and faithful friend of the South, to point to him as an example of the way the South was betrayed by Northern statesmen in all contests between the sections. This man Douglas was now the great leader of the Black Republican cause in Congress. He was more harmful to the South and the administration than a legion of abolitionists. He had never cared for Southern interests, had merely sought Southern support to advance his own political career. Between Douglas and a Republican, the latter was preferable, for an intriguing, deceitful, and insinuating wretch was more dangerous than an open, candid, avowed enemy. The South had nothing to gain from his defeating the Republican candidate Abraham Lincoln in the Illinois Senatorial contest, and Seward would be a better man for the Presidency.[32]

The stand of Douglas and his friends from the North Central States shook the confidence of some men who had put their trust in the national party. "This defection of Douglas [wrote W. D. Porter] has done more than all else to shake my confi-

[32] Lancaster *Ledger*, Nov. 17, 1858; Charleston *Mercury*, Dec. 12, 15, 16, 30, 1857, Jan. 5, Feb. 22, June 18, July 16, 20, 29, Aug. 20, Sept. 8, Oct. 25, 29, Nov. 23, 1858; Edgefield *Advertiser*, Dec. 23, 1857, Nov. 11, 1858; Newberry *Conservatist*, Nov. 23, 1858; Newberry *Rising Sun*, March 31, Sept. 1, 15, Oct. 3, 1858; Spartanburg *Carolina Spartan*, Nov. 11, 1858; Columbia *South Carolinian* (n.d.), quoted by Lancaster *Ledger*, Sept. 29, 1858; Sumter *Watchman*, Jan. 27, Feb. 17, 1858.

dence in northern men on the slavery issue, for I have always regarded him as one of our safest and most reliable friends." Benjamin F. Perry wrote that no recent political event had given him greater cause for regret than Douglas's stand on the Lecompton constitution. "I had confidence in Mr. Douglas [Perry said] and looked to him as our next President." Alfred Huger was "surprised and disappointed" at Douglas. He was John D. Ashmore's "favorite until his tergiversation on the Lecompton constitution showed his utter want of sincerity & fair dealing with the rights of the South." The Lancaster *Ledger* said that the division of the Democratic party on the Kansas issue "should teach the South that she must mainly rely upon her own strength and that there is danger in placing unreserved confidence in the profession of those who are not identified with us in interest."[33]

Acceptance by moderates of the charge that Douglas was a renegade was an advantage to the extremists comparable in importance to Buchanan's decision in 1857 to condone the Lecompton convention. It enabled them to undermine confidence in Northern Democrats and to widen the wedge between the two wings of the party.

Buchanan's support of the Lecompton constitution and his subsequent rejection of Douglas's bid for reconciliation led some of the isolationists to become more friendly to the administration and the Democratic party. The policy of this group of isolationists, represented by the Rhetts, McQueen, Miles, Keitt, and Boyce, was substantially what it had been at the beginning of the Pierce administration. They supported the President and advocated co-operation with the party without becoming merged in its organization. Although convinced that the Republican

[33] Letters to J. H. Hammond from W. D. Porter, Dec. 28, 1857, B. F. Perry, Jan. 8, 1858, J. D. Ashmore, Jan. 16, 1859; Alfred Huger to W. P. Miles, Dec. 19, 1857; Lancaster *Ledger*, Feb. 24, 1858. Arthur Simkins, editor of the Edgefield *Advertiser*, was one of the few moderates who defended Douglas. In an editorial of Aug. 8, 1860, Simkins asserted that he had reproved "the untiring efforts of the Administration and its allies to crush a man whose only political fault" was his "abstract opinion" on the territorial question.

party was becoming stronger and that no national party could protect Southern interests, they refused to assume a position of opposition to the Democratic party or the administration, and they did not breathe a word about forming a Southern sectional party.

The paradoxical alacrity with which some men who had formerly denounced national party politics now expressed their confidence in the President and his party was presumably prompted by a realization that the Buchanan-led Democratic party was nominally national but essentially Southern. The Charleston *Mercury* said on July 22: "We now support the Administration because it has cast off these renegade Democrats, defied Douglas, and is altogether worthy of our support against Americans, Douglasites and Black Republicans." Gilmore Simms thought that the Democratic party was, in fact, a Southern party and that the success of the Republicans would make it entirely so. At Whippy Swamps, October 2, Lawrence Keitt said that the decline of the Northern wing of the party was accompanied by a strengthening of the Southern. The policy and the whole machinery of the party, except the national convention, he said, were in Southern hands. "It is in view of this ascendency of the South in the counsels of the party, that I think the party purer than it has been, and that good policy requires our co-operation with it."[34]

[34] W. G. Simms to J. H. Hammond, Jan. 28, 1858; Keitt's speech reported by Lancaster *Ledger*, Oct. 20, 1858, and Newberry *Rising Sun*, Oct. 20, 1858. I. W. Hayne wrote to J. H. Hammond, Jan. 24, 1858: "God forbid that we should be 'merged' in the '*National Democracy*,' but while in the union we should if possible *control* the Democracy—and the only practicable plan for uniting the South is through the Democratic organ in the South. . . . My experience and observation teach me that all the attempts to form new parties are generally futile so far as reform is concerned. The true wisdom is to join the existing party nearest your own views and lend your energies toward controlling and directing its doctrines, principles and general policy." W. H. Trescot wrote to Hammond, March 20, 1858: "I certainly cannot express any affection for the Democratic party but in the position of an effective minority (although of course it could not maintain this position for more than one Presidential canvass) it might be made very useful for our ulterior purpose. Ought not the state therefore to give Mr. Buchanan's administration a hearty support and go into the coming contest as one with the National Democrats?"

Some isolationists, such as James Hopkins Adams and Maxcy Gregg, were apparently ignorant of or unimpressed with the division of the national Democratic party and Southern domination of the administration. Without exception men whose experience had been confined to local and state politics, spokesmen of this group analyzed the party situation just as they had before the Democratic party suffered open schism. They opposed the affiliation of South Carolina with the national party organization, advocated voting for Democratic measures when they were approved by the South, did not rely upon the party to protect Southern interests, and thought that the Republican party would ultimately gain control of the federal government. Their differences with other isolationists were numerous but superficial: They had no words of praise for Buchanan, were disposed to censure the administration and the Democratic party for the defeat of the Lecompton constitution and the passage of the English Bill, tried during the summer to make a hero of Bonham because he voted against the English Bill, were willing to agitate the slave-trade issue, and were determined to launch an offensive against the National Democrats in South Carolina.[35]

In 1858 isolationists of the Gregg-Adams type were obsessed with the belief that the National Democrats were gaining ground in South Carolina.[36] They became suspicious about the conciliatory statements uttered by Congressmen who had always stood firmly aloof from the national organization of the Democratic party. They thought they saw signs that even fiery Law-

[35] Charleston *Mercury*, Dec. 7, 1858; Newberry *Conservatist*, Sept. 6, 21, Oct. 5, Dec. 14, 1858; Newberry *Rising Sun*, Sept. 1, 1858; Sumter *Watchman*, July 7, Oct. 12, 1858; *An Appeal to the State Rights Party of South Carolina: in Several Letters on the Present Condition of Public Affairs* (Columbia, 1858); letters to J. H. Hammond from James Hopkins Adams, Sept. 22, Oct. 9, John A. Calhoun, Feb. 10, March 26, W. F. De Saussure, Feb. 13, Allan J. Green, June 1, 1858; J. H. Hammond to M. C. M. Hammond, Aug. 10, 1858.

[36] White, *Rhett*, p. 148; White, "National Democrats," p. 380; Newberry *Conservatist*, Dec. 14, 1858; Newberry *Rising Sun*, Sept. 1, 1858; correspondence from Columbia, by "A Visitor," Nov. 12, 1858, in the Spartanburg *Carolina Spartan*, Nov. 18, 1858; *An Appeal to the State Rights Party*; R. B. Rhett, Jr., to J. H. Hammond, Jan. 5, 1858.

rence Keitt was drifting into what they called the "national current." Had he not gone to a rally in the Fifth Congressional District that was sponsored by the National Democrats, had he not praised Orr in his speech there, and was his support of Buchanan and the party not unnecessarily strong? "The recent lion of the Third Congressional District [wrote James D. Tradewell], a while since the vehement denouncer of National Democracy, who refused to go into its caucus at Washington to vote for the nomination of its sweaty leader in South Carolina for Speaker, under alternate lashing and petting, has tamed down into its disgusting apologist, declaring that of its fidelity he should entertain no doubt in advance."[37] Milledge Bonham, whom they had extolled, disappointed them even more than Keitt. He not only professed support for the national party, said that the South had dependable friends in the North, and praised Buchanan; he also said that the state should be represented in the convention of 1860.[38] Above all, these doctrinaire isolationists were alarmed by what they considered the defection of Senator James Henry Hammond.

Hammond in 1858 was trying to steer a middle course that would meet the approval of all factions in the state. He refused to recognize the division of the state into National Democrats and State Rights Democrats. While seeking the friendship of the Orr group, he strove to keep up his connections with the isolationists, who were most responsible for putting him into office.[39]

In an informal dinner speech on July 22 and in a prepared speech at Barnwell Court House on October 29, Hammond urged the adoption by the South of a strictly defensive position. The slaveholding region should make no attempts to expand its frontiers, he argued. Lack of labor and lack of suitable lands

[37] *Appeal to the State Rights Party*, p. 22.
[38] Text of Bonham's speech at Edgefield, Sept. 2, 1858, in Newberry *Rising Sun*, Sept. 22, Pickens *Keowee Courier*, Sept. 18, Sumter *Watchman*, Sept. 15, 21, Lancaster *Ledger*, Sept. 15, 1858.
[39] Perry, *Reminiscences* (1883), pp. 107-110; J. H. Hammond to W. G. Simms, March 26, Aug. 13, 1858; J. H. Hammond to W. P. Miles, Nov. 23, 1858 (Miles Papers, University of North Carolina).

for slavery made it imperative that the South abandon its policy of territorial expansion as a means of gaining political power. The South need not, however, fear confinement to its established frontiers. A politically united South in coalition with Northern friends could still control the national government. If the South became convinced that his program of control through coalition was impossible, the alternative of secession was always available.[40]

Hammond seemed to think that he was striking out upon a new line of policy, that he was providing a new plan to take the place of the old Calhoun idea of preserving the balance between the free and slave states. Actually he had merely adopted the fundamental policy of the National Democrats. Francis W. Pickens, at the Columbia convention of 1856, had stated the program of coalition with Northern friends in much the same terms as Hammond did this year.[41]

Conscious or not of his kinship in policy to the National Democrats, Hammond deliberately attempted to be benevolently neutral toward them. Although privately opposed to the system of party conventions, he refused to make any public declarations against them, and he avoided discussing the relationship of the state to national parties. In Washington he was friendly to Orr, and in a public letter in August he said kind words about him.[42]

[40] Charleston *Courier*, Nov. 3, 1858; Washington [D. C.] *States*, July 29, Nov. 5, 10, 1858; J. H. Hammond to M. C. M. Hammond, Aug. 10, Nov. 28 and to W. G. Simms, Aug. 2, 13, 1858; J. H. Hammond to W. P. Miles, Nov. 5, 1858 (Miles Papers, University of North Carolina); W. H. Trescot to J. H. Hammond, July 25, 27, Aug. 15, 1858.

[41] Benjamin F. Perry made a clear statement of this policy in a letter to Hammond, April 18, 1858: "No matter what issue may come it is all important to keep the South united. If this can be done I apprehend no danger. We can dictate our own terms. There will always be a minority at the North, honest enough & wise enough to sustain the constitutional rights of the Republic. By keeping the South united we may with that minority be able to maintain our equality in the Union or independence out of it." In letters to B. F. Perry, April 24 and November 21, 1859, Pickens commented upon the similarity of Hammond's policy to his own (Perry, *Reminiscences*, 1883, pp. 173-178).

[42] Kibler, *Perry*, pp. 287-291; Perry, *Reminiscences* (1883), pp. 107-110; J. H. Hammond to W. G. Simms, July 3 and to M. C. M. Hammond, Nov. 28, 1858; J. H. Hammond to Craytonville Dinner Committee, Aug. 4, 1858, quoted by the Pickens *Keowee Courier*, Aug. 28, 1858.

National Democrats and other moderates were exuberant because of Hammond's apparent adoption of their policy.[43] "I am glad you made a conservative speech," wrote Orr. "Your course in the Senate I think meets the universal approval of my constituents."[44]

The very fact that National Democrats applauded Hammond was sufficient reason for some extremists to condemn him. "The State Rights party were astounded," Maxcy Gregg said of Hammond's July speech. "Something like despair was caused by so heavy a blow coming from such a quarter. The National Democrats, and the lovers, open or secret, of the Union, were delighted and triumphant."[45] Gregg, Adams, and the other ultra-isolationists were alarmed at what they considered the Union tendencies of Hammond's speeches. R. B. Rhett, Jr., told Hammond that these men found fault with his views "as calculated to give aid and comfort and strength to unmitigated unionists and submissionists like Col. Yeadon, while depressing and weakening the earnest advocates of resistance like Col. Gregg."[46] John Cunningham made a similar explanation of the dissatisfaction of the isolationists: "The State Rights party are dissatisfied with your Beech Island Speech, because you *appear* to abandon all claim of a Southern share of the Territories, and to ignore the probable necessity or propriety of their effort to unite the South in favour of a Southern confederacy, as an alternative to Northern aggression."[47]

While not pleased with Hammond's stand, the pro-administration isolationists did not publicly put him into the class of Union-savers or National Democrats. The *Mercury's* comment

---

[43] Perry, *Reminiscences* (1883), pp. 110, 174-176; White, "National Democrats," p. 380; Lancaster *Ledger*, Oct. 20, Nov. 10, 1858; Edgefield *Advertiser*, Aug. 4, 25, 29, Nov. 10, 1858; Pickens *Keowee Courier*, Aug. 7, Oct. 9, Nov. 13, 1858; Spartanburg *Carolina Spartan*, Nov. 11, 1858; letters to J. H. Hammond from J. D. Ashmore, Nov. 9, R. Buchanan, Nov. 11, Franklin Gaillard, Dec. 9, Samuel McGowan, Nov. 3, W. D. Porter, July 29, Nov. 3, and Richard Yeadon, Aug. 30, 1858.

[44] James L. Orr to J. H. Hammond, July 25, 1858.

[45] *Appeal to the State Rights Party*, p. vii.

[46] R. B. Rhett, Jr., to J. H. Hammond, Aug. 2, 1858.

[47] John Cunningham to J. H. Hammond, Oct. 9, 1858.

upon his Barnwell speech was one of friendly disagreement: "He thinks our position one of strength—we think it one of weakness. He thinks it one of progressive power—we think it one of increasing weakness to inevitable overthrow." Their disagreement, the Charleston paper said, was not basic but inferential, and time alone would prove which was right.[48] John Cunningham did not especially disapprove of any points in his speech; he did not expect that Hammond, in his position, could go as far as he did.[49]

During the year 1858 the broad outlines of factional alignments in South Carolina remained the same as they had been since the beginning of 1856. Divisions within these factions, however, created a situation of greater complexity than had existed in 1856 and 1857.

Another Senatorial election reflected the changes which took place during the year.[50] The National Democrats were rather evenly divided between two candidates until the seventh ballot, when they united on a single candidate.[51] The isolationists, who

[48] Charleston *Mercury*, Nov. 2, 1858. R. B. Rhett, Jr., wrote to Hammond, Nov. 5, 1858: "I am glad you approve of the line of my editorial note. The fact is, agreeing as we do in principle it would be captious and wholly without sense to quarrel on a matter of fact that time will decide before any question can arise to divide us. We can, therefore, differing in opinion as to the position of the South, yet cooperate quietly and harmoniously in the same policy of preparation and instruction. South Carolina will never again, I take it, attempt separate secession and when the other Southern States are ready to take some step there will be no difference of opinion in South Carolina, I am sure."

[49] John Cunningham to J. H. Hammond, Nov. 13, 1858.

[50] This account of the Senatorial election is based upon the following sources: White, *Rhett*, pp. 151-152; correspondence from Columbia, Nov. 27, in Charleston *Courier*, Nov. 30, 1858; Charleston *Evening News* (n.d.), quoted by the Washington [D. C.] *National Intelligencer*, Dec. 9, 1858; Columbia correspondence of the Charleston *Evening News*, Dec. 4, 1858, quoted by the Charleston *Mercury*, Dec. 9, 1858; Pickens *Keowee Courier*, Dec. 4, 11, 1858; Camden *Journal* (n.d.), quoted by Lancaster *Ledger*, Jan. 12, 1859; Augusta [Ga.] *Daily Constitutionalist*, Nov. 28, Dec. 2, 4, 1858; Washington [D. C.] *States*, Dec. 4, 1858; letters to J. H. Hammond from John D. Ashmore, Jan. 16, 1859, and from W. G. Simms, May 8, 1858; J. H. Hammond to M. C. M. Hammond, Nov. 28, 1858; *House Journal* (1858), pp. 69, 74, 80, 85, 88, 92, 97, 98, 105, 107, 110, 114, 116, 120, 122.

[51] The two men supported by the National Democrats were C. G. Memminger and John Lawrence Manning. The vote for Memminger on suc-

had quickly united behind the candidacy of Hammond the year before, were divided several ways in 1858. One group, which acknowledged at the most a perfunctory support of Buchanan's administration and which was not opposed to the agitation for reviving the foreign slave trade, voted throughout the ten ballotings for one candidate.[52] A second group of isolationists, which warmly supported Buchanan and which discouraged agitation of the slave-trade issue, were divided between three candidates.[53] A portion of the votes from this second group, on the ninth ballot, switched to James Chesnut, the sole candidate representing the middle position of noncommittals. When the National Democrats on the next ballot decided to support Chesnut, he was elected.[54]

As in 1857, the uncommitted candidate was victorious. Unlike the year before, however, the election of the middle-ground candidate was made possible by division within the ranks of the isolationists. In 1857 all the isolationists plus some neutrals had brought about the election of the victorious candidate. In 1858 all the National Democrats plus neutrals and isolationists brought about the election of Chesnut. The net result was the same—the elevation of a man who was associated with neither of the major factions.

The total strength of the isolationists in the legislature in 1858 seems to have been greater than the previous year. In 1857 they were not numerous enough to elect a man of their own faction and were successful only because they put up a

---

cessive ballots was 23, 30, 27, 31, 29, 26, 6, 2, 1, 0; the vote for Manning was 24, 20, 21, 26, 24, 24, 42, 53, 50, 0.

[52] James Hopkins Adams, whose vote was 36, 37, 45, 47, 42, 42, 47, 47, 55, 44. Out of the six men who had at least 20 votes on the first ballot, Adams with 36 had the largest number.

[53] At first this group was divided between two candidates, R. B. Rhett, Sr., and John McQueen. The vote for Rhett on successive ballots was 23, 24, 19, 10, 3, 4, 0, 1, 3, 4. McQueen's vote was steady until the ninth ballot: 23, 22, 19, 22, 18, 23, 29, 21, 0, 2. The third candidate associated with this group appeared on the fourth ballot; this was Lawrence Keitt, whose vote on successive ballots was 4, 19, 26, 30, 29, 1, 0. Keitt's gains probably came for the most part from Rhett and Chesnut supporters.

[54] Chesnut's vote was 21, 21, 18, 17, 13, 6, 2, 0, 46, 92. Most of the Keitt and McQueen votes switched to Chesnut on the ninth ballot.

popular, uncommitted candidate who was able to win over most of the middle-ground electors. If they had united on one candidate in 1858, they would have had a good chance of success, even without support from Chesnut. On the first ballot, the three isolationists [Adams, Rhett, McQueen] polled a total of 82 votes, which was 48½ per cent of the total possible votes; the total for the two National Democratic candidates was 57, which was 33½ per cent of the possible votes. Of the votes actually cast on the first ballot, the three isolationist candidates had 52½ per cent, while the two National Democrats had 36½ per cent.

CHAPTER IX

DEFIANCE OR FORBEARANCE, 1859

FREE OF THE Kansas problem, President Buchanan turned his attention to foreign affairs. His message of December, 1858, disclosed his desire for the United States to purchase Cuba and to assume a protectorate over the northern part of Mexico. In 1859, in February, he requested Congress to authorize the President to use the armed forces to prevent "lawless violence" from obstructing the transit routes across Central America; and, in December, he asked for an invasion of Mexico to restore order. None of his requests were granted, however, and Buchanan's aggressive policy in the Caribbean and Gulf regions was no more successful than that of his predecessor.

Few South Carolinians agreed with that part of the Democratic platform which declared that there were questions of foreign policy "inferior to no domestic questions whatever." The slavery controversy, which was generally viewed as a domestic question, overshadowed all other questions, and the grievances of South Carolina against the North and the Union were seldom linked to foreign policy. Most South Carolinians were as hostile to imperialism in Buchanan's administration as they had been in Pierce's. The public reacted to Buchanan's Mexican policy with indifference. Filibustering was generally opposed, and the notorious William Walker, who had sympathizers in other Southern states, had few defenders in South Carolina. The search of American ships by British vessels engaged in the suppression of the slave trade stirred up some excitement but apparently not so much as the proponents of the foreign slave trade desired. Lawrence Keitt was the only member of the South

Carolina delegation who spoke in Congress for the acquisition of Cuba.[1]

Some isolationists thought that Buchanan's foreign policy was merely a device to sidetrack the South from important domestic questions. "Don't touch Cuba," W. Gilmore Simms wrote to Congressman Miles, February 3, 1859. "She is the bait which the Democratic party holds out to the South. Beware how you enter this field. The Democratic party has but one chance left for life, that of involving us in a foreign war. . . . It is the only process for bolstering up the Democratic party, and while that party lives the South can never be secure." A *Mercury* editorial entitled "The Red Rag of Cuba for the South" said that suggestions for acquiring Cuba were "pleasing deceits—baits manufactured for party purpose—to quiet the South in the progress of the North to mastery in the Union."[2] The *Mercury* also argued that the heads of the Democratic party desired war as a diversion from sectional antagonism: "For by war, the people of the United States may be united, and diverted from the deadly progress of sectionalism, to its dreaded consummation of a dissolution of the Union."[3] The Newberry *Rising Sun* said that the proposal to purchase Cuba was "a scheme gotten up by some of the hungry, wire pulling democrats about Washington."[4]

In the short session of Congress, the extremists of both sections tried to pump life into the territorial question by a sort of

---

[1] Lancaster *Ledger*, Jan. 6, 13, 20, 1858, Feb. 2, 1859; Charleston *Mercury*, March 10, 12, 1857, June 10, July 10, Dec. 9, 1858, Jan. 24, Dec. 29, 1859; Edgefield *Advertiser*, Feb. 2, 9, 1859; Newberry *Conservatist*, Oct. 12, 1858; Newberry *Rising Sun*, Feb. 9, 23, March 2, 1859; Pickens *Keowee Courier*, Jan. 29, 1859; Spartanburg *Carolina Spartan*, Feb. 3, 1859, Oct. 4, 1860; Washington [D. C.] *States*, Jan. 27, 1859; *Congressional Globe*, 35 Cong., 1 Sess., p. 2746, 2 Sess., pp. 453-457; letters to J. H. Hammond from E. B. Bryan, May 24, James Gadsden, May 20, 24, Allen J. Green, June 1, I. W. Hayne, Jan. 24, R. B. Rhett, Jr., July 25, John Russell, June 7, Waddy Thompson, Aug. 17, 1858; letters from J. H. Hammond to M. C. M. Hammond, Jan. 19, 1858, Dec. 11, 1858, and to W. G. Simms, April 8, 1860; letters to W. P. Miles from Alfred Huger, Jan. 23, W. H. Trescot, May 30, and W. T. Wragg, June 3, 1858.

[2] Charleston *Mercury*, Feb. 26, 1858.

[3] *Ibid.*, June 15, 1858.

[4] Jan. 26, 1859.

argumentative artificial respiration.   John P. Hale, on the Republican side, asked for repeal of that provision of the English Act which made the admission of Kansas contingent upon a population equal to the number necessary for one Representative in Congress.   Albert Gallatin Brown, an extreme Southern Rights advocate, on the other hand, raised the demand for congressional legislation to protect slave property in the territories. The stand of this Mississippi Senator was a reply to Douglas's contention that a territorial legislature could effectively exclude slavery by refraining from enacting protective laws.

South Carolina moderates were annoyed by this demand for protective legislation.   The Spartanburg *Carolina Spartan* thought that agitation of the subject was unfortunate: "It is an abstraction, and can benefit in no way but to keep up agitation, and perhaps save the fortunes of some Democratic aspirants before the Charleston Convention, or aid in a Black Republican triumph in the Presidential election of 1860."[5]   The Columbia *South Carolinian* said that it was a "dangerous doctrine," and argued that protection could not be given by the federal government in opposition to local opinion.[6]   Senator Hammond thought that the demand for congressional protection was "ideal, impracticable & injurious to all."[7]   John D. Ashmore, the newly elected Representative from the Fifth District, called the new doctrine a "miserable humbug."[8]   James L. Orr, also exasperated with this "transparent and atrocious" proposal, thought that a congressional slave code, if attainable, would not be executed by the courts and juries of a territory whose refusal to enact legislation protecting slavery had rendered such congressional legislation necessary.[9]   Francis W. Pickens thought it "an error in any portion of the South, to assume that there must be Congressional legislation in advance, to protect slavery by law, in

[5] Undated editorial quoted by the Washington [D. C.] *States*, April 19, 1859.
[6] Undated editorial quoted by the Pickens *Keowee Courier*, April 2, 1859, and by the Lancaster *Ledger*, April 27, 1859.
[7] J. H. Hammond to W. G. Simms, March 13, 1859.
[8] J. D. Ashmore to J. H. Hammond, Aug. 25, 1859.
[9] J. L. Orr to J. H. Hammond, Sept. 17, 1859.

the new Territories."[10]　Senator James Chesnut, in a speech at Camden, September 28, declared that a slave code for the territories was "the last thing that should be asked of Congress."[11]

The doctrine of congressional protection for slavery in the territories offered no escape for Northern Democrats. Here at last was one Southern demand that no Northern man could justify before his constituents. "I would never vote for a slave code in the territories by Congress," Douglas declared, "and I have yet to learn that there is a man in a free state of this Union, or any party, who would."[12]

The demand for a congressional slave code was another move on the part of the extremists that tended to split the Democratic party. It was the disruptive effect of the slave code proposal that nettled the conditional Unionists in South Carolina. A purely academic issue, it nevertheless might ruin the last chances for preserving the Union. The advocates of the slave code, Hammond wrote, were stripping the South of every supporter in the free states.[13]

Another demand that could never be supported in the North was being agitated by the proponents of the slave trade. Despite strong economic and moral objections to reopening the trade and despite the desire of most leaders not to agitate the question, their movement did not appear, in the first quarter of 1859, to be losing ground.[14]

[10] Quoted by the Augusta [Ga.] *Daily Constitutionalist*, Oct. 15, 1859.

[11] Quoted by Augusta [Ga.] *Daily Constitutionalist*, Sept. 30 and Oct. 15, 1859, and by Washington [D. C.] *States*, Oct. 5, 1859. B. F. Perry's view of the slave code can be found in his *Biographical Sketches* (1887), pp. 146-148, 159-165. The Edgefield *Advertiser*, May 4, April 20, Aug. 3, Sept. 21, 1859, was critical of the slave-code proposal. See also White, "National Democrats," p. 382, and Boucher, "South Carolina and the South on the Eve of Secession," pp. 126-127.

[12] *Congressional Globe*, 35 Cong., 2 Sess., p. 1242.

[13] J. H. Hammond to W. G. Simms, March 13, 1859.

[14] The Pickens *Keowee Courier* reported, Jan. 22, that the slave trade was being discussed in the state. The Newberry *Rising Sun*, Jan. 12, said that the pertinacious and persevering advocates of the slave trade were forcing the indifferent people to pay attention to the subject. Some people, it said, were persuaded by "the dazzling front of argument presented." Andrew Gordon Magrath wrote to J. H. Hammond, Jan. 21, 1859: "The slave trade agitation, of which you have written me, is as you will see, still continued. In the hands of a small minority, it is yet made to wear the proportion of a

L. W. Spratt, the original advocate of the foreign slave trade, was encouraged by the failure to suppress the question. In February, 1859, he still believed that Southern members of Congress, regardless of their personal views on the subject, would be constrained to defend it against Northern assailants. Spratt did not believe that Congress would ever reopen the slave trade; his strategy was to force the Southern members to fight to the bitter end the arguments which Northern men brought to bear against the slave trade and to demand for the South complete legal control over the institution of slavery.[15]

The slave trade came before Congress in the short session in connection with an appropriation bill. Both Lawrence Keitt and William P. Miles protested against granting money for support of the Negroes who had been sent to Liberia from the captured ship *Echo*. Keitt objected on the grounds that the appropriation was for the benefit of the Colonization Society. The question of reopening the slave trade, he said, should not enter the discussion of this appropriation.

That question I will meet whenever it comes up. I deprecate its agitation because it is disturbing, and can now result in no practical action. . . . In the meantime, I would sweep from the statute-book every interference with slavery. I would repeal the law declaring the slave trade piracy; I would withdraw our slave squadron from the coast of Africa; and I would leave slavery unintervened against, wherever the power of the country stretches.[16]

Miles took a similar stand. He doubted whether he would ever be ready to agitate for reopening the slave trade; but he was highly incensed by the federal laws that he thought put a stigma upon Southern institutions. He was prepared to advocate with

question, greatly dividing the State. And the violence of its advocates does, in fact, go far to supply the numerical deficiencies, which exist. The majority of the State, in numbers overwhelmingly no doubt is opposed." John C. Hope, of Lexington district, wrote to Hammond, Feb. 26, 1859, that a majority in South Carolina was opposed to reopening the trade, but that zealous advocates of the measure were "gaining some grounds for encouragement."

[15] L. W. Spratt to W. P. Miles, Feb. 12, 1859.
[16] *Congressional Globe*, 35 Cong., 2 Sess., p. 615.

all his mind and strength sweeping these laws from the statute books.[17]

Spratt was pleased with the speeches of the two Congressmen. "You cover all the grounds necessary to be taken," he wrote to Miles, February 12.

The question of policy is subordinate to the one of right. Whether there is occasion for more slaves is a matter upon which the states can determine for themselves and at their leisure, but whether they have the right to decide upon it for themselves is one of your immediate concern and I have confidence that you have indicated the position upon which the entire delegation from the slaveholding states will have to stand.

Opposition to agitation of the slave-trade question came from the same circles as the year before. One wing of the extremists, represented by the Rhetts, Cunningham, Keitt, and Boyce, opposed the question because it divided their own group as well as the South as a whole. Moderates saw that this subject divided the South, and they were afraid that its continued agitation would inevitably alienate Northern friends. In the minds of Hammond, Orr, and Ashmore, the slave trade was coupled with the slave-code question. Both questions deprived the South of supporters in the North and promoted the election of a Republican to the Presidency.[18]

In the summer and fall both secessionists and conditional Unionists made strong appeals for the suppression of the slave-trade agitation. But when the legislature met in November, L. W. Spratt and Edward B. Bryan were present with resolutions and speeches. These men found, however, that the temper of the legislature had changed markedly since 1858.

[17] *Ibid.*, p. 619.

[18] Charleston *Mercury*, Oct. 25, 1859; Edgefield *Advertiser*, Jan. 19, March 30, 1859; speeches of W. W. Boyce at Chester, July 4, and at Ebenezer, Sept. 1, quoted by Washington [D. C.] *States*, July 12, 1859, and Sept. 10, 1859, by Sumter *Watchman*, Sept. 20, 1859, by Charleston *Mercury*, Sept. 3, 1859; speech of James Chesnut, Sept. 28, 1859, quoted by Washington [D. C.] *States*, Oct. 5, 1859, and by Augusta [Ga.] *Daily Constitutionalist*, Sept. 30, and Oct. 15, 1859; letters to J. H. Hammond from John D. Ashmore, Aug. 25, and from John Cunningham, Jan. 15, 1859; J. H. Hammond to W. G. Simms, March 13, April 22, July 30, 1859.

Excited by the recent raid of fanatical abolitionists in Virginia, the members had no desire to debate such a factious and secondary measure. Resolutions which sanctioned repeal of federal laws restricting the slave trade failed to come to a vote. In the Senate a motion to table all matter connected with the subject

FIG. 10. This graph shows how senators from three groups of state districts, ranked according to slave population, voted in 1859 on a motion to table reports and all other matter connected with the subject of the slave trade.

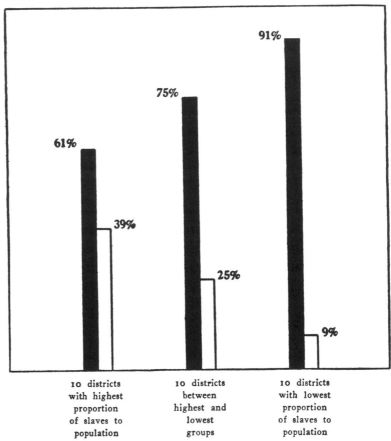

Proportion of votes for tabling to total cast by senators from the districts comprised in each group.

Proportion of votes against tabling to total cast by senators from the districts comprised in each group.

passed by a vote of 30 to 12.[19] Thus, as the year 1859 closed, the leaders in South Carolina came to an approximate agreement on the suppression of this question. The agreement was engineered by secession leaders, who persuaded some of the advocates of the slave trade that unity was worth more at the moment than continued agitation of their proposal. Under the circumstances, the disappearance of the issue from the political scene hardly strengthened the bond between South Carolina and the Union.

The hope of some moderates that the Republican party would suffer from the removal of the Kansas issue was not fulfilled in 1859. The results of state elections this year showed that the Republicans were still strong in the North. Extremists cited the elections to verify their predictions that the antislavery party would grow stronger and stronger until it ultimately triumphed. After reviewing the elections of 1859, the *Mercury* asked:

When the people of the North, *at three successive annual elections*, shall have proven that the generous estimate of their forbearance, justice, or sagacity is fallacious, will not their persevering and insolent aggressions be met with a courage and decision which shall forever secure to the South redemption and deliverance? Will not all doubters or speculators in Northern fidelity and integrity acknowledge their error?[20]

An important element in the thinking of those who viewed the triumph of the Republican party as inevitable was the belief that its leaders were able and skilled politicians. The irreconcilables of South Carolina never showed contempt for the political skill of the Republican leaders, never believed that they were all fanatical fools, never fell back upon the complacent hope that they would be outmaneuvered by Southern leaders. Sheer sympathy in the North for Republican aims would not insure victory for the antislavery party, they thought;

[19] *House Journal* (1859), p. 32; *Senate Journal* (1859), pp. 5, 75.
[20] Charleston *Mercury*, Nov. 26, 1859.

the ability of a group of politicians who knew how to exploit Northern opinion would play its role in the eventual outcome.

William H. Seward was regarded in South Carolina as the type of leader who had given the antislavery movement its great political power. Even in the days when he belonged to the old Whig party, Seward was thought of as the leading antislavery Senator; and since 1856 he had been looked upon as the undisputed leader of the Republican party. Most South Carolinians assumed that he would be the Republican presidential candidate in 1860. Neither his character nor his political ability was attacked by the press of the state. The disgust that Sumner's name always provoked was notably absent in references to Seward. It was to the New York Senator that South Carolina leaders looked to ascertain the next move of the Republican party. In Senator Hammond's discussions of a strategy to defeat the Republican party, Seward was mentioned more frequently than any other leader. Seward's "irrepressible conflict" speech of 1858 was, in the judgment of the extremists, no less than an official declaration of the Republican party, and they tried to persuade South Carolina and the South that it exposed the end sought by "Black Republicanism."[21] The *Mercury* publicized him as the leader of the party that could not be beaten:

Wm. H. Seward is the undoubted head of that party which now has possession of the northern States. He is no mere fanatic. He is a cool and able statesman, whose policy is sectional mastership and the adaptation of the tributary South to northern views of "freedom

[21] Charleston *Mercury*, Jan. 10, 1860; Newberry *Rising Sun*, March 17, 1858, Oct. 17, 1860; Spartanburg *Carolina Spartan*, Nov. 25, 1858; Sumter *Watchman*, March 17, 1858; speech of W. W. Boyce at Ebenezer, Sept. 1, 1859, quoted by Sumter *Watchman*, Sept. 20, *Mercury*, Sept. 3, Washington [D. C.] *States*, Sept. 10, 1859; speech of James Chesnut in the U. S. Senate, Dec. 7, 8, 1859, in *Congressional Globe*, 36 Cong., 1 Sess., pp. 37, 59; speech of J. H. Hammond, March 4, 1858, in the *Congressional Globe*, 35 Cong., 1 Sess., pp. 959-962; *An Appeal to the State Rights Party*, p. 9; letters to J. H. Hammond from B. H. Brown, April 7, Peyton G. Bowman, March 15, James Gadsden, March 11, Allen J. Green, March 7, 1858; J. H. Hammond to M. C. M. Hammond, March 9, 1858; J. H. Hammond to W. P. Miles, Nov. 5, Nov. 23, 1858 (Miles Papers, University of North Carolina).

and the rights of man." He organized and has led Black Republicanism to victory, and constituted the ruling spirit of that organization. His views are their views. His designs, those which they
will seek to compass. He is a little in advance in his declarations of
policy, but as they advance in power the practice of these will inevitably follow.[22]

For many South Carolina extremists, Northern Democrats
were enemies equally as dangerous as "Black Republicans."
The old arguments were repeated in 1859: There were no real
Democrats in the North, that is, no Democrats who lived up
to the principles of the party. Whenever a sectional issue arose
between the North and South, Democrats enough had always
been found to support Northern sectionalism. The defection of
Northern leaders was necessitated by the demands of their constituents; if they upheld the South, they would suffer defeat
at the hands of the Republicans.[23]

The belief that the presidential election of 1860 would decide the fate of the Union was firmly fixed in the minds of the
leaders of all factions. Newspapers and politicians who had for
several years opposed close ties with the national party renewed
their promise to secede if a Republican were elected President.
Speeches of John McQueen, W. W. Boyce, and R. Barnwell
Rhett, Sr., expressed determination to make the ultimatum of
Republican defeat or disunion the sole issue before the South.[24]

[22] Charleston *Mercury*, Oct. 22, 1859.

James Chesnut, in the U. S. Senate, Dec. 8, 1859, said that Seward's
"irrepressible conflict" speech of 1858 "had had more effect than all the
speeches which have ever been made by the advocates of southern rights to
bring the southern mind to the condition in which we find it" (*Congressional
Globe*, 36 Cong., 1 Sess., p. 60).

[23] Charleston *Mercury*, Feb. 8, March 26, April 1, May 10, June 28,
1859; Sumter *Watchman*, Aug. 30, 1859.

[24] White, *Rhett*, pp. 154-155; Lancaster *Ledger*, July 6, 1859; speech of
John McQueen at Lancaster Oct. 18, 1859, reported in Lancaster *Ledger*,
Oct. 26, 1859; report of letter (n.d.) written by John McQueen in reply to
an invitation to attend public dinner for James Chesnut, in Washington
[D. C.] *States*, Oct. 20, 1859; speech of Milledge Bonham in the House,
Dec. 16, 1859, in *Congressional Globe*, 36 Cong., 1 Sess., p. 167; speech of
W. W. Boyce at Ebenezer, Sept. 1, quoted by *Mercury*, Sept. 3, *Watchman*,
Sept. 20, Washington [D. C.] *States*, Sept. 10, 1859; speech of W. W. Boyce
at Sumter, Nov. 8, 1859, in Sumter *Watchman*, Nov. 15, 1859; synopsis

The most clear-cut objective of the isolationists in regard to the campaign of 1860 was to block the nomination of Stephen A. Douglas. Harping upon the theme that there was nothing to choose between Douglas and a Republican, the extremist press conducted what appears to have been a highly effective attack, for there were no forthright and unequivocal defenders of Douglas among the leaders of the state. The Sumter *Watchman* noted that even the press of "Orr Nationalism" had not supported him, although the welfare of national Democracy was at stake. The usual assumption in 1859 was that Douglas would not receive the nomination.[25]

For almost ten months in 1859 the politicians in South Carolina directed most of their thinking and their talking to the

---

of remarks made by W. W. Boyce at Chester, July 4, in Washington [D. C.] *States*, July 12, 1859; speech of R. Barnwell Rhett, Sr., at Grahamville, July 4, 1859, in the *Mercury*, July 7, 1859; letters to J. H. Hammond from Lawrence Keitt, April 11, and John Cunningham, April 18, 1859.

[25] Lancaster *Ledger*, July 20, Aug. 17, 1859; Cheraw *Gazette* (n.d.), quoted by the Lancaster *Ledger*, July 20, 1859; Charleston *Mercury*, March 22, May 20, June 15, Aug. 22, 24, Sept. 14, 15, 17, Oct. 11, 1859; Columbia *Guardian* (n.d.), quoted by Sumter *Watchman*, Aug. 16, 1859; Sumter *Watchman*, Aug. 23, 1859; John Cunningham to J. H. Hammond, Aug. 27, 1859; J. H. Hammond to W. G. Simms, April 8, 1860.

James L. Orr wrote to Hammond, Sept. 17, 1859: "Douglas I think has settled his prospects for the Presidency and when the inquisition is held the verdict will be *felo de se*." John E. Carew, of the *Mercury* staff, wrote to Miles, Feb. 28, 1859, that Douglas could be considered shelved as far as the presidential nomination was concerned. J. H. Hammond wrote to W. G. Simms, April 8, 1860: "Over two years ago I told Douglas he had thrown away his chances for the Presidency. I have since told him so 20 times."

There was perhaps a dormant sympathy for Douglas in the state. Edward Noble, of Abbeville, wrote to F. W. Pickens, Aug. 10, 1859, that there was an evident design to bring the state to support Douglas. He was not certain how successful it would be; the Douglas men would be slow coming out, would feel the pulse of the state and slowly prepare it for his nomination. He had heard that Simkins, of the Edgefield *Advertiser*, was for Douglas as the only available Democrat and he thought that the Columbia *South Carolinian* might be made to lean his way (letter in Duke University Library). The Edgefield *Advertiser* denied that it agreed with Douglas's interpretation of popular sovereignty, but it pointed out his advantages as an available candidate for the Democratic nomination in 1860 and praised his "fairness and independence" (editorials of July 13, July 20, Aug. 10, Sept. 7, 1859). Opinions favorable to Douglas were expressed in letters written by pseudonymous writers reputed to be South Carolinians which appeared in the Augusta [Ga.] *Daily Constitutionalist*, March 22, 1860, and Washington [D. C.] *States and Union*, April 6 and 19, 1860.

subject of the next presidential election. Then, suddenly, in the last half of October, the complexion of politics in South Carolina changed. A single event precipitated a somersault from speculation about president-making to the immediate safety of South Carolina and the South. On the night of October 16 John Brown and eighteen followers captured the arsenal at Harper's Ferry, Virginia, the first step in their fantastic plan to liberate the slaves of the South.

For the rest of the year John Brown was the main subject for discussion in South Carolina. Many columns of the newspapers were taken up with the story of the Virginia raid. People read how places in South Carolina had been marked on Brown's map for uprisings. Rumors of disturbances in other slave states were circulated. Public meetings, most of them weeks after the event, were called to organize vigilance committees. Resolutions adopted at these "public safety" meetings announced that transients from the North would have to account for their presence in the state. Two Northern school teachers, an emigrant ditch-digger, and several other residents were requested to leave the state.[26]

Except to petrify already ingrained opinions about the sectional conflict, the Harper's Ferry incident had little effect upon the minds of a very considerable fraction of those citizens who had some voice in the public affairs of South Carolina. For those who had already made up their minds that Southern security in the Federal Union was impossible, the invasion was neither surprising nor of unique importance.[27] It was merely a sign of the times, a logical outcome of Republican preachings such as Seward's Rochester speech, a prelude to what would

[26] Boucher, "South Carolina and the South on the Eve of Secession," pp. 129-130; Lancaster *Ledger*, Nov. 9, Dec. 7, 1859, Jan. 1, 4, 1860; Charleston *Mercury*, Oct. 19, 31, Nov. 1, 2, 3, 8, 14, 28, 30, Dec. 5, 1859, Jan. 6, 1860; Kingstree *Star* (n.d.), quoted by the Charleston *Mercury*, Jan. 6, 1860; Pickens *Keowee Courier*, Oct. 29, Nov. 5, Dec. 10, 1859; Spartanburg *Carolina Spartan*, Nov. 24, 1859; Sumter *Watchman*, Nov. 1, 15, 22, 29, Dec. 24, 1859, Jan. 17, 1860.
[27] The *Mercury*, Nov. 14, said: "We have made no fuss about this Harper's Ferry business. We regard it as a small affair, except as a sign of the times and of the temper and intentions of the northern majority."

occur again and again, a preview for Southerners of the destiny that awaited them in the Union. They had warned the South to expect such incidents, had tried to persuade the citizenry that they could not be safe in the Union. Now perhaps their warning would be heeded.

A few of our most zealous statesmen [said the Lancaster *Ledger*] warned us time and again of the probability of such a condition of affairs being experienced in the South at some time in the future, if the tide of abolition fury at the North was not checked. Many of us hooted at the idea and thought that the danger existed in the imaginations of some of our fire-eating politicians; but the prophecy does not now seem so absurd.[28]

No man in 1859 did the work of the South Carolina disunionist so well as Old Brown of Osawatomie. Newspapers that had formerly expressed moderate opinions began to write frankly about the necessity or probability of disunion. The Pickens *Keowee Courier* said that if the "cut throats at Harper's Ferry are to be sustained, then the sooner we get out of the Union the better."[29] The Spartanburg *Carolina Spartan*, which had supported the convention movement in 1856, presented an editorial on November 24 which demonstrated the effect of the raid on South Carolina opinion: "We do not care a fig about the Convention or the election of another President, as we are convinced the safety of the South lies only outside the present Union—and this we believe to be the judgment of a large majority of our people." The Lancaster *Ledger*, another newspaper that had supported participation in national party politics, said on November 2: "Let us endeavor to move in concert, set our houses in order, looking to the grand event which has been mooted for years and which circumstances now indicate as affording the only haven of security, viz., a dissolution of the Union." The Edgefield *Advertiser*, edited by Arthur Simkins, one of the few moderates who had refused to denounce Douglas in 1859, said: "Neither justice nor patriotism requires that she [the South] forbear longer, unless a change of Northern senti-

[28] Lancaster *Ledger*, Nov. 2, 1859.
[29] Pickens *Keowee Courier*, Oct. 29, 1859.

ment and policy be shown by the Presidential election of the coming year."[30]

Disunionists were pleased with the change of opinion in the state. Union men were becoming convinced, said the *Watchman*, that the Constitution could not protect them.[31] "The staunchest Union men, heretofore, are becoming the sternest in the vindication of the rights of the South," said the *Mercury*.[32] In the state legislature D. H. Hamilton approvingly reported that he had heard "a rank Union man," who had "never expected to live to see the day when he would come to regard the Union as a nuisance," say that "he was ready for Disunion now."[33]

William Henry Gist, the governor of South Carolina in 1859, was an outright disunionist.[34] Throughout his political career he consistently stood on the side of the insurgent faction of the state. Although born in Charleston, he had spent most of his fifty-two years in Union District, where lived many other planters who preferred Southern sectionalism to the constitutional nationalism of their Representative, James L. Orr. His election to the governorship in December, 1858, was called a victory for those who refused "to chain South Carolina to the car of national parties."[35] Although a disunionist, Gist, unlike many of his ultra friends, was neither proscriptive nor factious. He did not want to make the party convention an issue in the state and thought that the isolationists should be neutral toward those who preferred to elect delegates to the Democratic convention. He disagreed with Spratt, Bryan, and all others who defended violators of the slave-trade laws.[36] In September, in a public letter, he advised secession if a Republican were elected in 1860. "If the South have gained any victories," he wrote,

[30] Edgefield *Advertiser*, Dec. 14, 1859.

[31] Sumter *Watchman*, Dec. 24, 1859.

[32] Charleston *Mercury*, Dec. 5, 1859.

[33] D. H. Hamilton to W. P. Miles, Dec. 9, 1859.

[34] There is a sketch of Gist by Francis Butler Simkins in the *Dictionary of American Biography*, VII, 322.

[35] Correspondence from Columbia, Dec. 10, 1858, in Sumter *Watchman*, Dec. 21, 1858.

[36] W. H. Gist to J. H. Hammond, Feb. 16, 1859.

"they may properly be styled spiritual victories, such as loving our enemies, doing good for evil, when smitten on one cheek turning the other for a like infliction."[37]

When the John Brown raid occurred, Gist thought that the time had arrived to stop excusing inaction on the grounds of conservatism, moderation, and statesmanship; and in his message to the legislature, November 29, he included explicit statements about the impossibility of living in the Union "in peace and harmony" and the necessity of secession in 1860 if defeated in the presidential election. Although convinced that the legislature was ready for extreme measures, he was too uncertain about the course of the other Southern states to make specific recommendations. He could only appeal to the legislature to exhaust every means to get the co-operation of the other Southern states.

Most of the governor's statements on federal relations were devoted to the growing antislavery movement in the North and to the presidential election of 1860. He pointed to a set of resolutions that he had received from the Vermont legislature as representative of opinion in all nonslaveholding states. These resolutions affirmed the right and duty of Congress to exclude slavery from the territories and the District of Columbia and declared that Vermont would resist the admission of new slave states into the Union. With few exceptions, Gist said, the entire North was arrayed against them, and the war against the South was proceeding relentlessly. Harper's Ferry was the crossing of the Rubicon for the abolitionists, and if the South did not unite, it would deserve the execration of posterity. Faced with great dangers, South Carolina would be foolish to rely upon the Democratic party or any presidential candidate for protection.

As well might we rely on a paste-board barque to protect us from ocean storms. South Carolina should be careful not to commit herself, directly or indirectly, to any Presidential aspirant, and be forced by party trammels to support a party nominee. An open and undisguised enemy is infinitely preferable to a pretended friend, and we should scorn the alternative of a choice of evils, as being but the

[37] Quoted in Spartanburg *Carolina Spartan*, Oct. 13, 1859.

poor privilege of a slave to choose his master. We have sunk very low, indeed, if our liberties are to depend upon the fortunate selection of a candidate for the Presidency, who, on account of his popularity, or his mysterious manner of expressing his opinions, makes himself acceptable to both sections, or is what is generally termed

FIG. 11. This graph shows how senators from three groups of state districts, ranked according to slave population, voted in 1859 on a resolution which invited the slaveholding states "to inaugurate the movement of Southern separation."

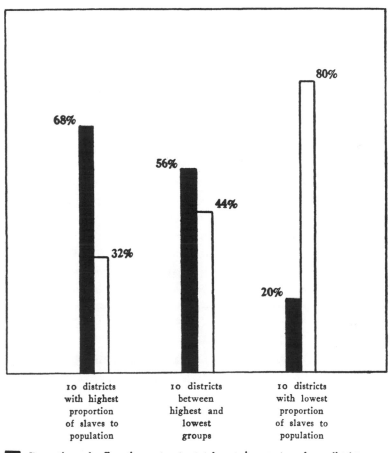

| | 10 districts with highest proportion of slaves to population | 10 districts between highest and lowest groups | 10 districts with lowest proportion of slaves to population |

■ Proportion of affirmative votes to total cast by senators from districts comprised in each group.

□ Proportion of negative votes to total cast by senators from districts comprised in each group.

available. It is unbecoming a free people to stake their liberties upon the successful jugglery of party politicians and interested office seekers, rather than a bold and determined resolution to maintain them at every hazard.[38]

A militant legislature received this message. Even Benjamin F. Perry, staunch National Democrat, presented resolutions which threatened the North with disunion.[39] The Senate, where the extremists benefited most from the apportionment, passed by a vote of 22 to 19 a resolution that invited the slaveholding states "to inaugurate the movement of Southern separation."[40] The House would not accept the Senate resolution, and a conference was necessary before agreement was reached. The resolution that finally passed both houses did not explicitly mention separation. It merely invited the slaveholding states to meet together in order "to concert measures for united action."[41]

The adopted resolution, a combination of one introduced in the House by Christopher G. Memminger and the preamble to the Senate resolution, included three other sections. The second requested the governors of the slaveholding states to appoint deputies for a Southern conference and to adopt any other suitable measure for the promotion of the meeting. The third provided for a special commissioner to Virginia "to express to the authorities of that State, the cordial sympathy of the people of South Carolina with the people of Virginia, and their earnest desire to unite with them in measures of common defence." The fourth section appropriated $100,000 for military contingencies.[42]

What proportion of the members of the legislature wanted to leave the Union in 1859? It may be conjectured from votes

[38] Message of Nov. 29, 1859, in the *House Journal* (1859), pp. 12-24 and *Senate Journal* (1859), pp. 11-23.

[39] B. F. Perry, *Biographical Sketches* (1887), pp. 180-185; Kibler, *Perry*, pp. 296-297; *House Journal* (1859), pp. 72-73.

[40] *House Journal* (1859), p. 263; *Senate Journal* (1859), p. 135.

[41] *House Journal* (1859), pp. 196-197, 199, 201, 202, 204, 263, 268, 274, 276; *Reports and Resolutions of the General Assembly of the State of South Carolina, Passed at the Annual Session of 1859* (Columbia, 1859), p. 579.

[42] *Reports and Resolutions* (1859), p. 579.

on several resolutions that referred to disunion that at least 50
per cent of the Senate[43] and at least 40 per cent of the House[44]
desired disunion.   Such a conjecture, there is some reason to
suppose, is an underestimation of disunion strength in the legislature.   If every member who voted for resolutions favorable
to disunion really desired to leave the Union and if some genuine secessionists declined to support such resolutions for strategic reasons, i.e., because they might antagonize the other
Southern states, the number that voted for disunion resolutions
was lower than the number that actually preferred a Southern confederacy.   Furthermore, a higher estimate of disunion
strength in the House might be reached by selecting resolutions

[43] By a vote of 22 to 19 a resolution was adopted which read: "Resolved,
That South Carolina, still deferring to her Southern sisters, nevertheless re-
spectfully announces to them that, in her judgment, the safety and honor
of the slaveholding States imperatively demand a speedy separation from other
States of the Confederacy, and earnestly invites the slaveholding States to
inaugurate the movement of Southern separation, in which she pledges herself promptly to unite" (*Senate Journal*, p. 135; *House Journal*, p. 262).

[44] This estimate of disunion strength in the House is based primarily on
the vote on a resolution offered by William Whaley, of St. Philip's and St.
Michael's.   The statement on the Union in Whaley's resolution, which asked
for an appropriation of $100,000 for the discretional use of the governor, was
in the preamble: "That, whereas, The Constitution of the United States, or-
dained and established to 'insure domestic tranquility,' has proven a failure,
and the union of these States, so far as the fraternal relations are concerned,
is dissolved; and, whereas, the highest interests of the slaveholding States demand that this dissolution shall, in form be consummated, which consummation
will probably involve the necessity of a resort to arms; therefore, . . ."   On
Dec. 14, this resolution was ordered to lie on the table by a vote of 66 to
44 (*House Journal*, pp. 174-175).

Two other resolutions that referred favorably to disunion and that came
to some kind of vote are given below:

(1) Offered by John C. Hope, of Lexington: "Resolved, That it is the
sense of the Legislature not to take steps for the immediate formation of a
Southern Confederacy; but, when any of the neighboring slave States enter
upon the proper course, to appoint deputies to meet others, similarly ap-
pointed, in Convention, to deliberate and agree upon a plan for such formation,
South Carolina will be ready to do her part in this gigantic movement."   On
Dec. 6, the House voted 60 to 38 against postponement of this resolution
(*House Journal*, pp. 99-100).

(2) Offered by W. S. Mullins, of Marion: "That the State of South
Carolina is now ready to act with the slaveholding States of this Confederacy,
or with such of them as desire present action in the formation of a Southern
Confederacy."   On Dec. 15 a motion to lay this resolution on the table failed
by a vote of 51 to 61.   Mullins withdrew his resolution when Memminger
offered his on Dec. 16 (*House Journal*, pp. 176, 191).

FIG. 12. This graph shows how representatives from three groups of state districts, ranked according to slave population, voted in 1859 on a motion to table William Whaley's resolution which stated that the Union should be dissolved and which called for an appropriation of $100,000 for military purposes.

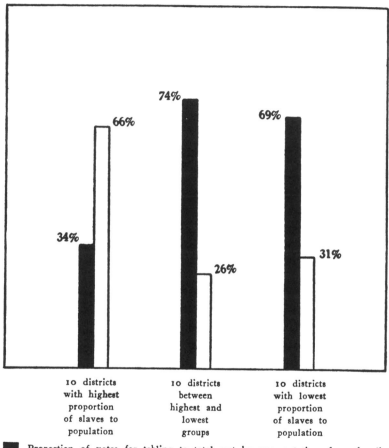

| | 10 districts with highest proportion of slaves to population | 10 districts between highest and lowest groups | 10 districts with lowest proportion of slaves to population |

■ Proportion of votes for tabling to total cast by representatives from the districts comprised in each group.

□ Proportion of votes against tabling to total cast by representatives from the districts comprised in each group.

other than the one upon which the figure given here is based.

South Carolina, in December, 1859, was back where it had been eight years before. Most of the elective officials in the state were dissatisfied with their position in the Union, and a large majority could see no practical, quick way to redress their grievances.[45]   There were, however, at least three important differences in the two situations:

FIG. 13.   This graph shows how representatives from three groups of state districts, ranked according to slave population, voted in 1859 on a motion to table W. S. Mullins's resolution which stated that South Carolina was ready to act with the slaveholding states in the formation of a Southern confederacy.

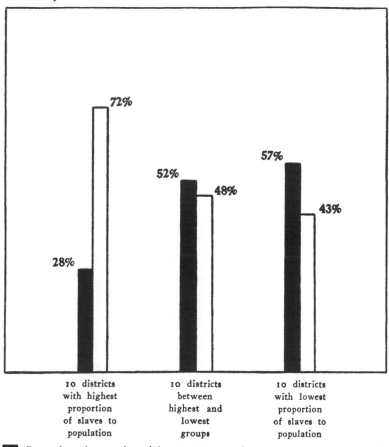

| 10 districts with highest proportion of slaves to population | 10 districts between highest and lowest groups | 10 districts with lowest proportion of slaves to population |

◼ Proportion of votes for tabling to total cast by representatives from the districts comprised in each group.

☐ Proportion of votes against tabling to total cast by representatives from the districts comprised in each group.

[45] C. G. Memminger wrote to W. P. Miles, Dec. 27, 1859: "All of us are persuaded that in this Union, there is no security—and either there must

(1) In December, 1851, South Carolina was approaching the termination of a cycle of heated agitation. In December, 1859, it was in the beginning phase of another cycle of intense agitation.

(2) In 1851 the legislature was sharply divided over the question of whether the state should attempt secession without outside support. In 1859 the legislature unitedly assumed that South Carolina should not secede or adopt other insurgent measures independently of the other Southern states. In 1859 not even the most blatant hotspurs proposed independent action. Their failure in 1851 had taught the secessionists a lesson that they remembered well eight years later, and their wording of resolutions on federal relations showed a punctilious deference to the other slaveholding states.

(3) In 1859 the South Carolina secessionists were more hopeful about achieving Southern independence than they had been eight years before. In December, 1851, they knew that an overwhelming majority of the leaders in the slaveholding states were opposed to secession. In December, 1859, they knew that numerous Southern leaders were disposed to favor secession in 1860 upon certain conditions.

---

be new terms established or a Southern Confederacy is our only hope of safety." W. H. Gist wrote to Miles, Dec. 20, 1859: "I have not the least doubt that South Carolina would sustain her members [in Congress] in almost anything they might do in concerted action with the Southern members, or any considerable portion of them." I. W. Hayne wrote to J. H. Hammond, Jan. 5, 1860: "The masses of this State would, you may be assured, rejoice in any movement tending to disunion, either on the part of Virginia or Georgia, and would be glad to move *pari passu* with either, and run the hazard of any further cooperation."

FIG. 14. This graph illustrates the vote in 1859 on John C. Hope's resolution which stated: "Resolved, That it is the sense of the Legislature not to take steps for the immediate formation of a Southern Confederacy; but, when any of the neighboring slave States enter upon the proper course, to appoint deputies to meet others, similarly appointed, in Convention, to deliberate and agree upon a plan for such formation, South Carolina will be ready to do her part in this gigantic movement."

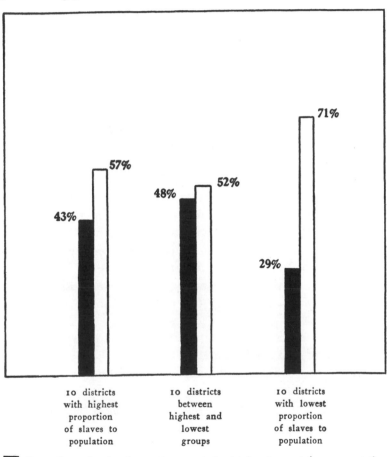

Proportion of votes for postponement to total votes cast by representatives from districts comprised in each group.

Proportion of votes against postponement to total votes cast by representatives from districts comprised in each group.

CHAPTER X

INSURGENCY, 1860

CHRISTOPHER G. MEMMINGER was South Carolina's special commissioner to Virginia. Fifty-six years old, German-born and Charleston-reared, lawyer by profession, chairman of the Ways and Means Committee of the state House of Representatives, promoter of educational and financial reforms, Memminger was one of the state's most valuable citizens.[1] Both his temperament and his politics made him suitable for the Virginia mission. He was mild in manner, without the fire-eating qualities so unpopular in Virginia. He was a good speaker, clear, forcible, mild, persuasive, not of the South Carolina bombastic school. Throughout his career he had been associated with the moderate faction in the state. He had opposed nullification in 1832 and separate secession in 1851, had urged reconciliation with Northern Democrats in 1852, had supported the convention movement in 1856, and had been one of two candidates put up by the moderates in the Senatorial election in 1858.[2]

The resolutions that Memminger carried to Virginia made no mention of disunion, but a large portion of the members who voted for them were secessionists who thought that they were committing South Carolina to a policy of co-operation with the slaveholding states for the purpose of forming a Southern con-

[1] A short biographical sketch of Memminger by Charles W. Ramsdell is in the *Dictionary of American Biography*, XII, 527.

[2] The Charleston *Mercury*, Dec. 29, 1859, said: "The choice is eminently proper, not only from this gentleman's great ability, but from his connection with and leadership, in the more moderate party of South Carolina. This must make his embassadorship more acceptable to Virginia, and lend power to the words he may speak there." I. W. Hayne wrote to W. P. Miles, Jan. 5, 1860: "The fact that Mr. Memminger was an old Union man and anti-secessionist, and that he has been charged by some with *too much* of moderation and caution will render him only the more effective."

federacy. The language used in the resolutions, in the minds of the secessionists, was euphemistic and diplomatic, designed to reassure Southerners who were averse to discussion of disunion. Memminger himself subscribed to this interpretation of the South Carolina resolutions.[3]

Memminger was in Richmond from January 12 to February 8.[4] Before he left Charleston, the South Carolina delegation in Washington had met with the Virginia delegation at his request to consult about the mission and to prepare the way by writing letters to certain leaders in Richmond. With him was his "beautiful and charming" daughter, who was helpful in his social life there.

Memminger was well received. Governor John Letcher thought that he was "a gentleman of unusually fine intelligence, admirable conversational talents, and most polished manners." The Virginia newspapers which were friendly to the mission emphasized his connection with the moderate faction in South Carolina. "Although from a State said to contain many fire-

[3] Memminger wrote to W. P. Miles, Jan. 3, 1860: "My opinion and I think the opinion of our state is that the Union cannot be preserved; and that a sectional government such as we have is not worthy of preservation. New terms, fresh constitutional guarantees might make another Union desirable. But in this, we will soon be deprived of every defence against the Northern section. While I am not disposed to thrust these views upon the Virginians it seems to me that justice to our state requires that they should be presented frankly, if I am invited to address them. They form a leading inducement to the lead which we wish Virginia to take in the matter; and I think they can be presented as our view without the slightest attempt to dictate."

[4] The following account of the Memminger mission is based upon these authorities and sources: Dwight L. Dumond, *The Secession Movement, 1860-1861* (New York, 1931), pp. 27-31; Ollinger Crenshaw, "Christopher G. Memminger's Mission to Virginia, 1860," *Journal of Southern History*, VIII (Aug., 1942), pp. 334-349; Charleston *Mercury*, Jan. 4, 1860; Edgefield *Advertiser*, Jan. 25, March 31, 1860; Pickens *Keowee Courier*, Feb. 4, 18, 1860; Augusta [Ga.] *Daily Constitutionalist*, Jan. 21, Feb. 15, 1860; Richmond correspondence of the Petersburg [Va.] *Express* (n.d.), quoted by the *Keowee Courier*, Jan. 21, 1860; Richmond [Va.] *Dispatch* (n.d.), quoted by the *Keowee Courier*, Feb. 4, 1860; C. G. Memminger to W. P. Miles, Dec. 27, 1859, Jan. 3, 16, 30, Feb. 4, 6, 1860; John Letcher to W. P. Miles, Jan. 12, 15, 1860; C. G. Memminger to R. B. Rhett, Jr., Jan. 28, 1860 (in Library of Congress); C. G. Memminger to John Letcher, Feb. 8, and C. G. Memminger to W. H. Gist, Feb. 8, 1860, in Pickens *Keowee Courier*, March 17, 1860; text of Memminger's address to the Virginia legislature in *De Bow's Review*, XXIX (Dec., 1860), 751-771.

eaters," a Petersburg correspondent wrote, "it must not be inferred that Mr. Memminger is a man of this class. Bold, chivalrous, high-toned, spirited, and as necessity requires, as full of metal [*sic*] as the war-horse which snuffs the battle from afar, he is yet mild as a lamb, meek as a Christian, which he really is, and would sooner pour oil on the troubled waters than add fuel to the flame."[5]

But whatever his qualifications as a politician or diplomat, it is doubtful whether any South Carolinian could have persuaded Virginia to support a Southern conference at that time. Most of the politicians and their constituents were suspicious of the South Carolina proposal. They thought it was a move toward the formation of a Southern confederacy. The Whig politicians, strongly opposed to secession, tried to capitalize on the widespread pro-Union sentiment by branding advocates of a Southern conference as disunionists. Even the few defenders of a Southern conference avowed that its purpose was to protect Southern interests in the Union and thereby prevent secession.[6] Memminger found that even the most extreme leaders were reluctant to give public endorsement to a Southern conference. Presidential politics was one reason for their reticence. Supporters of Virginia's aspirants for the Democratic nomination were anxious to avoid taking any action which might react to the disadvantage of their candidates.

The Virginians were hospitable. They graciously entertained Memminger and his daughter; they listened politely when he told about the dangers of the South in the Union; and their resolution declining a Southern conference included an expression of appreciation for South Carolina's "fraternal regard and affection."

Long before the legislature finally acted upon the proposal for a Southern conference, Memminger had realized that he could do nothing in Richmond and had returned to Charleston.

[5] Correspondence of Petersburg [Va.] *Express* (n.d.) quoted by Pickens *Keowee Courier*, Jan. 21, 1860.

[6] Memminger wrote to Miles, Jan. 3, 1860, that the Richmond [Va.] *Enquirer* was mistaken in representing his mission as one to preserve the Union.

The apprehension that the proposal for a conference must lead to disunion, Memminger concluded, was the main hindrance to its adoption.

For the secessionists of South Carolina, the course of Alabama and Mississippi was far more important than that of Virginia. The support of these states was indispensable, that of Virginia merely desirable. The failure of the Memminger mission was, therefore, not a great disappointment to secessionists of the Rhett school. Since 1857 the *Mercury* had descanted upon the folly of depending upon Virginia or any border state to take the lead in a "resistance" movement.[7] On March 10 it referred to its previous stand and argued that the rejection of a Southern conference by Virginia proved that the Cotton States would have to assume the leadership in a secession movement. In a personal letter to Congressman Miles, R. B. Rhett, Jr., editor of the *Mercury*, wrote that Mississippi, Alabama, and South Carolina were "quite enough to break down the spoils Democracy and, on the election of a Black Republican, to dissolve the Union."[8]

News from Alabama and Mississippi in the first quarter of 1860 was encouraging to the South Carolina secessionists. In Alabama the legislature provided for the convocation of a special state convention upon the election of a Republican to the Presidency, and the Democratic state convention instructed its delegates to withdraw from the national convention if the party platform failed to recognize the right of Congress to protect slavery in the territories. In Mississippi the legislature agreed to the proposal for a Southern conference, and many delegates to the Democratic convention supported the Alabama platform.[9]

[7] Charleston *Mercury*, March 19, April 28, July 25, 1857, Aug. 2, 14, 1858, June 11, 30, July 21, 23, 1859; R. B. Rhett, Jr., to J. H. Hammond, Aug. 2, 1858.

[8] R. B. Rhett, Jr., to W. P. Miles, Jan. 29, 1860.

[9] Craven, *Coming of the Civil War*, pp. 413-414; Denman, *Secession in Alabama*, pp. 79-81; Dumond, *The Secession Movement*, pp. 28-34; Milton, *Douglas*, p. 404; Rainwater, *Mississippi: Storm Center of Secession*, pp. 105-106, 114, 117, 120; Randall, *Civil War*, p. 175; *Official Proceedings of the Democratic National Convention, Held in 1860, at Charleston and Baltimore* (Cleveland, 1860), pp. 56-57; message of William H. Gist, Nov. 27, 1860,

While the South Carolina legislature debated the question of Southern security and while Memminger was in Richmond, the South Carolina press was conducting an intensive propaganda for Southern self-sufficiency.[10] That the security of slavery was menaced by association with Northerners was the main theme of a campaign for nonintercourse that began about the middle of December, 1859, and lasted until March, 1860. Many Northern merchants with whom Southern merchants and planters traded supported the antislavery movement. South Carolinians should therefore trade with merchants in their own state or some other slaveholding state. Northern colleges and universities and Northern teachers in the South taught abolition doctrines to Southern students. Therefore Southern youth should be educated by Southern teachers in Southern schools. Northern magazines and newspapers held that slavery was wrong. Therefore Southern people should read only those journals published in the South by Southern owners and Southern editors. So the argument went.

The immediate consequences of this agitation for nonintercourse with the North were few in the winter of 1859-1860. Some South Carolina medical students resigned from Philadelphia schools. A group of Charleston merchants sponsored an advertisement campaign which failed in its purpose of persuading up-country buyers to cease trading with New York firms. The legislature did little to promote this movement for eco-

in *House Journal* (1860), p. 20 and *Senate Journal* (1860), p. 16; Charleston *Mercury*, Jan. 11, 14, 16, 20, April 3, 1860.

[10] The summary given here of the movement for self-sufficiency is based upon these sources: Lancaster *Ledger*, Jan. 25, Feb. 29, 1860; Charleston *Mercury*, Jan. 2, 6, 12, 17, March 2, 1860; Spartanburg *Express*, Jan. 18, 25, Feb. 1, Aug. 8, 1860; Spartanburg *Carolina Spartan*, Jan. 19, 26, March 1, 1860; Columbia *Guardian* (n.d.), quoted by the *Mercury*, Jan. 6, 1860; Sumter *Watchman*, Dec. 20, 24, 1859, Jan. 10, 24, Feb. 22, 1860; letter by "Several Constituents" in Charleston *Mercury*, Jan. 10, 1860; letter by "Southerner" in *Mercury*, Jan. 5, 1860; letter by "Fairfield" in the Winnsboro *Register* (n.d.), quoted by *Mercury*, Jan. 9, 1860; Washington [D. C.] *States and Union*, Jan. 22, 1860; *House Journal* (1859), pp. 178, 248, 270, 278; *Senate Journal* (1859), pp. 52, 94, 159; *Acts of the General Assembly of the State of South Carolina passed in December, 1859* (Columbia, 1859), pp. 768, 769.

nomic and cultural independence; it merely sought to prevent outsiders from spreading subversive ideas in the state by requiring a license of traveling salesmen and itinerant peddlers and by forbidding the circulation of books and magazines calculated to create disaffection among the slaves.

The practical results of the agitation for sectional self-sufficiency were meager, but for the secessionist per se, who had little or nothing to lose by such agitation, failure may have been as advantageous as success. Merchants, bankers, educators, and journalists, who perhaps began to hope that they might gain what Northerners would lose from Southern self-sufficiency, could easily blame their frustrations upon the continued existence of the Union. In a Southern confederacy their expectations might be fulfilled.

While the press agitated for nonintercourse with the North, a bitter sectional and party struggle was taking place in Congress. The South Carolinians in Washington saw a disorderly, rowdy, wrangling, fighting session. Senator Hammond said that everyone carried a revolver and that a "great slaughter" might occur any day. "There are no relations [Hammond wrote]— not absolutely indispensable for the conduct of joint business— between the North and South in either House. No two nations on earth are or ever were more distinctly separated and hostile than we are here. Not Carthage and Rome, England and France at any period. How can the thing go on?"[11]

The South Carolina delegation was well-behaved. In the wildest session any of the members had ever seen, none of them became involved in the numerous personal altercations on the floor. Even excitable Lawrence Keitt let Southerners from other states do the fist waving.

Although more restrained than delegations of other years, this one of 1860 was less disposed to believe in the continuation of the Union. The stand of its members in the speakership election demonstrated the growth of insurgency in South Caro-

[11] J. H. Hammond to M. C. M. Hammond, April 22, 1860; similar statement to Francis Lieber, April 29, 1860, in *Life and Letters of Francis Lieber*, pp. 310-311.

lina in four years. In 1856 three of the six members of the House were outside the pale of the Democratic party organization. In 1860 five of the six members acted independently of the party organization. In 1856 the three isolationists voted for the Northern candidate of the national Democratic party. In 1860 the five isolationists voted for Southern or Far-western Democrats, Americans, or old-line Whigs. In 1856 the organization Democrats voted for the Democratic candidate only. In 1860 the one organization Democrat voted for Democrats, Americans, and old-line Whigs. In 1856 the delegation acquiesced in the decision of the Democratic party to accept a plurality election. In 1860 the delegation was pledged to resist a plurality election.[12]

The positions of the two newest members of the South Carolina delegation, James Chesnut and John D. Ashmore, likewise showed the drift toward disruption. Senator Chesnut had always stood on the very border line between the group that worked for disunion and the group that worked for preservation of the Union. He was now in the Senate primarily because he had managed to avoid making a stand on the question of the national Democratic party and because he had personal friends in all factions. His position "on the fence" made him a particularly good barometer of the trend of opinion in his state. His impromptu remarks and his single prepared speech in this session put him into the camp of the Southern extremists, although perhaps not yet in the ranks of the South Carolina irreconcilables. Most significant was his complete concurrence with resolutions introduced by Jefferson Davis which said that Congress was obliged to protect slavery in the territories. These he termed "just" and "wise."[13]

[12] Correspondence from Washington, D. C., Nov. 29, Dec. 1, in Charleston *Courier*, Dec. 1, 6, 1855; Charleston *Mercury*, Jan. 29, 1856; Columbia *Carolina Times*, Jan. 14, 22, Feb. 22, 1856; letter from Washington, D. C. (n.d.), in the Columbia *South Carolinian* (n.d.), quoted by the Lancaster *Ledger*, Feb. 13, 1856; Lawrence Keitt to Sue Sparks, Jan. 10, Feb. 2, 1856; *Congressional Globe*, 34 Cong., 1 Sess., pp. 77, 96, 156, 157-158, 189, 246, 320, 335-336, 36 Cong., 1 Sess., pp. 166, 219-220, 274-275, 352, 365, 477, 533, 610, 961-962.

[13] *Congressional Globe*, 36 Cong., 1 Sess., pp. 37, 1613-1619.

John D. Ashmore was associated with the most moderate faction in the state.   In temperament and methods he closely resembled James L. Orr, whose vacated seat he now occupied.[14] Ashmore agreed with most of his colleagues on the questions before Congress, but he was still the least sectional member of the delegation.   Once, during the speakership contest, he parted company with his five colleagues and four Alabamans when he voted for John Alexander McClernand, a Douglas man from Illinois.   In two other important ways, Ashmore showed that he had not yet locked arms with McQueen, Miles, Keitt, Bonham, and Boyce.   He refrained from demanding that the Democratic nominee endorse the theory that Congress was obligated to protect slavery in the territories, and he pledged himself to support any candidate nominated by "the delegates in convention from the South and the true Democracy of the North."[15]

For years Ashmore had looked upon the growing distrust between the North and South with the darkest forebodings. He had hoped that some combination of fortuitous circumstances might bring about a settlement of the controversy, but in March, 1860, he had little hope that the slavery question would be settled in the Union.

Ashmore was impressed with the distrust of the Northern and Southern people for each other.   He feared that open conflict could not be avoided because the differences of opinions had reached the point where each side viewed the opinions and sentiments of the other as insincere exaggerations.   Ashmore had no desire to indulge in threats, but he was anxious to make clear to the Northern Congressmen the state of public opinion in the South.

Threats of disunion had been made so many times in the South that many Northern leaders had begun to take them

[14] *Ibid.*, p. 958; Anderson *Gazette*, Oct. 20, quoted by the Augusta [Ga.] *Daily Constitutionalist*, Oct. 23 and the Pickens *Keowee Courier*, Oct. 30, 1858; *Biographical Directory of the American Congress* (Washington, 1928), p. 652.

[15] Charleston *Mercury*, Feb. 2, 4, 11, March 7, 23, April 5, 1860; Pickens *Keowee Courier*, Feb. 25, 1860; Spartanburg *Carolina Spartan*, Feb. 16, 1860; *Congressional Globe*, 36 Cong., 1 Sess., pp. 960-962.

lightly, to meet them with derision and scorn. Ashmore was afraid that the Northern leaders would make the fatal mistake of dismissing the many disunion threats made since October, 1859, as just so much Southern bravado. This Northern mis-judgment of Southern opinion, in his mind, was the great danger in 1860.

He warned the Northern members not to make the mistake of judging Southern opinion by the threats which were being made by disunionists who had been making them for years. He asked them rather to consider the feelings of the quiet, domestic, hard-working people of the South, such as his own constituents. The decision of these sober-minded people for or against the Union, he said, depended upon their judgment of Northern opinion. Once they became convinced that hostility toward the South was the dominant feeling of Northerners, they would leave the Union.

If [Ashmore said] the sentiment of sympathy we see daily ex-pressed with the fate of John Brown, after his invasion of Virginia; if the sentiment contained in the Helper book; if the programme marked out by Seward and his satellites; if the numerous Repub-lican and Abolition meetings, of which I see an account in the news-paper press, be a fair index of public opinion at the North, then I announce it here, as my deliberate opinion, that nineteen out of every twenty of my constituents are in favor of disunion, without one hour's unnecessary delay; and if you continue to pursue this course of insult and aggression, I, though I claim to be a constitutional, union-loving man, will return to my constituents and sound the alarm, and with my own hands kindle the beacon-fires from hill-side and mountain-top that will rally them to the defense of their rights.[16]

Was the antislavery party destined to be the ruling power in the North? In 1860 the way a person answered that question still determined his decision for or against the Union. Since 1852 some had said that the triumph of the antislavery party was inevitable. They had either frankly advocated or covertly

[16] Speech of March 1, 1860, in *Congressional Globe*, 36 Cong., 1 Sess., pp. 958-962.

sympathized with secession. Others had said that the Northern antislavery party could be defeated and eventually suppressed. They had worked to preserve the Union. But steadily, for the last four years, the confidence of the conditional Unionists had been undermined. The Brooks assault, the nomination of Buchanan instead of Pierce, the slim margin of victory of the Democrats in the presidential election of 1856, the sustained strength of the Republican party in Congress, the apparent desertion of Northern Democrats such as Douglas in 1857 and 1858, the doctrine of an "irrepressible conflict" popularized by Seward's Rochester speech of 1858, the beginning of a campaign to pit the nonslaveholder against the slaveholder as exemplified by a book written by Hinton Rowan Helper called *The Impending Crisis,* and finally John Brown's raid had shattered their confidence in the power of their Northern allies.

The testimony of a Charleston bookseller reveals the inner workings of the mind that was losing hope in early 1860. James McCarter wrote to his Congressman:

> You are aware that I have always been a great lover of the Union, and have clung to it, with a sincere devotion; and even now, I do not give up any hope that some fortunate person may find out some way of escape from the evils of dissolution! But my fears are now greatly in advance of my hopes, and I begin to think the only chance of saving it, is to bring about some collision, which will show us the strength of the conservative element in the North. This element, I have always considered as large enough to keep the Democratic party in power with the aid of the South. If I am mistaken in this, my hope is gone.[17]

The upsurgence of disunion opinion in South Carolina following the John Brown raid weakened but did not wipe out support for the national convention of the Democratic party.[18]

[17] James McCarter to W. P. Miles, Jan. 16, 1860.
[18] The story of the convention party up until the time of the national convention in Charleston is based upon these sources: Kibler, *Perry,* pp. 297-301; White, "National Democrats," pp. 382-384; Perry, *Biographical Sketches* (1887), pp. 145-151, 153-170, 187; Perry, *Reminiscences* (1883), p. 176; Lancaster *Ledger,* March 21, 1860; Laurensville *Herald* (n.d.), quoted by the Pickens *Keowee Courier,* Jan. 28, 1860; Pickens *Keowee Courier,* April

In December, 1859, thirty-seven members of the legislature signed a public announcement in favor of sending delegates to the national convention in 1860. Only eleven more had made a similar declaration in December, 1855. Most of the National Democrats, although much less confident of the power of their Northern allies and the preservation of the Union than they had been in 1856, were still willing to make a last-ditch stand in the presidential election of 1860. They still preferred to avoid disunion if possible. Only defeat of the Republican party could prevent disunion, they felt, and only a national Democratic party could defeat the Republican party. They therefore continued to support the convention as a means of using South Carolina's influence to keep the party intact.

The numerical strength of the convention party was bolstered by recruits from two groups that had not previously supported the national Democracy. One of these groups joined the convention movement because it wanted to do something to preserve the Union. Its members were the remnants of the old-line Whigs in the state, the most staunchly Union men in the state. Richard Yeadon, editor of the Charleston *Courier*, and William Gregg, the Graniteville manufacturer, were repre-

---

7, 1860; Edgefield *Advertiser*, Dec. 12, 1859, Jan. 4, Feb. 8, 15, 29, March 28, April 11, 25, Aug. 8, 1860; Spartanburg *Carolina Spartan*, Aug. 18, Oct. 20, 1859, Feb. 23, March 8, 1860; Columbia *South Carolinian* (n.d.), quoted by Lancaster *Ledger*, Feb. 8, 1860; speech of James L. Orr at the Democratic state convention, April 16, 1860, reported by the Pickens *Keowee Courier*, May 5, 1860; speech of James D. Ashmore, March 1, 1860, in *Congressional Globe*, 36 Cong., 1 Sess., p. 960; speech of T. Y. Simons, Jr., in the state Senate, quoted by Charleston *Mercury*, Jan. 5, 1860; speeches at public meeting in Charleston, Feb. 23, 1860, reported by Charleston *Mercury*, Feb. 24, 1860; letter by J. Funderburk in Lancaster *Ledger*, April 18, 1860; letter by pseudonymous writer ["One of the Committee"] in Lancaster *Ledger*, April 18, 1860; proceedings of a public meeting at Lancaster, April 2, reported by Lancaster *Ledger*, April 4, 1860; proceedings of the Democratic state convention, April 16, 1860, reported by Pickens *Keowee Courier*, April 21, 28, 1860, and the Lancaster *Ledger*, April 25, 1860; Washington [D. C.] *States and Union*, Jan. 24, 1860; Augusta [Ga.] *Daily Constitutionalist*, Feb. 25, 1860; W. H. Trescot to W. P. Miles, Jan. 22, 1860; John C. Hope to J. H. Hammond, March 10, 1860. The list of members of the legislature who signed the public pronouncement in favor of the convention was published in the Charleston *Mercury*, Dec. 24, 1859, and Pickens *Keowee Courier*, Jan. 7, 1860.

FIG. 15. This graph is based upon the list of members who signed a pronouncement in 1855 in favor of representation in the national Democratic convention and a similar list issued in 1859.

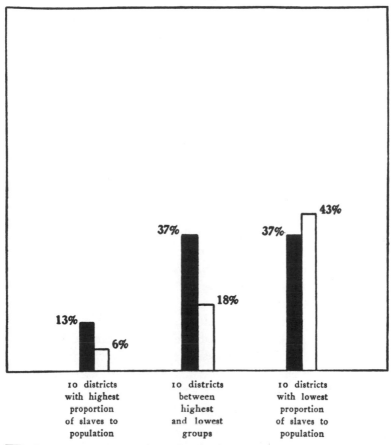

10 districts with highest proportion of slaves to population

10 districts between highest and lowest groups

10 districts with lowest proportion of slaves to population

■ 1855: proportion of members who signed to total number of representatives and senators apportioned to the districts comprised in each group.

□ 1859: proportion of members who signed to total number of representatives and senators apportioned to the districts comprised in each group.

sentative of this group. The other group joined the convention movement in order to break up the national Democratic party. These men wanted to elect a Southern President upon the Alabama platform or leave the Union. They were eager for South Carolina to send delegates to Charleston who would withdraw from the national convention if the platform failed to state that Congress was obligated to protect slavery in the territories. Milledge Bonham, Congressman from the Fourth District, was the most prominent representative of this group. Bonham, in 1860, was an avowed secessionist and an opponent of the system of nominating conventions. Yet he favored representation at the convention this year, because "recent political events" made it, "for various reasons, a matter of vast consequence that the State should be correctly represented in the Charleston Convention."[19]

Most avowed disunionists declined to support Milledge Bonham's stratagem. They continued to argue that most Northern Democrats were hostile to the interests of the South, that Northern Democrats would control the convention, that no Southern man could receive the nomination unless he were "a trimming demagogue or double-faced border State man," that Southern aspirants for the Presidency necessarily compromised the interests of the South in order to obtain Northern support, that the method of nominating by conventions enabled office-seeking politicians to name the candidates and tended to break down State Rights.[20]

What with most irreconcilables still remaining aloof from the convention party, control of the state convention that met in Columbia on April 16 was easily retained by the genuine supporters of the national Democracy. James L. Orr still had a firm hold on the convention Democrats; he presided over the state convention, was named first choice of the South Carolina

[19] M. P. Bonham to Joseph Abney, Feb. 24, 1860, in Pickens *Keowee Courier*, March 10, Sumter *Watchman*, March 7, Lancaster *Ledger*, May 20, 1860.

[20] Kingstree *Star* (n.d.), quoted by Orangeburg *Southron*, March 14, 1860; Charleston *Mercury*, March 2, May 20, June 6, Oct. 13, Nov. 29, Dec. 1-6, 12, 15, 29, 1859, Jan. 9, 11, 13, 19, 27, 30, 31, Feb. 11, 14, 17, 21, 27, 29, March 1, 12, 13, 16, 19, 26, 27, 30, 1860; Orangeburg *Southron*, Feb. 15, 1860; Newberry *Conservatist*, Jan. 14, 28, 31, March 6, 13, April 3, 10, 1860; Sumter *Watchman*, July 19, 1859; letters by Dixon Barnes and W. C. Cauthen in Lancaster *Ledger*, April 11, 1860; letters to W. P. Miles from A. O. Andrews, April 11, John Cunningham, March 10, April 5, Henry Gourdin, April 4, D. H. Hamilton, April 4, I. W. Hayne, April 11, R. B. Rhett, Jr., Jan. 29, March 28, April 11, and W. H. Trescot, March 10, 1860; John Cunningham to J. H. Hammond, Oct. 14, 1859.

delegation for the presidential nomination, and the resolutions adopted were in harmony with his ideas. The only concession made to the strongly sectional opinions of a few of the delegates was a resolution stating that a territorial government could not directly or by unfriendly legislation exclude slavery. The delegation was given a free hand in the national convention. It was not bound to vote for any particular candidate indefinitely, nor was it instructed to withdraw from the convention upon stipulated conditions. "The convention has been an Orr affair," R. B. Rhett, Jr., telegraphed to Congressman Miles.[21]

Although the irreconcilables opposed South Carolina's representation in the Charleston convention, they were very much concerned about decisions to be made there, for they wanted to defeat the nomination of Stephen A. Douglas, and they wanted South Carolina to follow the lead of Alabama in the convention. They were confident that no South Carolina delegation would dare vote for Douglas in the convention, but they were uncertain as to whether it might not accept his nomination and urge his election. A greater fear, however, was the possibility that the delegation would fail to give encouragement to Alabama and Mississippi. If these states were supported by other Southern delegations, they knew that the nomination of Douglas could be prevented, the national Democratic party could be destroyed, and disunion might be achieved in 1860. R. B. Rhett, Jr., believed that revolutionary leadership alone was needed to bring about a breakup of the national party and the Union.[22]

[21] Telegram from R. B. Rhett, Jr., to W. P. Miles, April 17, 1860.

[22] R. B. Rhett, Jr., wrote to Miles, Jan. 29, 1860: "My belief is that the weakness is with the public men of the South, who themselves 'have no stomach for the fight.' Is it not, that they are too much of partizans and aspirants, afraid of failure and party proscriptions, and unwilling to hazard anything in an effort to direct and shape the Southern sentiment to practical action? Is it not that they fear to lead and prefer to follow their people, safely? Are they men who dare attempt to *make* public opinion? Such men are statesmen. . . . The fact is that, from party contact at Washington, the courage of Southern representatives, for any practical measure requiring nerve, oozes out at their fingers ends in proportion as the sessions advance. So long as the Democratic party, as a 'National' organization, exists in power at the South, and so long as our public men trim their sails with an eye to either

Ironically, Rhett and other South Carolina secessionists could not themselves provide the daring leadership they desired in the Charleston convention.   By default, the very men who desired to precipitate disruption had allowed the National Democrats to select the delegation.   Rhett and his friends could only continue their old role as agitators; their assignment in a revolt, if there were to be one, would be to arouse opinion and to apply pressure directly on the South Carolina delegation.

At the national convention in Charleston, the Alabama delegation, led by William Lowndes Yancey, assumed leadership of the Southern extremists.   On April 30, the seventh day of the convention, the Alabama delegation withdrew from the Democratic convention after a majority of the delegates refused to endorse a platform resolution stating that Congress was con-

---

its favor or enmity, just so long must we hope for no southern action for our disenthrallment and security.   The South must dissever itself from the rotten northern element.   After the Charleston Convention we must have a Southern State-Rights Democratic party, organized on principles and with State-Rights candidates upon whom to rally.   This will insure the defeat of the double-hand 'National'-Democracy so called—and make up the issue between the sections with a resistance party already formed to meet the event of a Black Republican President elected by the North.   There is no hope of the State-Rights men controlling the Charleston Convention.   Hence the importance of obtaining the secession of the Alabama and Mississippi delegations, on the issue of Squatter Sovereignty and the construction of the Dred Scott decision. If they will but do it, the people I am sure will come up to scratch, and the game will be ours. . . .   Of course, measures depend upon men.   If the State-Rights men in Alabama and Mississippi will only bend themselves to the work, this purpose can be accomplished.   But they certainly cannot ride two horses in different directions.   Their timidity melts away the spirit of resistance in their people.   It is useless to talk about checking the North or dissolving the Union with unanimity and without division at the South.   Those who are not prepared to face opposition at home are not fit for the crisis. The South must go through a trying ordeal before she will ever achieve her deliverance, and men having both nerve and self-sacrificing patriotism must head the movement and shape its course, controlling and compelling their inferior contemporaries.   In my mind there is now a feeling abroad throughout our borders that could be used successfully by a few bold, strong men. I believe that with such a party the spoils-men and unionists could be thoroughly and effectually overcome both in Alabama and Mississippi.   The demagogues and short-sighted would fail, and the State-Rights men would triumph.   But these public men must cut loose from party ties and yield all party aspirations, and rise to the requirements of difficult times.   Of course, if enough men of power, courage and devotion cannot be found to lead the van of the revolution and hold the confidence of their people, then no revolution or action will arise to put the Southern people in their true position."

stitutionally obligated to protect slavery in the territories. Delegations from other states of the Lower South followed Alabama. In order, they were Mississippi, Louisiana, South Carolina, Florida, Texas, Arkansas, and Georgia.[23]

The South Carolina delegates were followers at Charleston. They showed no initiative in demanding the Alabama platform, nor did they ever raise the cry for a Southern nominee. If withdrawal of the Southern delegates had depended upon their taking the first step, the Charleston convention would not have broken up.[24]

The decision of South Carolina to follow Alabama and Mississippi was influenced by their commitments to co-operate with the other Southern states in the party convention. In 1856 and 1860 advocates of the convention had argued that South Carolina could best secure the co-operation of the other Southern states by participating in the Democratic convention. Presented with a practical opportunity for such co-operation, the delegates

[23] Craven, *Coming of the Civil War*, pp. 415-416; Denman, *Secession in Alabama*, pp. 81-82; Dumond, *Secession Movement*, pp. 35-54; Kibler, *Perry*, p. 314; Milton, *Douglas*, pp. 433-441; Rainwater, *Mississippi*, pp. 121-124; Randall, *Civil War*, p. 175; Rhodes, *History of the United States*, II, 440-452; Schouler, *History of the United States*, V, 454-456; Sitterson, *North Carolina Secession*, pp. 162-165; Smith, *Parties*, pp. 109-113; White, "National Democrats," pp. 384-385; White, *Rhett*, pp. 163-164; *Official Proceedings of the Democratic National Convention: Held in 1860, at Charleston and Baltimore* (Cleveland, 1860), pp. 55-65.

The Charleston *Mercury*, May 3, 1860, said: "The events of that day [April 30] will probably be the most important which have taken place since the Revolution of 1776. The last party, pretending to be a National party, is broken up; and the antagonism of the two sections of the Union has nothing to arrest its fierce collisions."

[24] R. B. Rhett, Jr., wrote to Miles, May 12, 1860, that when the delegation came to Charleston "they had no more idea of going out than of flying. They would not even go to the Southern caucus." James L. Orr said in a public letter dated July 23, 1860, that "the secession of the southern delegates from the Charleston convention was unwise and impolitic" (quoted in Lancaster *Ledger*, Aug. 8, Spartanburg *Carolina Spartan*, Aug. 9, Augusta [Ga.] *Daily Constitutionalist*, Aug. 7, 1860; Arthur Simkins, one of the delegates who did not sign the South Carolina announcement of withdrawal, said that he had "felt strong opposition to the rash resolve of Alabama, which all knew would result in breaking up the assemblage, and which many believed would terminate in disunion" (Edgefield *Advertiser*, Aug. 8, 1860). Three members of the South Carolina delegation did not sign the announcement of withdrawal from the convention.

of South Carolina could do little else than accept it. Wavering members of the, delegation were influenced by the state of public opinion in South Carolina and by demonstrations staged by the fire-eaters who had congregated at Charleston.[25]

The seceders at Charleston agreed to meet in convention at Richmond on June 11.[26] Now was the time, the extremists decided, to put aside the policy of self-denial; now was the time to make a bid for power in the state. No longer were they content to let the National Democrats determine the political destiny of the state, the South, the Union. At Charleston the South Carolina delegation had "moved with too much caution,

[25] The Newberry *Conservatist*, May 1, 1860, reported " a great disposition to freely and severely criticize the Delegation of the South Carolina Conventionists."   R. B. Rhett, Jr., wrote Miles in a letter dated May 12 "that the withdrawal of the South Carolina delegation was brought about by the outside pressure and indignation expressed at the course of the Columbia convention. . . . If they had not retired, they would have been mobbed." Benjamin F. Perry, one of the South Carolina delegates who refused to withdraw from the convention, said that "outside pressure" at the convention was tremendous.   In a letter to Franklin Gaillard, May 15, Perry told of meetings of Southern delegates every night, of public speeches at hotels, of inflammatory speeches and caucuses, of consultations and arrangements as to what should be done in certain emergencies, and of crowds of visitors hissing from the galleries (letter printed in Pickens *Keowee Courier*, June 2, 1860).

[26] The following account of events between the Charleston convention and the second session of the Richmond convention is based upon these authorities and sources: Craven, *Coming of the Civil War*, pp. 416-417; Dumond, *Secession Movement*, pp. 75-96; Kibler, *Perry*, pp. 316-321; Milton, *Douglas*, pp. 450-451, 457, 469-478; Perry, *Biographical Sketches* (1887), pp. 153-170; Randall, *Civil War*, pp. 176-180; Rhodes, *History of the United States*, II, 454, 470-471, 473-475; White, *Rhett*, pp. 164-168; White, "National Democrats," pp. 385-389; *Official Proceedings of the Democratic National Convention*, pp. 144-152; Lancaster *Ledger*, May 30, June 6, 13, 20, 1860; Charleston *Mercury*, May 5, 8, 10, 12, 16, 18, 23-25, June 4-6, 9, 11, 13, 18, 30, 1860; Edgefield *Advertiser*, May 9, 16, 30, 1860; Newberry *Conservatist*, May 15, 22, June 5, 12, 19, 26, July 3, 10, 31, 1860; Newberry *Rising Sun*, May 16, 22, 29, 30, June 6, 20, 27, 1860; Pickens *Keowee Courier*, June 2, 9, 16, 1860; Spartanburg *Express*, May 28, 1860; Spartanburg *Carolina Spartan*, May 24, June 7, 14, 21, 1860; Columbia *South Carolinian* (n.d.), quoted by the Newberry *Conservatist*, May 8, Lancaster *Ledger*, May 9, *Keowee Courier*, May 19, June 16, 1860; Camden *Journal*, May 15, 1860; Augusta [Ga.] *Daily Constitutionalist*, June 1, 2, 12, 17, 23, 1860; public letter by R. B. Rhett, Sr., May 10, in Charleston *Mercury*, May 16, Pickens *Keowee Courier*, June 2, 1860; letters to J. H. Hammond from James Gilliam, June 4, Isaac W. Hayne, June 3, 1860; letters to W. P. Miles from Robert N. Gourdin, May 10, D. H. Hamilton, May 29, William E. Martin, May 9, W. D. Porter, May 6, R. B. Rhett, Jr., May 10, 12, and William Trescot, May 8, 1860.

with too little nerve." At Richmond, they feared, the same delegation might be receptive to the appeal that the convention postpone action until an attempt had been made to unite the national Democracy on a Southern platform. The course of South Carolina at Richmond must be as advanced as that of Alabama and Mississippi. A delegation that would actively use its influence against a reunion of the national party must be elected. Thus, the isolationists, who had denounced the convention system for a decade, now began to take part in the district meetings preliminary to a second state convention to be held in Columbia. They were not inconsistent, they argued, for the Richmond convention was to be a Southern convention, not a national one. In April few genuine opponents of the national party had attended the district meetings to appoint delegates; in May the isolationists attended the meetings in full force and flooded the second Columbia convention with delegates of strong disunion proclivities.

Some of the isolationists were willing to send to Richmond the same delegation that had represented the state at Charleston. At the convention that assembled in Columbia on May 30, William S. Lyles, an outspoken disunionist and anti-conventionist, nominated the old delegation; and John Hugh Means, chairman of the convention, was in favor of this proposal. Most of the isolationists at this second state convention, however, demanded a delegation that should include representatives of the anti-convention group. Aided by the disproportionate number of votes which the legislative apportionment gave them, they achieved a stunning setback to the regular conventionists on the first ballot for one of the four delegates at large: they elected Robert Barnwell Rhett! Without a contest, they then elected the three other delegates at large and most of the delegates from the congressional districts.

The regular convention Democrats at the May convention in Columbia took the stand that the Charleston delegation should be sent to Richmond. That delegation, they said, had proved that it could act with Alabama and Mississippi, and its withdrawal from the convention had been approved by the whole state, including the isolationists.   Not a single act of the delegation at Charleston, they argued, justified the lack of confidence that the anti-conventionists demonstrated by demanding a new delegation.

The Orr-led Democrats were defeated with a vengeance at this Columbia convention.   Their own candidate against Rhett— I. W. Hayne—was a disunionist and opponent of the convention system; yet they were defeated by their most celebrated enemy. After this humiliation, they announced that they could not work in harmony with Rhett and his followers, and, by refusing to make additional nominations, voluntarily handed over the delegation to the isolationists.

The struggle for power in the May convention was between the two extremes.   The middle-ground leaders were merely spectators.   Harmony in the state, which all leaders professed to desire at this portentous juncture, could be achieved only by permitting neither of the two extremes to triumph.   But at Columbia in May the middle ground was not to win out as it had in the senatorial elections of 1857 and 1858.   I. W. Hayne, who attempted to occupy an intermediary position, could do nothing.   When he tried to bring about a conference between the two factions, he "had the cold shoulder from *each* side." He found that each side, at first, believed that it was in the ascendancy.   Hayne was put up by the National Democrats to oppose Rhett, but he had known nothing of their intentions "until two minutes or less, before it was announced."   He was sure that Rhett's election would be unpopular in the South and, in the faint hope that he might defeat him, consented to run. He withdrew afterwards to give a chance for a compromise, but it was then too late.[27]

By capturing control of the Richmond delegation, the isolationists made sure that they would be active participants at the next convention rather than mere observers and agitators as they had been at Charleston.   But they thereby ignored the precept

[27] I. W. Hayne to J. H. Hammond, June 3, 1860.

generally subscribed to since 1852 that men reputed to be South Carolina fire-eaters were ill-suited to lead a political movement requiring widespread support in the other slaveholding states. The National or convention Democrats were still, in May, 1860, more "available" as representatives for South Carolina in a concerted Southern movement. Barnwell Rhett was no more qualified to promote united Southern action at Richmond in June than he would have been in January. The same circumstances that prompted Governor Gist to appoint Memminger to the Virginia mission still obtained.

The isolationists stirred up hard feelings among the leaders and brought about a serious division in the state and in the end accomplished nothing by their actions. At Richmond the intransigent South Carolina delegation was virtually deserted when delegates from every other Southern state except Florida agreed to seek readmission to the convention of the national Democratic party, which reconvened at Baltimore on June 18.

Most of the men who went to Baltimore were refused seats in the convention. When they reassembled at Richmond on June 26, their ranks were augmented by the majority of the delegates from Virginia, North Carolina, Maryland, Kentucky, Tennessee, Oregon, and California. Virginia had led a new secession at Baltimore because the convention refused to admit the Charleston seceders.

The enlarged Richmond convention ratified the nomination of John C. Breckinridge, who had been selected in Baltimore by a meeting of party bolters. Already three other men had received nominations. Stephen A. Douglas had been elected by the national Democratic party after the second secession in Baltimore; John Bell was the candidate of the Constitutional Union party, which was supported by old-line Whigs and Americans whose sole aim in 1860 was to preserve the Union; and Abraham Lincoln had been selected as the Republican nominee.

There was no presidential campaign in South Carolina. Breckinridge was unopposed in the state, but only a few men thought that he had a chance of success. After October 9, the date of state elections in Pennsylvania and Indiana, most of the leaders made up their minds that Lincoln would be elected in November.[28]

From July to November, the main question before South Carolina was the course of the state and the South upon the election of the Republican candidate. The leaders almost unanimously favored some form of resistance, and the over-whelming majority favored the formation of a Southern con-federacy. National Democrats as well as isolationists openly committed themselves to disunion. By early October it was clear that the time had arrived to fulfil their promise, which they had made as early as 1856, to leave the Union if the anti-slavery party triumphed.[29]

[28] Boucher, "South Carolina and the South on the Eve of Secession," p. 139; Charles Edward Cauthen, "South Carolina's Decision to Lead the Secession Movement," *North Carolina Historical Review*, XVIII (Oct., 1941), 360-372; Perry, *Biographical Sketches* (1887), pp. 171-172; Lancaster *Ledger*, July 4, Sept. 5, Oct. 31, 1860; Edgefield *Advertiser*, June 20, July 11, 18, Aug. 8, 15, Sept. 5, 12, 26, Oct. 3, 31, 1860; Newberry *Conservatist*, Oct. 30, 1860; Spartanburg *Carolina Spartan*, Aug. 16, Oct. 18, 1860; speeches at Williamston, Aug. 9, reported in Pickens *Keowee Courier*, Aug. 18, 1860; public letter of James L. Orr, July 23, 1860, quoted by Lancaster *Ledger*, Aug. 8, Spartanburg *Carolina Spartan*, Aug. 9, Augusta [Ga.] *Daily Constitutionalist*, Aug. 7, 1860; synopsis of speech by James L. Orr at Green-ville in Washington [D. C.] *States and Union*, Nov. 1, 1860; synopsis of speech by James Chesnut, Nov. 5, 1860, in Washington [D. C.] *States and Union*, Nov. 8, 1860; public letter of P. T. Mobley, in Lancaster *Ledger*, Aug. 8, 1860; letters to J. H. Hammond from John D. Ashmore, July 10, James Chesnut, Oct. 17, John Cunningham, July 30, I. W. Hayne, Sept. 15, Lawrence Keitt, Aug. 4, Oct. 23, W. P. Miles, Aug. 5, W. D. Porter, n.d., probably in September; J. H. Hammond to W. G. Simms, Sept. 23, 1860; let-ters to W. P. Miles from John D. Ashmore, July 30, Lawrence Keitt, Oct. 3, W. G. Simms, July 15, 1860; J. D. Wright to John Wistar Simpson, Sept. 13, 1860 (Duke University Library).

[29] Boucher, "South Carolina and the South on the Eve of Secession," p. 141; Cauthen, "South Carolina's Decision to Lead the Secession Movement," pp. 360-361, 365-366; Kibler, *Perry*, pp. 323-325; White, *Rhett*, pp. 169-170; Lancaster *Ledger*, Sept. 12, 19, Oct. 31, Nov. 7, 1860; Charleston *Mercury*, Aug. 4, 6, 8, Sept. 24, Oct. 4, 8, 11, 12, 13, 15, 19, Nov. 1, 3, 1860; Orangeburg *Southron*, Nov. 14, 1860; Edgefield *Advertiser*, Aug. 8, 15, Sept. 26, 1860; Newberry *Conservatist*, July 31, Aug. 21, 28, 1860; Newberry *Rising Sun*, Sept. 19, 1860; Pickens *Keowee Courier*, Aug. 11, Sept. 1, 8, 15, 22, 29, Oct. 13, 1860; Spartanburg *Express*, Aug. 29, 1860; Camden *Journal*, Aug. 7, 14, Sept. 8, 18, 1860; statements of candidates for the legislature, quoted by Lancaster *Ledger*, Sept. 19, 26, Oct. 3, Camden

Benjamin F. Perry was the only prominent National Democrat who advised acceptance of the Republican administration. Perry could not overlook the fact that some Southern leaders had tried to break up the national Democratic party as a means of precipitating disunion. For years past, he wrote in a letter published in the newspapers in August, there had been a systematic organization in the South to weaken and drive from the Democratic party all who stood by it and fought for it in the Northern states. Perry, who had been a delegate at Charleston, was convinced that the disunionists had rejoiced at the breaking up of the Democratic convention. The Charleston convention, he said, should have been composed of national Democrats— Yancey had no more right to a seat than Rhett.[30]

Perry gave two main reasons why he thought the South should not leave the Union immediately after the election of Lincoln. First, he pointed out that the election would be in conformity with the Constitution. Secondly, he argued that Lincoln's election was not an immediate menace to slavery. The Republican administration, he said, would begin as a weak one. Two thirds of the voters would probably be opposed to it, and Lincoln would pursue "a very cautious, politic and wise course toward the South."[31]

Journal, Oct. 2, Pickens *Keowee Courier,* Sept. 8, Oct. 27, 1860; speeches at Williamston, Aug. 9, reported by Pickens *Keowee Courier,* Aug. 18, 1860; public letter by W. W. Boyce, Aug. 3, in Pickens *Keowee Courier,* Aug. 18, Camden *Journal,* Aug. 21, 1860; public letter of Lawrence Keitt, July 17, in Camden *Journal,* Aug. 7, 1860; public letter of James L. Orr, July 23, 1860, in Lancaster *Ledger,* Aug. 8, Spartanburg *Carolina Spartan,* Aug. 9, Augusta [Ga.] *Daily Constitutionalist,* Aug. 7, 1860; synopsis of speech by J. L. Orr at Greenville, in Washington [D. C.] *States and Union,* Nov. 1, 1860; William Henry Gist to Thomas O. Moore, October 5, in John G. Nicolay and John Hay, *Abraham Lincoln: A History* (10 vols.; New York, 1890), II, 306-307; McCarter's Journal, I, 612 (Library of Congress); letters to J. H. Hammond from J. D. Ashmore, July 10, Aug. 30, Lawrence Keitt, Aug. 4, Sept. 10, Oct. 23, W. D. Porter, n.d., and Nov. 11, 1860; Lawrence Keitt to W. P. Miles, Oct. 3, 1860.

[30] Kibler, *Perry,* pp. 325-328; the text of Perry's letter of Aug. 13 is in Perry, *Biographical Sketches* (1887), pp. 171-180.

[31] Perry, *Biographical Sketches* (1887), pp. 171-180.

Several prominent citizens, such as James L. Petigru, John Belton O'Neall, George S. Bryan, Edward Frost, and James Petigru Boyce were not in favor of secession. The story of these men is told by Lillian A. Kibler in "Unionist

Leaders who ardently desired Southern independence wanted to avoid discussion of the question of secession by South Carolina alone. The *Mercury*, in an editorial of August 10, asserted that the question of whether South Carolina should secede alone in case all the other Southern states submitted to the Republican administration should not be raised until attempts to get all, several, or even two of the other slaveholding states to join it in a secession movement had failed. This advice was generally accepted, and only a few prominent advocates of disunion, before November, publicly stated what their position would be if the other Southern states accepted the Republican administration. Lawrence Keitt and W. W. Boyce admitted that they would favor the independent secession of South Carolina.[32]

While the question of whether South Carolina should secede alone if the other Southern states acquiesced in the election of Lincoln was not prominently or extensively debated in South Carolina during the summer and fall of 1860, there was rather general agreement among all advocates of a confederacy that independence could be achieved only by the several slaveholding states seceding separately rather than through a convention composed of delegates from the Southern states. This general acceptance of separate state action as the proper method of secession, however, did not remove the old question as to whether South Carolina should assume leadership in the secession movement.[33]

Sentiment in South Carolina in 1860," *Journal of Southern History*, IV (Aug., 1938), 346-366. The few dissident Unionists had no political influence, and at no time did they organize an opposition to secession.

[32] Cauthen, "South Carolina's Decision to Lead the Secession Movement," pp. 361-362, 364; Kibler, *Perry*, p. 324; White, *Rhett*, pp. 170-171; W. W. Boyce to D. L. Provence and W. S. Lyles, Aug. 3, in Pickens *Keowee Courier*, Aug. 18 and Camden *Journal*, Aug. 21, 1860; Lawrence Keitt to A. G. Sally, Henry Elliot, and others, July 16, in Camden *Journal*, Aug. 7, 1860; Lawrence Keitt to W. P. Miles, Oct. 3, 1860; Lawrence Keitt to J. H. Hammond, Oct. 23, 1860; J. D. Ashmore to J. H. Hammond, Aug. 30, 1860.

[33] The question of South Carolina's assuming leadership in the secession movement is the subject of a special study by Charles E. Cauthen, "South Carolina's Decision to Lead the Secession Movement," *North Carolina Historical Review*, XVIII (Oct., 1941), 360-372.

Congressman Miles, "sick and disgusted" with bluster, threats, manifestoes, and resolutions, hoped that South Carolina would act swiftly with a minimum of talk if Lincoln were elected;[34] and Congressmen Keitt and Boyce, in publicly declaring for immediate secession in the event of Lincoln's election, showed that they were not opposed to South Carolina's acting first. While willing to act regardless of what course was adopted in the other Southern states, these men nevertheless hoped that the secession of South Carolina would be followed by that of other states. On the other hand, several prominent leaders followed a watchful and cautious course during the summer and early fall. The two Senators, Hammond and Chesnut, privately expressed their fears of the consequences of South Carolina's attempting to lead the South.[35] James L. Orr, likewise, in public statements, revealed doubts about his state's taking the lead. In a public letter dated July 23, Orr said that he would give assent to a policy of disunion if Georgia, Alabama, and Mississippi would unite with South Carolina "in a common secession upon the election of a Black Republican"; and in a speech at Greenville in late October he recommended the appointment of commissioners to consult with the other Southern states to ascertain their intended course in order that there might be concert of action.[36]

The question of whether South Carolina should lead became, of course, a pressing and practical matter only when it became clear that no other state would act first. At no time during the summer was there optimism about another state's

---

[34] W. P. Miles to J. H. Hammond, Aug. 5, 1860.

[35] James Chesnut to J. H. Hammond, Oct. 17, 1860; J. H. Hammond to I. W. Hayne, Sept. 19, 1860. Chesnut veered toward an advocacy of immediate secession between Oct. 17 and Oct. 27. On the latter date he wrote to Hammond: "I very much agree with you and what you said in your letter, except my mind is daily inclining to the necessity of trying the issue of secession, and the doctrine of coercion, even by the solitary movement of the state. But I wish to consult with you and other friends before I fully decide."

[36] Orr's letter of July 23 in Lancaster *Ledger*, Aug. 8, Spartanburg *Carolina Spartan*, Aug. 9, and Augusta [Ga.] *Daily Constitutionalist*, Aug. 7, 1860; Orr's speech in Greenville quoted by Charleston *Mercury*, Oct. 30, 1860, and Washington [D. C.] *States and Union*, Nov. 1, 1860.

taking the lead, and by the close of October virtually all leaders in touch with Southern politics realized that Mississippi, Alabama, or Georgia could not be counted upon to lead a secession movement.

For certain leaders in the state, one of the most reliable sources of confidential information about conditions in the other Southern states was Governor Gist, who, in early October, sent letters to six governors inquiring as to the probable action of their states in the event of Lincoln's election.[37] From not one of these governors did Gist receive a promise or prediction that his state would act first in a secession movement. The replies, however, provided some hopes for those who advocated the secession of South Carolina as a means of stimulating the other states to act. The governors of Mississippi, Alabama, and Florida intimated that their states would follow the lead of some other state or states, while the governors of North Carolina and Louisiana, who thought that their states would oppose secession, indicated that they would not permit federal coercion of a seceding state. The governor of Georgia thought that his state would await an "overt act," but he added that it might be influenced greatly by "the action of other States."

South Carolinians had learned, in the 1850's and before, that their destiny was not in their own hands alone. They had learned that they must co-operate with the other Southern states and that they must co-operate as followers, not leaders. South Carolina, distrusted more than any other slaveholding state by the Southern people, still seemed unfit to assume the leadership in the movement for Southern resistance. Champions of Southern independence in September and October did not have to look far back to see how the South distrusted South Carolina. Twice in this year of 1860 the counsel of their state had been ignored: the proposal for a Southern conference and the Richmond convention were recent memories. Yet when the legislature met in extra session on November 5 to select presidential electors,

[37] Gist's letter, dated Oct. 5, and the replies of the governors are printed in Nicolay and Hay, *Abraham Lincoln*, II, 306-314.

it was ready for South Carolina to risk another fiasco rather than acquiesce in a Republican administration.

On November 7 South Carolina knew that Lincoln had been elected. On November 10 both houses of the legislature agreed to a bill which provided for a state convention to meet on December 17. Not a single vote was cast in either house against the bill on the final reading.[38]

The men who passed this convention bill knew that South Carolina could not depend upon any other state's taking the lead in a secession movement through the process of separate state action. Opposed to a Southern conference and with no expectation that Alabama and Mississippi would secede first, a large majority of the members of the legislature favored prompt secession of South Carolina as a means of inciting the other states to take action.[39] If South Carolina seceded first, the other states

[38] *House Journal, Called Session* (1860), p. 35; *Senate Journal, Called Session* (1860), pp. 22-23.

There was no opposition in principle to calling a state convention expressed in the legislature. There was, however, considerable disagreement as to the time for calling, electing, and holding such a convention. A few members thought that South Carolina should not call a convention until some other state had acted. A great majority were willing to call a convention without delay, but were divided as to the dates for the election and assembling of delegates. The Senate at first (Nov. 9) agreed to a bill setting Jan. 8 and 15 as election and convocation dates respectively, but subsequently (Nov. 10) accepted an amendment proposed by the House which fixed the dates at Dec. 6 and 17. Formal ratification of the act occurred Nov. 13. For a detailed account of the drafting of the act providing for a state convention, see Cauthen, "South Carolina's Decision to Lead the Secession Movement," pp. 366-372.

[39] Cauthen, "South Carolina's Decision to Lead the Secession Movement," p. 365; Dumond, *Secession Movement*, p. 139; White, *Rhett*, pp. 179-180; Darlington *Flag* (n.d.), quoted by Camden *Journal*, Nov. 6, 1860; Charleston *Mercury*, Nov. 1, 3, 1860; correspondence from Columbia, Nov. 11, in Newberry *Conservatist*, Nov. 13, 1860; Yorkville *Enquirer* (n.d.), quoted by the Pickens *Keowee Courier*, Dec. 1, 1860; Augusta [Ga.] *Daily Constitutionalist*, Nov. 9, 11, 13, 1860; addresses by public men at Columbia, as reported in Columbia *South Carolinian*, Nov. 7, and quoted by Augusta [Ga.] *Daily Constitutionalist*, Nov. 8, 1860; speech of James L. Orr at Columbia, quoted by Washington [D. C.] *States and Union*, Nov. 17, 1860; correspondence from Charleston, Nov. 8, in Washington [D. C.] *States and Union*, Nov. 9, 1860; special dispatch from Charleston, Nov. 12, to New York *Daily World* (n.d.), quoted by Washington [D. C.] *States and Union*, Nov. 14, 1860; message of Governor Gist, Nov. 27, in *House Journal* (1860), pp. 26-27; W. D. Porter to J. H. Hammond, Nov. 11, 1860.

would follow, they had been told by Governor Gist in his message of November 5.[40] From A. P. Aldrich, Chairman of the House Committee on Federal Relations, they had learned that telegraphic messages were being received hourly urging South Carolina to act promptly.[41] And from numerous other sources they had heard of communications from Southern leaders advising South Carolina to assume the lead.[42]

The decision of the legislature to call a state convention was made with the enthusiastic approval of an electorate whose emotions had been aroused by two months of steady agitation. South Carolina was excited in September and October. In their newspapers the people read about new plots for slave insurrections in Texas and other Southern states. A fear of slave uprisings similar to that which had swept the state in November and December, 1859, was revived. Once more vigilance and public safety committees were organized. In some localities "Minute Men" were organized for the purpose of marching on Washington to prevent by force the inauguration of Lincoln. Newspapers and speakers at political meetings pictured the social horrors of abolition, the economic loss that would result from Republican rule, the glorious prospects in store for the people in a new slaveholding republic, the improbability of war resulting from secession. The martial spirit of the South Carolinians came into full bloom. Brass bands played at political meetings; parades were held; rifle clubs, cavalry units, and volunteer rifle companies were organized.[43]

[40] Message of Governor Gist, Nov. 5, in *Senate Journal, Called Session* (1860), p. 10 and *House Journal, Called Session* (1860), p. 10.

[41] Augusta [Ga.] *Daily Constitutionalist*, Nov. 13, 1860.

[42] Cauthen, "South Carolina's Decision to Lead the Secession Movement," p. 365.

[43] Lancaster *Ledger*, Aug. 15, Sept. 5, 12, Oct. 10, 31, Nov. 7, 14, 1860; Charleston *Mercury*, Aug. 29, Oct. 5, 11, 19, 25, 27, 1860; Edgefield *Advertiser*, Oct. 3, 31, 1860; Newberry *Conservatist*, Aug. 7, 28, Sept. 4, Oct. 16, 23, 30, Nov. 11, 13, Dec. 4, 1860; Newberry *Rising Sun*, Aug. 15, Oct. 3, 24, Nov. 7, 14, 1860; Pickens *Keowee Courier*, Aug. 18, Sept. 3, 8, Oct. 27, 1860; Spartanburg *Express*, Sept. 12, Oct. 3, 1860; Spartanburg *Carolina Spartan*, Sept. 6, 27, Oct. 4, 1860; Columbia *Guardian*, Nov. 6, quoted by Camden *Journal*, Nov. 13, 1860; Columbia *South Carolinian* (n.d.), quoted by the Newberry *Conservatist*, Nov. 13, 1860; Camden *Journal*, Nov. 6,

The news of Lincoln's election and the passage of the convention bill were followed by sensational events. On November 7 two federal officials, Judge A. G. Magrath and District Attorney James Conner, both associated with the moderate faction of the state, announced their resignations; and in the next few days most of the federal officeholders gave up their positions. On November 10 Senator James Chesnut submitted his resignation to the legislature.[44] Senator James Henry Hammond, carried along by the tide of opinion, with some misgivings resigned three days later: "I thought Magrath and all those fellows were great asses for resigning and have done it myself," wrote Hammond. "It is an epidemic and very foolish."[45]

Neither Hammond nor any other leader in the state could have held back the avalanche precipitated by Lincoln's election and the convention bill. "At once the state fired up," A. P. Calhoun told the Alabama convention. "It was an upheaving of the people. No leader or leaders could have resisted it, or stemmed its impetuosity. The wave of public opinion swept over the lower, the middle, and leaped into the recess of the mountain districts."[46] On November 11 W. D. Porter wrote to Hammond: "In this State, I think no one can resist the current. We are too far committed." The few members of the legislature who harbored doubts about hasty action had "to remain in concealment" because of "the general enthusiasm of the people & especially of the members of the Legislature."[47] The more moderate found it useless to urge wise counsel, a correspondent for a New York newspaper wrote from Charleston on November 12.[48] Even the professed secessionist, when

---

1860; Augusta [Ga.] *Daily Constitutionalist*, Oct. 16, 1860; letters to J. H. Hammond from G. D. Tillman, Oct. 9, and Lawrence Keitt, Sept. 10, 1860.

[44] Charleston *Mercury*, Nov. 8, 1860; Newberry *Conservatist*, Nov. 27, 1860; *House Journal, Called Session* (1860), pp. 33, 45; *Senate Journal, Called Session* (1860), pp. 21, 27-28; James Chesnut to J. H. Hammond, Nov. 15, 1860.

[45] J. H. Hammond to M. C. M. Hammond, Nov. 12, 1860.

[46] William R. Smith (ed.), *The History and Debates of the Convention of the People of Alabama, Begun and Held in the City of Montgomery, on the Seventh Day of January, 1861* (Montgomery, 1867), pp. 31-32.

[47] McCarter's Journal, I, 14.

[48] Quoted by the Washington [D. C.] *States and Union*, Nov. 14, 1860.

he mentioned military dangers ahead, was "listened to with impatience."[49]   Sympathizers from the North who thought of coming to South Carolina to urge a change of purpose were told by former moderates that they would not be welcome.   "Our purpose is fixed: our course is certain," they declared.[50]   People complained "bitterly of slow and lukewarm public leaders" to Mrs. James Chesnut, who exclaimed: "And yet people talk of the politicians leading!"[51]

The election of delegates for the state convention took place on December 6.   Since an overwhelming majority of the voters assumed by this time that the convention would take South Carolina out of the Union, the question of secession was not a major issue in the election.   Indeed, issues, large or small, had little or no part in either the nominations or election of delegates to the convention.   With issues suspended and the factional lines which had divided men throughout the fifties effaced, personal influence, more than ever before, seems to have determined whether one individual rather than another was nominated and elected by the voters of a given district.[52]

    [49] McCarter's Journal, I, 12.
    [50] A. G. Magrath and H. Gourdin to Richard Lathers, Dec. 8, 1860 (Library of Congress).
    [51] Mary Boykin Chesnut, *A Diary from Dixie* (New York, 1905), p. 2.
    [52] Chesnut, *A Diary from Dixie*, pp. 2-4; Kibler, *Perry*, pp. 342-343; John A. Broadus, *Memoir of James Petigru Boyce* (Louisville, Ky., 1893), pp. 185-187; William P. Trent, *William Gilmore Simms* (New York, 1892), p. 253; White, *Rhett*, pp. 181-184; Lancaster *Ledger*, Nov. 21, 28, Dec. 5, 12, 19, 1860; Charleston *Mercury*, Nov. 13, 14, 15, 19, 26, 27, Dec. 3, 4, 5, 8, 1860; Edgefield *Advertiser*, Nov. 14, Dec. 3, 1860; Newberry *Conservatist*, Nov. 13, Dec. 25, 1860; Pickens *Keowee Courier*, Nov. 10, 17, 24, Dec. 1, 8, 1860; Newberry *Rising Sun*, Nov. 7, 14, 21, 28, Dec. 12, 19, 26; Greenville *Patriot and Mountaineer* (n.d.), quoted by the Spartanburg *Carolina Spartan*, Nov. 22, 1860; *Carolina Spartan*, Nov. 14, 22, 29, Dec. 6, 1860; Yorkville *Enquirer* (n.d.), quoted by the *Keowee Courier*, Dec. 1, 1860; Washington [D. C.] *States and Union*, Nov. 14, 15, 17, 19, 22, 24, Dec. 8, 1860; Augusta [Ga.] *Daily Constitutionalist*, Nov. 17, 18, 25, 28, Dec. 1, 2, 5, 1860; inaugural address of Governor Francis W. Pickens, Dec. 17, 1860, in Newberry *Conservatist*, Dec. 25, 1860; letters by A. B. Longstreet in Newberry *Conservatist*, Dec. 18, 25, *Keowee Courier*, Dec. 1, Spartanburg *Express*, Dec. 12, Spartanburg *Carolina Spartan*, Nov. 28, Dec. 5, 12, 1860; J. H. Hammond to W. H. Mitchell, Nov. 21, 1860, in Hammond Papers and quoted by *Keowee Courier*, Dec. 8, 1860; J. H. Hammond to R. F. Simpson, Nov. 22, 1860; A. P. Aldrich to J. H. Hammond, Nov. 25,

In contrast with their attitude toward the convention of 1852, the outstanding men of the state were eager to serve in the convention of 1860, for they realized that they would be the instruments for making events of great historical significance. The electors in general, likewise, were impressed with the import of the occasion and wanted only their most famous, able, respected, and trusted citizens to represent them in an assembly that they compared with the Continental Congress of 1776. This widespread belief in the momentous character of the December convention, combined with the impotence of issues and the disappearance of organized factions, resulted in the selection of a body of delegates who comprised the very elite of South Carolina.

Already prepared to take South Carolina out of the Union, delegates to the state convention assembled at the Baptist Church in Columbia on December 17. Profiting from the influence that derives from fulfilled prophecy, the extremists dominated the initial proceedings. For presidency of the convention, they elected David Flavel Jamison, who had advocated separate secession in 1851 and who had supported sectionalism and isolation from national parties during the fifties. Of sixteen candidates whose names appeared on the first tally, only James L. Orr had been a prominent supporter of the national Democracy. On none of the four ballots did Orr receive more than 20 per cent of the total votes cast.[53]

The convention did not delay in announcing South Carolina's decision to secede. On the first day, by a vote of 159 to 0, it adopted a secession resolution and provided a committee to draw up an ordinance. A smallpox "epidemic" in Columbia offered an excuse to transfer the convention to historic Charleston, where the final ceremony of making South Carolina an independent

Dec. 6, 1860; letters to W. P. Miles from J. D. Ashmore, Nov. 15, John R. Horsey, Dec. 10, W. G. Simms, Nov. 12, R. B. Rhett, Jr., Dec. 8, and W. H. Trescot, Nov. 8, 1860; A. G. Magrath and H. Gourdin to Richard Lathers, Dec. 8, 1860 (Library of Congress); McCarter's Journal, I, 9, 11, 21.

[53] *Journal of the Convention of the People of South Carolina, Held in 1860, 1861, and 1862, together with the Ordinances, Reports and Resolutions, Etc.* (Columbia, 1862), pp. 7-8.

republic could be carried out more appropriately in the "capital of Southern Civilization." In the early afternoon of December 20 the secession ordinance was adopted unanimously. That night at seven o'clock, in Institute Hall, a stately, two-hour ceremony was begun before 2,000 jubilant onlookers. One by one, the 170 delegates affixed their names to the document which dissolved "the Union between the State of South Carolina and other States United with her under the Compact Entitled 'The Constitution of the United States of America.' "[54]

This time there were fireworks, ringing bells, and parades— a great shouting, a flow of oratory, an abundance of bluster, many prophecies of great things to come. A newspaper correspondent who described the proceedings of the convention concluded his dispatch with these words:

And thus was passed, ratified and sanctioned in the city of Charleston, the 20th December, 1860, the glorious act of secession, which is to make the Southern States the greatest people under the sun, and South Carolina the greatest State of them all.[55]

[54] *Journal of the People of South Carolina*, pp. 10-12, 43-45, 48-49, 751-754; *Journal of the* [Mississippi] *State Convention and Ordinances and Resolutions Adopted in January, 1861* (Jackson, Miss., 1861), pp. 163-175; William R. Smith (ed.), *The History and Debates of the Convention of the People of Alabama*, pp. 389-394; Lancaster *Ledger*, Dec. 19, 24, 1860; Charleston *Mercury*, Dec. 21, 1860; Newberry *Conservatist*, Dec. 25, 1860; correspondence from Columbia, Dec. 17, and from Charleston, Dec. 18, in Pickens *Keowee Courier*, Dec. 22, 1860, Jan. 5, 1861; correspondence from Charleston, Dec. 20, in Spartanburg *Carolina Spartan*, Jan. 3, 1860; Edgefield *Advertiser*, Dec. 24, 1860; Augusta [Ga.] *Daily Constitutionalist*, Dec. 20, 21, 22, 23, 1860; A. P. Aldrich to J. H. Hammond.
[55] Spartanburg *Carolina Spartan*, Jan. 3, 1860.

CHAPTER XI

THE PARAMOUNT ISSUE

WAS THE ANTISLAVERY party destined to be the domi nant power in the federal government? This question wa the paramount issue in South Carolina politics in the 1850's.

One group of leaders was convinced throughout this decade that the antislavery party was destined to rule the nation. It had its strongest support in districts with the heaviest concentration of slaves. Its strength in the legislature ranged from about one third to one half of the membership during the period 1852 to 1859. It was weakest between 1852 and 1856, made slight gains in 1857 and 1858, and probably constituted a majority by the close of 1859. By November, 1860, virtually the entire legislature accepted its dictum about the eventual domination of the antislavery forces.

The irreconcilables—those leaders who refused to believe that the Compromise of 1850 or any other measures could provide a permanent settlement of the sectional conflict in the Union—interpreted the events of the 1850's to prove their proposition that the antislavery party must eventually triumph. *Uncle Tom's Cabin*, Northern opposition to the Kansas-Nebraska Act, Northern emigrant-aid societies, repeated frustrations of the Pierce foreign policy, defeat of the Democratic party in the congressional election of 1854, Northern defense of the unauthorized government established in Kansas by the antislavery party, the Brooks-Sumner affair, the failure of Pierce to receive the Democratic nomination in 1856, the strength of the Republicans in their first presidential election, the policy of Robert Walker as governor of Kansas Territory, the revolt of Northwestern Democrats against the Lecompton constitution, failure to admit Kansas as a slave state, Seward's "irrepressible conflict" speech, Republican victories in the elections of 1858, the John Brown raid, and finally the election of Lincoln in 1860 were cited as proof of their proposition that the antislavery party was destined to rule the country.

The irreconcilables either ignored or dismissed as unimportant any evidence which seemed to disprove their main proposition. The absence of legislation hostile to the South, the election of Pierce to the Presidency, the subsidence of the antislavery agitation between 1851 and 1854, the sponsorship by Northern Democrats of the repeal of the Missouri Compromise, a presidential policy during the Pierce administration designed to propitiate the South, the resurgence of Democratic power in 1855 after the overwhelming defeat of 1854, the success of the Democratic candidate in the presidential election of 1856, the Dred Scott decision, the election of James L. Orr to the Speakership of the House, loss of ground by the Republicans in the local elections of 1857, and the plurality election of Lincoln in 1860—none of these conditions, policies, or events ever shook the belief of the irreconcilables that the antislavery movement was gaining strength.

Some of the irreconcilables provoked Northerners into giving support to the antislavery and anti-Southern movement against which they complained so bitterly. Their demands for the admission of Kansas under a constitution adopted by a minority of the residents, for congressional protection of slavery in the territories, and for a revival of the foreign slave trade placed severe strains upon the friendship of Northern Democrats. The tendency of the irreconcilables to become provocative and aggressive was especially noticeable toward the close of 1857.

Another group of leaders in South Carolina was undecided about the inevitability of the domination of the antislavery party. Throughout the period 1852-1859 this group never ceased to hope that the advance of the antislavery movement might be checked. Unlike the irreconcilables, they were willing to give all assistance possible to their Northern friends. In order to strengthen the bond between the South and Northern friends, many of them gave support to the movement to enter the convention of the national Democratic party. Neither provocative nor aggressive, they opposed the demands for reviving the slave trade and for a slave code in the territories.

This conciliatory group reached the peak of its strength during the years 1855 and 1856. Between 1857 and 1859 an increasing number of its adherents began to waver in their confidence that the Republican party could be subdued. In November, 1860, most of them accepted the presidential election as sufficient proof that the antislavery party was destined to rule. Having arrived at this conclusion, they carried out their pledge to advocate secession.

The movement for Southern independence in South Carolina during the period 1852-1860 was primarily a process by which the conciliatory group in the state became convinced that the antislavery party must eventually gain the ascendancy in the federal government.

BIBLIOGRAPHY

I. MANUSCRIPTS

Papers of SAMUEL W. CRAWFORD, Library of Congress. Entries in diary for December comment on state of opinion at time of secession convention.

Papers of STEPHEN A. DOUGLAS, University of Chicago Library. Only a few letters from South Carolinians are in this large collection.

Letters to HENRY GOURDIN, Library of Congress. Letters in this small collection show what a prominent Charleston merchant was hearing from England, the North, and other Southern states during October and December, 1860.

Papers of JAMES HENRY HAMMOND, Library of Congress. The most valuable collection of letters for the purposes of this study; it contains hundreds of letters from prominent men in South Carolina and other states.

Letters of WADE HAMPTON, Duke University Library. Only a few addressed to Hampton of use for politics of this period.

Letters to GEORGE FREDERICK HOLMES, Library of Congress. Several letters from David Flavel Jamison are useful for the secession controversy of 1850–1852.

Doctoral dissertation by GEORGE V. IRONS, "The Secession Movement in Georgia, 1850–1861," Duke University, 1936, Duke University Library.

Papers of RICHARD LATHERS, Library of Congress. Letters, clippings, speeches having to do with Lathers's efforts to influence the moderates of South Carolina for compromise were of use for this study.

Doctoral dissertation by HAMPTON McNEELY JARRELL, "William Gilmore Simms, Realistic Romancer," Duke University, 1932, Duke University Library.

Correspondence of LAWRENCE KEITT, Duke University Library. Letters between Keitt and Sue Sparks. Some of these letters comment on the political situation, and all throw light on Keitt's personality.

Letters of E. J. LIDE, Duke University Library. Only a few of use for the politics of this period.

McCARTER's Journal, Library of Congress. Excellent for the excitement in South Carolina during November and December, 1860.

Letter by CHRISTOPHER G. MEMMINGER to R. B. Rhett, Jr., January 28, 1860, Library of Congress. Comments on attitude of Virginia legislature toward his mission.

Papers of WILLIAM PORCHER MILES, University of North Carolina Library. A large and valuable collection of letters by and to Miles.

Letters of FRANCIS W. PICKENS, Duke University Library. Several political letters of the 1850's.

Papers of ROBERT BARNWELL RHETT, in possession of Mrs. Joseph Ransom, Memphis, Tennessee. A large collection of letters addressed to Rhett while he was in Congress. A few letters between William R. Taber, Jr., an editor of the Charleston *Mercury*, and John Cunningham, editor of the Charleston *Evening News*, comment on the Know-Nothing party in Charleston.

Master's thesis by HAROLD S. SCHULTZ, "Movement to Revive the Foreign Slave Trade, 1853–1861," Duke University, 1940, Duke University Library.

Papers of WHITEMARSH B. SEABROOK. Letters in this collection are particularly good for the relationship of South Carolina to Mississippi and Georgia during the period 1849–1851.

Papers of JOHN WISTAR SIMPSON, Duke University Library. A few letters of value for politics in the 1850's.

Papers of RICHARD SINGLETON, Duke University Library. A few letters of value for politics of the 1850's.

II. NEWSPAPERS

Augusta [Ga.] *Daily Constitutionalist*, 1856–1860.

Camden *Journal*, 1853–1857, 1860.

Charleston *Courier*, 1851–1857.

Charleston *Evening News*, 1852–1855.

Charleston *Mercury*, 1852–1860.

Charleston *Standard*, 1856.

Cheraw *Gazette*, 1856.

Columbia *Banner*, 1853.

Columbia *Carolina Times*, 1856.

Columbia *South Carolinian*, 1852–1853.

Darlington *Flag*, 1852.

Edgefield *Advertiser*, 1852–1860.

Greenville, *Southern Patriot*, 1852.

Lancaster *Ledger*, 1853–1860.

Laurensville *Herald*, 1854–1855, 1858–1860.

Memphis [Tenn.] *Daily Appeal*, 1856, 1858–1859.

Newberry *Conservatist*, 1858–1860.

Newberry *Rising Sun*, 1858–1860.

[New York, N. Y.] *Frank Leslie's Illustrated Newspaper*, 1860–1861.

Orangeburg *Southron*, 1856, 1859–1860.

Pickens *Keowee Courier*, 1857–1860.

Spartanburg *Express*, 1860.

Spartanburg *Carolina Spartan*, 1856–1860.

Sumter *Banner*, 1852–1855.

Sumter *Black River Watchman*, 1852–1855.

Sumter *Watchman*, 1855–1860.

Washington [D. C.] *National Intelligencer*, 1858.

Washington [D. C.] *States*, 1857–1859.

Washington [D. C.] *States and Union*, 1859–1860.

III. PUBLISHED SOURCES

Acts of the General Assembly of the State of South Carolina (annually, Columbia, 1852–1860).

ADAMS, JAMES HOPKINS. *Response of James H. Adams to the Voters of Richland District, Made in Reply to Questions Propounded by his Fellow-Citizens, on the Electoral Question* (Columbia, 1854).

ADAMS, JAMES TRUSLOW, AND COLEMAN, R. B. (eds.). *Dictionary of American History* (5 vols.; New York, 1940).

An Appeal to the State Rights Party of South Carolina: in Several Letters on the Present Condition of Public Affairs (Columbia, 1858).

AYER, LEWIS M. *Patriotism and State Sovereignty: An Oration Delivered before the Two Societies of the South Carolina College, on the Fourth of December, 1858* (Charleston, 1859).

B., E. H. "Political Philosophy of South Carolina," *Southern Quarterly Review*, N.S. VII (Jan., 1853), 120-140.

BANCROFT, FREDERIC. *Calhoun and the South Carolina Nullification Movement* (Baltimore, 1928).

BEVERIDGE, ALBERT J. *Abraham Lincoln, 1809–1858* (2 vols.; New York and Boston, 1928).

Biographical Directory of the American Congress, 1774–1927 (Washington, 1928).

BOUCHER, CHAUNCEY SAMUEL. *The Nullification Controversy in South Carolina* (Chicago, 1916).

————. "Representation and the Electoral Question in Ante-Bellum South Carolina," *Proceedings of the Mississippi Valley Historical Association for 1915–1916*, IX (Cedar Rapids, Iowa, 1917), 110-125.

————. "The Secession and Co-operation Movements in South Carolina, 1848 to 1852," *Washington University Studies*, V, No. 2 (1918), 65-138.

————. "Sectionalism, Representation, and the Electoral Question in Ante-Bellum South Carolina," *Washington University Studies*, IV, Part 2, No. 1 (1916), 3-62.

————. "South Carolina and the South on the Eve of Secession, 1852–1860," *Washington University Studies, Humanistic Series*, VI, No. 2 (1919), 85-144.

BOUCHER, CHAUNCEY S., AND BROOKS, ROBERT P. (eds.). "Correspondence Addressed to John C. Calhoun, 1837–1849," *Proceedings of the American Historical Association for the Year 1929* (Washington, 1930).

BROADUS, JOHN A. *Memoir of James Petigru Boyce* (Louisville, 1893).

BROOKS, PRESTON SMITH. *Speech of Honorable Preston S. Brooks, Delivered at Columbia, South Carolina, August 29, 1856* (Boston, 1856).

————. "Statement by Preston S. Brooks," *Massachusetts Historical Society Proceedings*, LXI (Boston, 1928), 221-222.

CAPERS, HENRY D. *The Life and Times of C. G. Memminger* (Richmond, 1893).

CARNATHAN, W. J. "The Proposal to Reopen the African Slave Trade in the South, 1854–1860," *South Atlantic Quarterly,* XXV (Oct., 1926), 410-429.

CAUTHEN, CHARLES EDWARD. "South Carolina's Decision to Lead the Secession Movement," *North Carolina Historical Review,* XVIII (Oct., 1941), 360-372.

CHADWICK, FRENCH ENSOR. *Causes of the Civil War, 1859–1861* ([*The American Nation: A History,* Vol. XIX], New York, 1906).

CHESNUT, MARY B. *A Diary from Dixie* (New York, 1905).

CLAIBORNE, J. J. H. *Life and Correspondence of John A. Quitman* (2 vols.; New York, 1860).

COLE, ARTHUR C. *The Irrepressible Conflict, 1850–1865* ([*A History of American Life,* Vol. VII], New York, 1934).

Congressional Globe (Washington, 1852–1860).

CRAVEN, AVERY. *The Coming of the Civil War* (New York, 1942).

———. *Edmund Ruffin, Southerner: A Study in Secession* (New York, 1932).

CRENSHAW, OLLINGER. "Christopher G. Memminger's Mission to Virginia, 1860," *Journal of Southern History,* VIII (Aug., 1942), 334-349.

CURTIS, GEORGE TICKNOR. *Life of James Buchanan* (New York, 1883).

De Bow's Review, 1852–1860.

DE BOW, JAMES D. B. *Statistical View of the United States, Embracing its Territory, Population—White, Free Colored, and Slave—Moral and Social Condition, Industry, Property and Revenue, the Detailed Statistics of Cities, Towns, and Counties* ... (Washington, 1854).

DENMAN, CLARENCE PHILLIPS. *The Secession Movement in Alabama* (Montgomery, 1933).

DU BOSE, JOHN WITHERSPOON. *The Life and Times of William Lowndes Yancey* (Birmingham, 1892).

DUMOND, DWIGHT LOWELL. *Antislavery Origins of the Civil War in the United States* (Ann Arbor, 1939).

———. *The Secession Movement, 1860–61* (New York, 1931).

——— (ed.). *Southern Editorials on Secession* (New York, 1931).

ELLIOTT, STEPHEN. *Annual Address before the Clariosophic and Euphradian Societies of the South Carolina College. . . . Delivered Dec. 4, 1859* (Charleston, 1859).

FITE, EMERSON DAVID. *The Presidential Campaign of 1860* (New York, 1911).

FLEMING, WALTER F. "The Buford Expedition to Kansas," *American Historical Review*, VI (Oct., 1900), 38-48.

GRAYSON, WILLIAM JOHN. *The Union, Past and Future: How It Works, and How to Save It* (Charleston, 1850).

GREEN, EDWIN L. *A History of the University of South Carolina* (Columbia, 1916).

HALSTEAD, MURAT. *Caucuses of 1860. A History of the National Political Conventions of the current Presidential Campaign: being a complete Record of the Business of the Conventions; with Sketches of distinguished Men in Attendance upon them, and Descriptions of the most characteristic Scenes and Memorable Events* (Columbus, Ohio, 1860).

HAMER, PHILIP MAY. *The Secession Movement in South Carolina, 1847–1852* (Allentown, Pa., 1918).

HAMMOND, JAMES HENRY. *Selections from the Letters and Speeches of the Hon. James H. Hammond, of South Carolina* (New York, 1866).

HODGSON, JOSEPH. *The Cradle of the Confederacy; or, The Times of Troup, Quitman and Yancey. A Sketch of Southwestern Political History from the Formation of the Federal Government to A.D. 1861* (Mobile, 1876).

HOUSTON, DAVID FRANKLIN. *A Critical Study of Nullification* (New York, 1896).

HOWE, DANIEL W. *Political History of Secession, to the Beginning of the American Civil War* (New York, 1914).

HUNT, GAILLARD. *John C. Calhoun* (Philadelphia, 1908).

JAMESON, J. FRANKLIN (ed.). "The Correspondence of John C. Calhoun," *American Historical Association Report for the Year 1899* (Washington, 1900).

JENKINS, W. S. *Pro-Slavery Thought in the Old South* (Chapel Hill, 1935).

JERVEY, THEODORE D. *Robert Y. Hayne and His Times* (New York, 1909).

JOHNSON, ALLEN, AND MALONE, DUMAS (eds.). *Dictionary of American Biography* (20 vols.; New York, 1928-1937).

JOHNSON, ALLEN. *Stephen A. Douglas: A Study of American Politics* (New York, 1908).

Journal of the Conventions of the People of South Carolina, Held in 1860, 1861 and 1862, together with the Ordinances, Reports and Resolutions, Etc. (Columbia, 1862).

Journals of the Conventions of the People of South Carolina, Held in 1832, 1833, and 1852 (Columbia, 1860).

Journal of the House of Representatives of the State of South Carolina (annual and special sessions, Columbia, 1851-1860).

Journal of the Senate of the State of South Carolina (annual and special sessions, Columbia, 1851-1860).

Journal of the [Mississippi] *State Convention and Ordinances and Resolutions Adopted in January, 1861* (Jackson, Miss., 1861).

Journal of the State Convention of South Carolina; together with the Resolution and Ordinance (Columbia, 1852).

KIBLER, LILLIAN ADELE. *Benjamin F. Perry, South Carolina Unionist* (Durham, N. C., 1946).

"Kossuth and Intervention," *Southern Quarterly Review*, N.S. VI (July, 1852), 221-235.

LA BORDE, MAXIMILIAN. *History of the South Carolina College, from its Incorporation, Dec. 19, 1801, to Dec. 19, 1865, including Sketches of its Presidents and Professors. With an Appendix* (Charleston, 1874).

MALONE, DUMAS. *Public Life of Thomas Cooper, 1783–1839* (New Haven, 1926).

MASON, EDWARD G. "A Visit to South Carolina in 1860," *Atlantic Monthly*, LIII (Feb., 1884), 241-250.

MEIGS, WILLIAM M. *The Life of John Caldwell Calhoun* (2 vols.; New York, 1917).

MEMMINGER, CHRISTOPHER G. "Address to the General Assembly of Virginia, January 19, 1860," *De Bow's Review*, XXIX (Dec., 1860), 751-771.

MERRITT, ELIZABETH. *James Henry Hammond* ([*Johns Hopkins University Studies in Historical and Political Science*, Vol. XLI, No. 4], Baltimore, 1923).

MILTON, GEORGE FORT. *The Eve of the Conflict: Stephen A. Douglas and the Needless War* (New York, 1934).

Miscellaneous Documents of the Senate of the United States for the First and Second Sessions of the Thirty-fourth Congress, 1855–'56 (Washington, 1856).

NICHOLS, ROY F. *The Democratic Machine, 1850–1854* (New York, 1923).

————. *Franklin Pierce: Young Hickory of the Granite Hills* (Philadelphia, 1931).

NICOLAY, JOHN G., AND HAY, JOHN. *Abraham Lincoln, A History* (10 vols.; New York, 1890).

Officers and Members of the House of Representatives of the State of South Carolina: 1856–1857. With their Election Districts, Postoffices, and Professions (Columbia, 1856).

Official Proceedings of the National Democratic Convention held in Cincinnati, June 2-6, 1856 (Cincinnati, 1856).

ORR, JAMES LAWRENCE. *The Cincinnati Convention. Letter from James L. Orr to C. W. Dudley, on the Propriety of having the State of South Carolina Represented in the Democratic National Convention, to be Held in Cincinnati* (Washington, 1855).

"P." "The Judiciary System of South Carolina," *Southern Quarterly Review*, N.S. II (Nov., 1850), 464-486.

PARKHURST, JOHN G. (ed.). *Official Proceedings of the Democratic National Convention, Held in 1860, at Charleston and Baltimore* (Cleveland, 1860).

PERRY, BENJAMIN F. *Biographical Sketches of Eminent American Statesmen, with Speeches, Addresses and Letters by Ex-Governor B. F. Perry of Greenville, S. C.* (Philadelphia, 1887).

————. *Reminiscences of Public Men* (Philadelphia, 1883).

————. *Reminiscences of Public Men, with Speeches and Addresses* (Greenville, S. C., 1889).

PERRY, THOMAS SARGENT (ed.). *The Life and Letters of Francis Lieber* (Boston, 1882).

PHILLIPS, ULRICH B. *The Course of the South to Secession* (New York, 1939).

PIERCE, EDWARD L. *Memoir and Letters of Charles Sumner* (4 vols.; London, 1879-1893).

Population of the United States in 1860; Compiled from the Original Returns of the Eighth Census, under the Direction of the Secretary of Interior, by Joseph C. G. Kennedy, Superintendent of Census (Washington, 1864).

[PORCHER, FREDERICK W.] "Southern and Northern Civilization Contrasted," *Russell's Magazine*, I (May, 1857), 97-107.

PORTER, WILLIAM D. *State Sovereignty and the Doctrine of Coercion* (Charleston, 1860).

Proceedings of the Democratic State Convention of South Carolina, Held at Columbia, 5th and 6th of May, 1856, for the Purpose of Electing Delegates to the Democratic National Convention, to Meet in Cincinnati in June (Columbia, 1856).

Proceedings of the Great Southern Co-operation and Anti-Secession Meeting Held in Charleston, September 23, 1851 (Charleston, 1851).

Proceedings of the Meeting of Delegates from the Southern Rights Associations of South Carolina. Held at Charleston, May, 1851 (Columbia, 1851).

Proceedings of the National Democratic Convention Convened at Charleston, S. C., April 23, 1860 (Washington, 1860).

RAINWATER, PERCY LEE. *Mississippi: Storm Center of Secession, 1856–1861* (Baton Rouge, 1938).

RANDALL, JAMES GARFIELD. *The Civil War and Reconstruction* (New York, 1937).

Register of Officers and Agents, Civil, Military, and Naval in the Service of the United States . . . (biennial, Washington, 1853, 1855, 1857, 1859).

Report of the Minority of the Special Committee of Seven, to Whom Was Referred So Much of his Late Excellency's Message No. 1, As Relates to Slavery and the Slave Trade (Columbia, 1857).

Report of the Special Committee of the House of Representatives of South Carolina, on So Much of the Message of His Excellency Gov. James H. Adams, As Relates to Slavery and the Slave Trade (Columbia, 1857).

Reports and Resolutions of the General Assembly of the State of South Carolina (annual sessions, Columbia, 1852-1860).

Reports of Committees of the House of Representatives, Made during the First Session of the Thirty-fourth Congress, 1855–'56 (3 vols.; Washington, 1856).

"Review of 'Uncle Tom's Cabin,' " *Southern Quarterly Review,* N.S. VII (Jan., 1853), 81-120.

RHODES, JAMES FORD. *History of the United States from the Compromise of 1850* (8 vols.; New York, 1877-1906).

The Rules of the House of Representatives and of the Senate of the State of South Carolina. Various Acts and Resolutions, Containing Standing Orders of the House, the Constitution of the

State of South Carolina and the Constitution of the United States (Columbia, 1857).

RUSSELL, ROBERT ROYAL. *Economic Aspects of Southern Sectionalism, 1840–1861* ([*University of Illinois Studies in the Social Sciences*, Vol. XI, Nos. 1 and 2], Urbana, 1924).

SCHAPER, WILLIAM AUGUST. "Sectionalism and Representation in South Carolina," *Annual Report of the American Historical Association for the Year 1900*, I (Washington, 1901), 237-463.

SCHOULER, JAMES. *History of the United States of America under the Constitution* (7 vols.; New York, 1894-1913).

SHANKS, HENRY T. *The Secession Movement in Virginia, 1847–1861* (Richmond, 1934).

SHRYOCK, RICHARD H. *Georgia and the Union in 1850* (Durham, N. C., 1926).

SIMMS, HENRY H. *A Decade of Sectional Controversy* (Chapel Hill, 1942).

SITTERSON, JOSEPH CARLYLE. *The Secession Movement in North Carolina* (Chapel Hill, 1939).

SMITH, THEODORE CLARK. *Parties and Slavery, 1850–1859* ([*The American Nation: A History*, Vol. XVIII], New York, 1906).

SMITH, WILLIAM R. (ed.). *The History and Debates of the Convention of the People of Alabama, Begun and Held in the City of Montgomery, on the Seventh Day of January, 1861* (Montgomery, 1867).

"South Carolina—Her Agriculture, Etc." ["prepared by a gentleman of South Carolina"], *De Bow's Review*, XIX (Nov., 1855), 523-555.

The South Carolina Legislative Times; Being the Debates and Proceedings in the South Carolina Legislature at the Session Commencing Nov. 1855 (Columbia, 1855).

SPRATT, L. W. *The Foreign Slave Trade, the Source of Political Power—of Material Progress, of Social Integrity, and of Social Emancipation of the South* (Charleston, 1858).

———. *A Series of Articles on the Value of the Union to the South, Lately Published in the Charleston Standard* (Charleston, 1855).

"State of Parties and the Country," *Southern Quarterly Review*, N.S. VIII (July, 1853), 1-53.

STEPHENSON, NATHANIEL W. "Southern Nationalism in South

Carolina in 1851," *American Historical Review*, XXXVI (Jan., 1931), 314-335.

SYDNOR, CHARLES S. "The Southerner and the Laws," *Journal of Southern History*, VI (Feb., 1940), 3-23.

TAYLOR, ROSSER HOWARD. *Ante-Bellum South Carolina: A Social and Cultural History* (Chapel Hill, 1942).

————. "The Gentry of Ante-Bellum South Carolina," *North Carolina Historical Review*, XVII (April, 1940), 114-131.

THORNWELL, JAMES HENLEY. *Letter to His Excellency Governor Manning on Public Instruction in South Carolina* (Columbia, 1853).

TOPPING, W. H. "Hon. James L. Orr, of South Carolina," *National Democratic Review*, Vol. I, No. 4 (April, 1856).

TOWNSEND, JOHN. *The South Alone Should Govern the South and African Slavery by Those Friendly to It* (Charleston, 1860).

TRENT, WILLIAM PETERFIELD. *William Gilmore Simms* (New York, 1892).

TRESCOT, WILLIAM H. *The Annual Address before the Calliopean and Polytechnic Societies of the Citadel Academy* (Charleston, 1856).

[TRESCOT, WILLIAM H.] "The Bench and Bar," *Russell's Magazine*, VI (Jan., 1860), 289-297.

————. "Oration Delivered before the South Carolina Historical Society, May 19, 1858," *Russell's Magazine*, V (July, 1859), 289-307.

————. *The Position and Course of the South* (Charleston, 1850).

VAN DEUSEN, JOHN G. *The Ante-Bellum Southern Commercial Conventions* (Durham, N. C., 1926).

————. *Economic Bases of Disunion in South Carolina* (New York, 1928).

WALLACE, DAVID DUNCAN. *The History of South Carolina* (4 vols.; New York, 1934).

WENDER, HERBERT. *The Southern Commercial Conventions* ([*Johns Hopkins University Studies in Historical and Political Science*, Vol. XLVIII, No. 4], Baltimore, 1930).

WHITE, LAURA A. "The National Democrats in South Carolina, 1852–1860," *South Atlantic Quarterly*, XXVIII (Oct., 1929), 370-389.

————. *Robert Barnwell Rhett: Father of Secession* (New York, 1931).

INDEX

Abbeville district, 21

Abbeville *Banner*, withholds endorsement of Buchanan, 123

Abolition, *see* Antislavery movement

Adams, James H.: in nullification controversy, 9; governor, 24; resolution in convention of 1852, 39 n.; on antislavery agitation, 86, 125; on health and economic conditions, 86 n.; on election of 1856, 124-125; for foreign slave trade, 131; opinions in 1858, 171; alarmed by Hammond's speeches, 174; candidate for U. S. Senate, 176 n.

Aiken, William: at South Carolina College, 8; in Thirty-second Congress, 43, 45; censured for courtesy to Nathaniel P. Banks, 135

Alabama: repudiation of South Carolina course, 27, 30; reliance of South Carolina secessionists upon, 203; leadership in disruption of national Democratic party urged, 214 n.; co-operation in secession sought, 223-224; secession sentiment in, 224, 225

Aldrich, A. P.: discusses resistance measures, 32; view of convention of 1852, 34; reports on proposals that South Carolina lead secession movement in 1860, 226

Allston, Robert F. W., governor, 24

American party: in Charleston in 1854, 73; in South Carolina in 1855, 79-83

Anderson district, 21

Antislavery movement: feared in South Carolina, 9, 29, 38, 50, 61-64, 69-72, 74, 83, 86, 97, 207-208; and Kansas-Nebraska Bill, 58, 60, 64, 68-70, 74; and caning of Sumner, 118; effect on foreign policy criticized, 78; and Kansas, 111-112; strength of considered, 52, 58, 69-71, 185, 192; as reason for secession, 208-209, 220, 226, 231-233; *see also* Republican party

Ashmore, John D.: supports Orr, 23; opinion of Douglas, 169; on slave code in territories, 180; against slave-trade agitation, 183; position in early 1860, 207-208

Atchison, David R., for suspension of Kansas aid, 139

Baker, Alpheus, solicits aid for Kansas emigrants, 138

Baptist Church in Columbia, convention of 1860 in, 229

Barnwell Court House, Hammond speaks at, 172

Barnwell, R. W.: view of state convention of 1852, 34; on admission of Kansas, 154 n.

Bell, E. B., in Kansas in 1856, 108

Bellinger, John, for power of legislature to secede, 38-39

Biographical data on S. C. Senators, Representatives, and Governors, 7 n.

Bonham, Milledge L.: at South Carolina College, 8; on State Rights, 9 n.; in Congress, 24, 151; opposes English Bill, 153, 171; on Republicans, 166; disappoints extremists, 172; for representation in national convention of 1860, 212

Boyce, W. W.: in Thirty-third Congress, 56; on Kansas-Nebraska Bill, 62-63; on tariff, 67, 134; on Cuba, 77; against Know-Nothings, 81; against national convention, 85, 96; on Kansas, 108, 112; for

Buchanan, 122; for Lecompton constitution, 152; on slave trade, 183; for secession if Republican elected President, 166, 187, 222-223

Breckinridge, John C., presidential nominee, 219-220

Brooks, Preston: in Thirty-third Congress, 56; on Kansas-Nebraska Bill, 62-63; prefers constitutional to sectional arguments, 73, 116; against Know-Nothings, 82; on Kansas, 108; canes Charles Sumner, 115-120; supports Orr, 23, 87, 116; predicts disunion if Republican elected President, 123, 124 n.; against Orr's slave-trade resolution, 132; drifts from national party, 133; death commented upon, 134

Brown, John, effect of his raid: on agitation for economic and cultural independence of South, 204; on convention question, 190, 209-210; on slave-trade agitation, 184-185; on secession sentiment, 189-190, 209

Bryan, Edward B.: against national convention, 104; for foreign slave trade, 142-143, 183-184

Buchanan, James, opinion of in South Carolina, 103, 121-123, 140, 169-171, 176

Burt, Armistead: and convention of 1852, 34; in Thirty-second Congress, 43

Burt, Francis, auditor in Treasury Department, 55

Butler, Andrew P.: in Thirty-second Congress, 43-44, 45; on campaign of 1852, 47 n.; on Kansas-Nebraska Bill, 60-62; on land grants, 66; preference for constitutional rather than sectional arguments, 73; reluctantly endorses national convention, 87, 93; on Kansas, 112, 113; assailed by Charles Sumner, 114-115; on tariff, 134

Calhoun, A. P., opinion of Congress, 151

Calhoun, John C.: solicited for public office, 3; on duty of leadership, 3; mastery of South Carolina politics, 11-12; successors to, 12; encourages leadership of Mississippi, 19

Camden *Journal*: on state convention of 1852, 36; against national convention, 46; on William H. Seward, 46; for Buchanan, 122

Campaigns: of 1852, 47-49; of 1856, 112, 121-124; of 1860, 219-220

Carew, John E., on Douglas, 188 n.

Charleston: strongly supports Orr program, 23; federal officials in, 54; Know-Nothing party in, 79; Negroes from *Echo* in, 158-159; merchants of advertise against Northern trade, 204; site of Democratic national convention of 1860, 214; site of secession convention, 229-230

Charleston *Evening News*: against Kansas-Nebraska Bill, 63; on elections of 1854, 70; for Southern party, 71, 83; on Cuban policy, 77; for Know-Nothing party, 79-81; for Buchanan, 122; on tariff, 67

Charleston *Mercury*: and R. Barnwell Rhett, Sr., 14-15; against nominating conventions, 46; on Pierce, 47; on presidential patronage, 54; predicts trouble for Pierce, 57; on Kansas-Nebraska Bill, 58; on antislavery agitation, 64; on relationship of convention and electoral-reform questions, 99 n.; on Kansas, 65-66, 76, 106, 112, 140-141; on elections, 70-71, 146, 185; for isolation from parties, 72? on Know-Nothings, 80; sympathy for Southern party, 83; on sectionalism, 86 n.; for Buchanan, 122, 140-141; for disunion in 1856, 125; on Republicans, 144; on English Bill, 156; on foreign slave trade, 157; for harmony in 1858, 166; on Hammond's position in 1858, 175; on Democratic foreign policy and Cuba, 179; on Seward, 186-187; on John Brown raid, 189 n.; on Memminger, 200 n.; lacks confidence in disunionist potentialities of Upper South, 203; on disruption of Democratic national convention at Charleston, 215 n.; on separate state secession, 222

Chesnut, James: at South Carolina College, 8; middle-ground position, 24; view of state convention of 1852, 34; elected U. S. Senator, 176; on slave code in territories, 181; position in early 1860, 206; decision for secession, 223 n.; on South Carolina's leading secession movement, 223; resigns Senatorship, 227

Chesnut, Mrs. James, on popular clamor for secession, 228

Cheves, Langdon, and state convention of 1852, 34, 41

Cincinnati, site of Democratic national convention of 1856, 103, 121

Colcock, William F: at South Carolina College, 8; in Thirty-second Congress, 43; Collector of Port of Charleston, 54

Columbia, site of conventions: state convention in 1852, 37-41; Democratic state convention of 1856, 102-103; Democratic state conventions of 1860, 212-213, 217; state secession convention of 1860, 229

Columbia *Carolina Times*: sympathy for Southern party, 83; withholds endorsement of Buchanan, 123

Columbia *South Carolinian*: on state convention of 1852, 36; on ordinance of 1852, 42 n.; on Pierce, 47 n.; on antislavery sentiment, 50 n.; on slave code in territories, 180

Commercial conventions, 142, 158

Commissioner, to Virginia in 1860, 194, 200-203

Committee of Twenty-One, in state convention of 1852, 38-41

Compromise of 1850: opinion of in South Carolina, 26-27, 52, 121; considered in Thirty-second Congress, 43

Congress: representation of South Carolina in, 4, 42-45, 56, 60-63, 66-67, 112-118, 150-153, 205-208; criticized in South Carolina, 150-151

Congresses: Thirty-second, 13-14, 42-45; Thirty-third, 56-63, 75;

Thirty-fourth, 112-118, 131-133; Thirty-fifth, 138, 150-153, 179-180, 182-183; Thirty-sixth, 205-208

Conner, James, resigns office, 227

Constitution of South Carolina, defended by Butler, 44; democratic innovations absent from, 93; electoral provisions, 99

Constitution of the United States, strict interpretation of, 10, 55, 103

Convention of national Democratic party, South Carolina's participation in considered, 22-23, 46, 84-85, 87-105, 191, 209-212, 214 n.; opposed most strongly in rural districts of the southern division of the state, 104; opposed most strongly in districts with highest proportion of slaves to population, 90, 105, 211; and electoral-reform advocates, 99 n., 100 n.; at Cincinnati, 121; at Charleston, 214-216

Convention of the State of South Carolina: in 1852, 28, 33-42; in 1860, 225, 228-230

Conventions: commercial, 142, 158; of national Democratic party, 121, 214; of state Democratic party, 102, 212; at Richmond, 219; of State of South Carolina, 28, 33-42, 225, 228-230

Conventionists, *see* Convention of national Democratic party, National Democrats

Cooke, John W., on Democratic party as obstacle to disunion, 95

Cooper, Thomas, as molder of opinion, 8

Co-operationists: against separate state secession, 29, 30, 33; reject resistance measures, 32; maintain organization, 33; offices obtained by, 51, 55; and national convention of Democratic party, 92

Corruption, ascribed to Republicans, 135

Cuba, 67, 76-78, 179

Cunningham, John: urges Hammond to lead resistance movement, 32; a Know-Nothing leader, 79-80; on Kansas, 112; on Hammond's speeches of 1858, 174, 175; and slave-trade agitation, 183

Custom, as incentive for public service, 5

Darlington *Flag*, on economic conditions, 49 n.

De Bow's Review, on slave-trade agitation, 164 n.

De Leon, Edwin, Consul-General, 54

Democracy, Butler's interpretation of, 44; exaltation of in foreign relations opposed, 53; said to be promoted by National Democrats, 100

Democratic party: relationship of South Carolina to during Calhoun era, 22-23, 46, 84-85; usefulness to South considered, 70-71, 96-97, 121, 145-146, 165 n., 167-171, 187, 192, 212; isolation from national organization advocated, 46-47, 72, 86 n., 96-102, 146, 167-168, 170-171, 212; support for, 23, 48-49, 72, 84-85, 88-89, 121-122, 170, 209-211; as obstacle to disunion, 94-95, 100, 167, 209-210, 213, 215 n., 221, 232-233; reunion of seceders with opposed, 217; its foreign policy as diversion from sectional conflicts within, 179; and slave-trade agitation, 131-132; and conflicting interpretations of popular sovereignty, 132; *see also* Convention of national Democratic party, Northern Democrats, Parties

Democratic platforms: of 1856, 121, 178; of 1860, 214-215

Diseases, 73, 229

Districts, Congressional and state, 15

Disunion, *see* Secession, Southern confederacy

Douglas, Stephen A.: support for, 103, 121; National Democrats lose confidence in, 168-169; extremists oppose nomination, 188, 213

Dred Scott decision: reaction in South Carolina to, 135, possible conflict over as opportunity for secession from Charleston convention, 214 n.

Durkee, Charles, 45

Echo, captured slaver, 158, 182

Economic conditions, 49, 73, 86 n.

Economic independence of South, desire for as cause of secession, viii-ix; propaganda for, 204-205

Edgefield district, 21, 92

Economy, in federal expenditures: favored by South Carolina delegation, 43; referred to by Governor Manning, 55

Edgefield *Advertiser*: on fire-eaters, 18; on impotency of South Carolina, 36; on federal spoils, 46 n.; on federal government, 49 n.; on Kansas-Nebraska Bill, 63-64; on antislavery agitation, 64; on elections of 1854, 70; on national convention, 92; on Kansas as slave state, 65 n.; on sectionalism and national Democracy, 72 n.; on Democratic party, 165 n.; and Douglas, 169 n., 188 n.

Education, of political leaders, 7-8

Elections: in 1851 for delegates to state convention, 28; in 1851 for delegates to Southern congress, 30; in 1852 for Presidency, 45-50; in 1852 for state legislature, 51; in 1853 for Congressmen, 55; in North in 1854 viewed with apprehension, 64 n.; in 1854 for legislature, 73; in 1855 for Charleston officials, 81; in 1856 for Presidency, 121-125; in 1857 for Charleston delegate to legislature, 142; in North in 1857 commented upon, 145-146; in 1857 for U. S. Senator, 147-149; in North in 1858, 165; in 1858 for U. S. Senator, 175-177; in North in 1859, 185; in 1860 for Presidency, 187, 224-225; in North in 1860, 220; in 1860 for delegates to state convention, 228

Electoral laws, changes in advocated, 80, 99-100

Elliott, George P., on English Bill, 156

Elliott, Stephen, extols civic virtues, 4-5

Emigration to Kansas, 106, 108-112, 138-139

English Bill, opinion of in South Carolina, 153-156

Evans, Benjamin, opinion of Congress, 151

Evans, Josiah J.: elected U. S. Senator, 51; against administration candidate for printer to Senate, 56; on Kansas-Nebraska Bill, 62 n.; for national convention, 87, 93; on admission of Kansas, 154 n.

Evans, Thomas, U. S. District Attorney, 55

Excitement, popular, in 1860, 226

Expansion (territorial), attitude of South Carolina toward, 53; *see also* Imperialism

Extremists, *see* Irreconcilables, Secessionists

Factions: under Calhoun, 11-12; in 1850's, 23-25; in 1854, 74; in 1855, 85; in 1856, 87, 121-122; in 1857, 142; in 1858, 147, 149, 157, 175-177; in 1859, 195; in 1860, 210-212, 217-218, 229

Farrow, James: supports Orr, 23; on reliability of Northern Democrats, 122

Federal offices: Edgefield *Advertiser* on, 46 n.; in South Carolina, 54; influence on Southern leadership, 46, 97-98, 193-194; resignations from in 1860, 227

Filibustering, 178

Fillmore, Millard, 26

Fifth Congressional District, strongly supports Orr-led Democrats, 23

Fire-eaters: their qualities, 15-16; typified by Lawrence M. Keitt, 16-18; criticized in South Carolina, 18, 146; viewed adversely in South, 19; awkward position of after 1852, 24; suitability for Southern leadership in early 1860, 219; *see also* Irreconcilables, Secessionists

Florida, secession sentiment in, 224

Foote, Henry S.: governor of Mississippi, 26; critical of South Carolina's constitution, 44

Foreign policy, views in South Carolina on, 53, 67, 76-78, 121, 178-179

Freeport Doctrine, anticipated by James L. Orr, 132

Free Trade, *see* Tariff

Frémont, John C., united opposition to, 123

Fugitive-slave law: repeal opposed, 44; resolution of Democratic state convention on, 103

Gadberry, J. M., delegate to Cincinnati convention, 103

Gadsden, James: minister to Mexico, 54; negotiates treaty with Mexico, 67

Gaillard, Franklin: supports Orr, 23; on Kansas policy, 141

Georgia: distrusts South Carolina leadership, 19; rejects secession, 26, 28, 30; and co-operation with South Carolina, 198 n., 223-224

Gist, William H.: at South Carolina College, 8; governor, 24; resolution in 1851 on state convention, 34; position in 1859, 191-194; communicates with Southern governors in 1860, 224; recommends immediate secession, 225-226

Gregg, Maxcy: on state allegiance, 29; for resistance measures, 31, 35; submits report in convention of 1852, 40; opinions in 1858, 171; alarmed by Hammond's speeches of 1858, 174

Gregg, William, 210

Green, Allan J., on admission of Kansas, 154 n.

Greenville *Mountaineer*, on Pierce, 53 n.

Hamilton, D. H.: comments on illegal slave trade, 158-159; on effect of John Brown's raid, 191

Hammond, James H.: solicited for public office, 3; at South Carolina College, 8; in nullification controversy, 9; candidate for U. S. Senate, 13; middle-ground position, 24; resistance measures proposed in 1851, 31-32; comments on ordinance of 1852, 41; elected U. S. Senator, 147-149, 151; for Lecompton constitution, 152; for coalition of South with Northern friends, 172-173; resembles National Democrats in his position, 173; response to his speeches of 1858, 174-175; on slave-trade agitation, 183; on slave-code agitation, 180, 181; on Seward, 186; on Douglas, 188 n.; on North-South relations in Congress, 205; on South Carolina's leading secession movement, 223; resigns Senatorship, 227

Hayne, Arthur P., in U. S. Senate, 151

Hayne, I. W.: on state convention of 1852, 34; on admission of Kansas, 154 n.; on Democratic party, 170 n.; on disunion sentiment in 1859, 198 n.; on Memminger, 200 n.; in Democratic state convention of May, 1860, 218

Health, of South Carolina, 73-74, 86 n.; of Preston Brooks, 116

Heart, John, on Rhett's relationship to *Mercury*, 15

Homestead legislation, opposed by South Carolina delegation in Congress, 43, 66

Hope, John C.: on slave-trade agitation, 182 n.; resolution on Southern confederacy, 195 n.

Houston, Samuel, criticizes South Carolina's constitution, 44

Huger, Alfred, on Calhoun's domination of South Carolina politics, 12 n.; on Douglas, 169

Immigrants, issue between Know-Nothings and their opponents in 1855, 80, 82

Imperialism, dislike for in South Carolina, 68, 121, 178

Institute Hall, 230

Insurrections, rumors of in 1860, 226

Insurgency: declines in 1852, 49, 51; revives in 1859, 189-191, 194-196; growth of in 1860, 205-206, 223-228; *see also* Secession

Intransigents, *see* Irreconcilables

Irreconcilables: views at close of 1852, 51, at close of 1853, 57, in 1854, 70; course of in 1854, 71-72; strength of in 1854, 74; relation to Know-Nothings, 79-80, 81; position at close of 1855, 85-86; attitude toward national convention of Democratic party, 96, 211-212; attitude toward Republicans, 120, 144-145, 165; reaction to election

of 1856, 124, 134; in 1856 confess desire for disunion, 125; on Kansas policy, 139-140, 156; unconcerned about Orr's election to Speakership, 150; and Speakership election of 1860, 206; suspicious of Buchanan's foreign policy, 179; and slave-trade agitation, 157, 183; and John Brown raid, 189; significance of Democratic split interpreted variously by, 170-171; alarmed by Hammond's speeches of 1858, 174-175; in Senatorial election of 1857, 147, and Senatorial election of 1858, 175-176; strength in legislature of 1858, 177; concerned about Douglas's candidacy for nomination, 213; desire to influence South Carolina delegation at Charleston convention, 213-214; at Charleston convention of 1860, 214-215; seek control of Richmond delegation, 216-217; in Democratic state convention of May, 1860, 217; oppose reunion of Democratic wings, 217; suitability for Southern leadership questioned, 218-219; at Richmond convention, 219; for secession, 220, 222; dominate secession convention, 229; course of reviewed, 231-232; *see also* Secessionists

Isolationists, *see* Irreconcilables

Jamison, David Flavel, chairman of secession convention, 229

Jones, James, urges Hammond to take lead, 32

Kansas: reaction in South Carolina to events in, 65-66, 76, 107-112, 139-142; suitability for slavery doubted, 62, 65 n., 111-112, 154; emigrants to, 106, 108-110, 138-139, 150; admission as a state considered, 62, 139-140, 152-155; and national convention of Democratic party, 105-106; reaction in South Carolina to Buchanan's policy in, 140-141; debated in Congress, 112-118; and secession, 154 n.; summary of controversy over, 156

Kansas-Nebraska Bill, passage of, 58; debated by South Carolina delegation, 60-63; South Carolina press on, 63-64; approved by Democratic state convention of 1856, 103, and by delegation in national convention, 121; and revival of antislavery agitation, 58, 60, 64, 68-70, 74; *see also* Missouri Compromise, Popular sovereignty

Keitt, Lawrence M.: praises South Carolina leadership, 5; a representative fire-eater, 16-18; in Congress, 24; resolution on state convention in legislature of 1851, 34; in Thirty-third Congress, 56; on Kansas-Nebraska Bill, 62-63; against Know-Nothings, 81; against representation in national convention, 85, 96; on Kansas, 108, 140; for Buchanan, 122; against Orr's slave-trade resolution, 132; on tariff, 134; on Republicans, 144, 166; for Lecompton constitution, 152; for co-operation with Buchanan-led Democratic party, 170; suspected of nationalistic tendencies in 1858, 172; candidate for U. S. Senator, 176 n.; on Cuba, 178; on slave trade, 182, 183; for secession in 1860, 222, 223

Know-Nothing party, *see* American party

Knoxville, commercial convention in, 142

Kossuth, Louis, lack of enthusiasm for in South Carolina, 45

Lancaster *Ledger*, on economic conditions, 49 n.; on Kansas, 111, 141; on Douglas, 169; on John Brown raid, 190

Law, training for common among leaders, 7

Leadership in South Carolina: regard for, 3; a patriotic obligation, 3; as compensation for deficiencies, 4-5; disregard for, 5-6; background of leaders, 7; influence of South Carolina College upon, 8; events witnessed by leaders, 9-10; lessons of 1830's for, 10; influence of Calhoun and nullifiers on, 10-12;

successors to Calhoun, 12-15; temperament as a factor in, 15; fire-eaters, 15-16; moderates, 16-23; factional structure within in 1850's, 24-25; type desired by R. B. Rhett, Jr., in 1860, 213 n.

Leadership of South Carolina, distrusted by other states, 13-14, 19-20, 200-203, 223-224

Lecompton constitution: opinion of in South Carolina, 152-153, 154 n.; and the reliability of Northern Democrats, 167-169; Buchanan's endorsement of pleases South Carolina extremists, 169-171

Legislature of South Carolina: provides for state convention and calls for Southern congress, 28; sets date for state convention, 34-35; elects governor and U. S. Senator, 51; absorbed with state problems in 1853, 55; tables anti-convention resolution, 104; acts upon disunion resolutions, 126-129, 194-199; acts upon slave-trade resolutions, 131, 143-144, 159-164, 183-185; elects U. S. Senators, 147-148, 175-177; and movement for cultural and economic independence of South, 205; provides for state convention in 1860, 225; receives resignations of U. S. Senators, 227

Letcher, John, on Memminger, 201

Lieber, Francis, on preoccupation with politics in South Carolina, 6 n.

Lincoln, Abraham: Senatorial candidate, 168; presidential nominee, 220-221, 222, 223, 225; his election precipitates resignation of federal officials, 227, and secession, 225, 229-230, 233

Lobbying, 135

Louisiana, secession sentiment in, 224

Low country: and South Carolina leadership, 21; and political parties, 85 n.; strongly opposed to national convention of Democratic party, 102, 104; propensity for disunion, 126

Lyles, William S., at Democratic state convention of May, 1860, 217

McCarter, James, loses confidence in survival of Union, 209

McDuffie, George, interpretation of the Constitution, 10

"Malachi" [pseudonymous writer], on Calhoun's domination of South Carolina politics, 12 n.

McQueen, John: in Congress, 24, 43; against Know-Nothings, 81; against national convention, 85, 96; on Kansas, 108, 140; for Buchanan, 122; on Republicans, 144-145, 166; candidate for U. S. Senate, 176 n.; for secession if Republican elected President, 187

Magrath, A. G.: supports Orr, 23; delegate to national convention, 103; on Kansas as a slave state, 65 n.; on slave-trade agitation, 181 n.; resigns judgeship, 227

Manifest Destiny, 77

Manning, John Lawrence: governor, 51; message of 1853, 55; on elections of 1854, 64 n.; on foreign policy, 68; delegate to Cincinnati convention, 103; candidate for U. S. Senate, 175 n.

Mazyck, Alexander: resolution for Southern confederacy, 128-129; resolution on slave trade, 164

Means, John Hugh: at South Carolina College, 8; message of 1851, 34; predicts secession in 1851, 37; chairman of 1852 convention, 37; on economic conditions, 49 n.; message of 1852, 50; at Democratic state convention of May, 1860, 217

Memminger, Christopher G.: and state convention of 1852, 34; for participation in national politics, 48-49; candidate for U. S. Senate, 175 n.; resolution in legislature of 1859, 194; on insecurity of South in Union, 197 n., 198 n.; doubts survival of Union, 201 n., 202 n.; commissioner to Virginia, 200-203

Mexico, 67, 178

Middleton, John Izard, introduces secession resolution, 129

Miles, William P.: in Congress, 151; on Buchanan's Kansas policy, 138; for Lecompton constitution, 152, 153; on slavery in Kansas, 65 n.; on admission of Kansas, 154 n.; on slave trade, 182, 183; for Southern confederacy in 1858, 152; for se-

cession if Republican elected President, 166; for immediate secession in 1860, 223

Minnesota, 134

"Minute Men," 226

Mississippi: leadership of South encouraged by Calhoun, 19; acceptance of Compromise of 1850, 26; against secession in 1851, 30; reliance of South Carolina secessionists upon in 1860, 203; withdrawal of delegation from Charleston convention proposed, 214 n.; support in secession movement desired by Orr in 1860, 223; secession sentiment in, 224-225

Missouri Compromise, report of a proposal to repeal, 57; repeal supported by South Carolina, 62-64, 103; Senator Evans on, 62 n.; *see also* Kansas-Nebraska Bill

Moderates: favored by circumstances after 1852, 20; James L. Orr as representative leader of, 20-22; in campaign of 1852, 48; support for Democratic party and Pierce in 1854, 72; against Know-Nothings, 81; organization of in 1856, 87; favorable to disunion in 1856 if Republican elected President, 123; discouraged by Republican strength in 1856, 124; criticize extremists, 146; and admission of Kansas, 155-157; and Douglas, 169; and slave-code agitation, 180; and slave-trade agitation, 183; and Republican party, 185; and John Brown raid, 190; lose confidence in survival of Union in early 1860, 208-209; *see also* National Democrats

Montgomery: site of proposed Southern congress, 28; commercial convention in, 158

Mullins, W. S., resolution on Southern confederacy, 195 n.

National Democrats: strength of, viii, 87, 103-104, 142, 147-149, 177, 209-210, 217, 233; geographical distribution of, 23, 102, 104; in Senatorial election of 1857, 147-149; in Senatorial election of 1858, 175-176; in Speakership election of 1860, 206; Edgefield *Advertiser* on, 72 n.; hold state convention in 1856, 101-103; in presidential campaign of 1856, 121-122; control state Democratic convention of April, 1860, 212; lose control of convention of May, 217; in national convention at Charleston, 214-216; withdraw from Charleston convention, 215-216; and delegation to Richmond, 218; and electoral reform, 99 n., 100 n.; against Know-Nothings, 81; for national convention, 23, 87; appraise antislavery movement, 97; and Brooks-Sumner affair, 120-121; attitude toward Republican party, 124, 146, 165-166; on Kansas policy, 141-142, 156; oppose slave-trade agitation, 131-132, 142, 157, 183; effect of slave-trade agitation on, 133, 183; effect of disagreements about popular sovereignty on, 133; annoyed by slave-code proposal, 180; relationship to Hammond, 173-174; availability for Southern leadership, 219; criticized in South Carolina, 171-172, 214 n.; Unionist proclivities of, 94, 102, 129-130, 146; conditionally favor secession in 1856, 123; declining confidence in Union, 209; for secession in 1860, 220; in secession convention, 229; course of reviewed, 232-233; *see also* Convention of national Democratic party, Democratic party, Moderates

Nationalism: Pierce's interpretation of approved, 72-73; conflict with sectionalism, 72-73, 106; said to be promoted by national conventions, 100; disapproval for, 116

Nativism, *see* American party

Naturalization, revision of laws governing proposed, 80

Negroes, illegal importations of, 158

Newberry *Conservatist*, on South Carolina delegation in Charleston convention of 1860, 216 n.

Newberry *Mirror*: withholds endorsement of Buchanan, 123; on Orr's statement about disunion, 124 n.

Newberry *Rising Sun*: on fire-eaters, 18; on Congress, 151; on Cuba,

179; on slave-trade agitation, 181 n.

Newberry *Sentinel*, on convention of 1852, 36

New Orleans, commercial convention in, 130

New York, disputes over federal patronage in, 53-54

Nicaragua, 67

Noble, Edward, on Douglas, 188 n.

Nominating convention: desirability of argued, 93, 98; geographic distribution of opponents of, 104; Hammond's opinion of, 173; opposition to in 1860, 212; *see also* Convention of national Democratic party

Nonintercourse, campaign for in 1859-1860, 204-205

North, views as to anti-Southern and antislavery feelings in, 49, 64, 70-71, 89, 146

North Carolina, secession sentiment in, 224

Northern Democrats: question of the desirability of Southern co-operation with, 48-49, 70, 89-90, 94, 96, 102, 121-122, 145-146, 167-169, 173 n., 187, 209, 212, 214 n.

Nullification, effect on South Carolina politics, 10-11; and dissemination of State Rights doctrine, 9 n.

Occupations, of political leaders, 7

Orr, James L.: sketch of, 20-22; organizes moderates, 23; and Speakership, 21-22, 56, 150; and state convention of 1852, 34; in Thirty-second Congress, 43-47; in presidential campaign of 1852, 47, 48; in Thirty-third Congress, 66; favors representation in national convention, 84, 87, 89, 92, 93, 94; speaks at state Democratic convention of 1856, 103; dominant at state Democratic convention of April, 1860, 212-213; loses control of state Democratic convention of May, 1860, 218; and agitation for revival of foreign slave trade, 132; on Congressional jurisdiction over slavery in territories, 132, 180; relationship to Hammond, 173; on

Douglas, 188 n.; predicts secession if Republican elected President in 1856, 124 n.; on the secession of Southern delegates from Charleston convention, 215 n.; on Democratic party as obstacle to disunion, 95 n.; predicts disunion if Democratic candidate defeated in 1860, 166; on leadership of South Carolina in secession movement of 1860, 223; candidate for chairmanship of secession convention, 229; criticized in South Carolina, 23, 106

Offices, tabulation of those commonly held by South Carolina leaders, 7 n.; *see also* Federal offices

O'Neall, John Belton, scorns emphasis on politics, 6

Orangeburg *Southron*: withholds endorsement of Buchanan, 123; for secession in 1856, 125

Ordinances: of convention of 1852, 41; of convention of 1860, 230

Oregon, 134

Parties, distrust for in South Carolina, 84, 85 n.; F. W. Pickens on, 102; irreconcilables change policy toward, 217; *see also* Democratic party, Whigs, Convention of national Democratic party

Patriotism: for state, as incentive for public service, 3; for South, 30, 73; for United States among National Democrats, 94

Patronage: Pierce's policy in New York and South Carolina, 53-54; as incentive for advocates of national convention, 95; baneful effects of asserted, 98

Peddlers, licensing of, 205

Perry, Benjamin F.: for national convention, 94, 101; on officeholding secessionists, 95; on Kansas policy, 141, 154 n.; on Douglas, 169; on Democratic convention at Charleston, 216 n.; opposes secession in 1851, 29; explains opposition to secession in report to convention of 1852, 40; resolution of 1859 threatens disunion, 194; opposes secession in 1860, 221

Pettigrew, J. Johnston, reports on slave trade, 144

Philadelphia, American party convention in, 79

Pickens, Francis W.: at South Carolina College, 8; and nullification controversy, 9; retirement from office, 11; and Calhoun, 13; statement on South Carolina's extremism, 19; supports Orr, 23; on parties in South Carolina, 85 n.; speaks at Democratic state convention of 1856, 102-103; at Cincinnati convention, 103; candidate for U. S. Senate, 147; and Hammond's position in 1858, 173; on slave code, 180

Pickens *Keowee Courier*: on Kansas policy, 141; on slave-trade agitation, 181 n.; on John Brown raid, 190

Pierce, Franklin: patronage policy criticized, 53; support for in South Carolina, 47-48, 55, 72, 88, 96, 103, 121

Pinckney, Henry L., retirement from public office, 11

Planters, statesmanship of praised, 6

Platform of Democratic party, 47, 121, 178, 214-215

Politics, how regarded in South Carolina, 3-6; *see also* South Carolina politics

Popular sovereignty, South Carolina interpretation of, 61-62, 121, 132-133, 213

Porter, W. D., supports Orr program, 23; on Douglas, 168; on upsurgence of secession sentiment in November, 1860, 227; on admission of Kansas, 155

Presidency: value to South questioned, 46, 47 n., 96, 192-193; Southern man for proposed, 84

Pressley, B. C., Assistant Treasurer of the U. S., 55

Preston, John Smith, supports Orr program, 23

Preston, William C., retirement from public life, 11

Progress, attitude toward in South Carolina, 93-94

Public lands, grants for railroads, 43-44, 66

Railroads, *see* Public lands

Reconciliation, advocated in 1852, 48-49

Reform, 49, 94, 99

Republican party: leadership appraised, 185-186; strength appraised, 127-128, 145, 165, 167, 169, 185, 221; alarms South Carolinians, 120, 123-125, 135, 144, 146, 167, 171, 220-230; as reason for secession, 123, 124 n., 191, 192, 210, 214 n., 220-226, 231-233

Resistance measures, advocated by secessionists in 1851-1852, 30-35, 38-40

Reynolds, George N., supports Orr program, 23

Rhett, Edmund, resolution at Convention of 1852, 39

Rhett, R. B., Jr.: fears Orr organization, 23; conciliatory comments on Hammond's speeches in 1858, 174; on harmony in South Carolina, 175 n.; strategy for secessionists, 203; on Democratic state convention of April, 1860, 213; desires revolutionary leadership, 213; on national Democratic party as obstacle to disunion, 213 n.; on withdrawal of South Carolina delegation from Charleston convention, 215 n., 216 n.

Rhett, Robert Barnwell, Sr.: and nullification, 9, 10; relationship to Calhoun, 11; a secessionist Senator, 13; hostility toward, 13-14; resigns from Senate, 14; criticism of in 1850's, 14; in Thirty-second Congress, 43; candidate for U. S. Senate in 1857, 147; at Montgomery commercial convention, 158; candidate for U. S. Senate in 1858, 176 n.; and slave-trade agitation, 183; for secession if Republican elected President, 187; elected delegate to Richmond convention, 217; unfitness to promote united Southern action, 219

Richardson, F. D., Know-Nothing candidate for mayor of Charleston, 79

Richmond bolters from Charleston convention assemble in, 219

River and harbor legislation, 43-44

Roman Catholic Church, as issue in 1855, 80, 82

Savannah, commercial convention in, 130

Seabrook, W. B., on distrust of South Carolina in other Southern states, 19 n.

Secession: opposed in Upper South, 203; reports in 1860 of uncertain Southern support for, 223-224, 225; proclaimed a right by co-operationist caucus, 33, and by state convention of 1852, 41; support for in South Carolina, 13-16, 27-30, 123-129, 152, 193-199, 197 n., 198 n., 220-230; map showing vote in legislature on resolution favorable toward, 126; resolutions favorable to strongly supported in districts with highest proportion of slaves to population, 127, 128, 193, 197, 199; by separate state action an issue, 16, 27-30, 175 n., 222, 225-226; and Northern antislavery opinion, 208-209, 220, 226, 231-233; and rejection of Lecompton constitution, 155; sentiment for promoted by John Brown raid, 190; threatened in case of Republican victory in presidential election, 123, 124 n., 166, 187, 191-192, 220, 222-225; obstructed by national Democratic party, 94-95, 100, 167, 209-210, 213, 215 n., 221, 232-233; a second choice for National Democrats, 103, 127, 146, 208-210; impending in 1858, 166; resolutions favorable to, 129, 195 n., 196 n.; and resolutions adopted by legislature of 1859, 200-201; leadership of South Carolina in movement of 1860, 226; calling of convention to act upon, 225; provided for by resolution of state convention of 1860, 229; accomplished by ordinance, 229-230; cause of, ix-x

Secessionists: temperamental characteristics of, 15-16; distrusted in South, 19; in office in 1850's, 24; continuation of division among in 1850's, 24-25; division of in 1852, 27; movement of 1851 fails, 27-30; for resistance, 31-34; face dilemma in 1852, 35; discouraged by prospects for convention of 1852, 36; secession by authority of legislature advocated by some, 38; praised by Butler, 44; federal offices obtained in 1853, 54, 95; on national party politics, 96, 100, 125; during and after presidential campaign of 1856, 123, 125, 129; pleased with reaction to John Brown raid, 189-191; attitude toward national convention of 1860, 211-212; role at Charleston convention, 214-215; desire for disruption of national Democratic party, 213, 221; during presidential campaign of 1860, 220, 222-223, 225, 228-230; geographical distribution of, 126; most numerous in districts with highest proportion of slaves to population, 127, 128, 193, 197, 199

Sectionalism: conflict with Constitutional nationalism, 72-73; advocated by South Carolina Know-Nothings, 81; Preston Brooks criticized for repudiation of, 116; advocated by *Mercury*, 86 n.; promoted by Brooks's caning of Sumner, 117-118; Edgefield *Advertiser* on, 72 n.; Democratic foreign policy as diversion from, 179; and W. H. Gist, 191; promoted by agitation for economic and cultural independence of South, 204-205

Seward, William H.: candidate for Presidency, 46; how viewed in South Carolina, 186

Simkins, Arthur: supports Orr, 23, on Kansas policy, 141; said to be sympathetic to Douglas, 188 n.; on John Brown raid, 190-191; on withdrawal of Alabama delegation from Charleston convention, 215 n.

Simms, W. Gilmore, on Cuba, 179; on Kansas as a slave state, 154 n.; on Southern influence in Democratic party, 170

Simons, T. Y., Jr., supports Orr program, 23

Slave code in territories: agitation for annoys moderates, 180; divides Democratic party, 181

Slavery: question of jurisdiction over in territories, 62-63, 103, 132-133, 135, 180, 213, 214-215; practicability of in Kansas questioned, 62, 65 n., 111-112, 154 n.; and foreign affairs, 178; a vital interest, 10; as paramount issue, 67 n., 82. For security of slavery as a political issue, *see* Antislavery movement, Republican party, Secession

Slaves: map and table showing proportion of slaves to total population in state districts, 89, 91; graphs showing the relationship between the proportion of slaves to total population in three groups of state districts and support for (or opposition to) revival of foreign slave trade, 143, 160, 161, 162, 163, 184, participation in national conventions, 90, 105, 211, and secession, 127, 128, 193, 196, 197, 199

Slave trade (foreign): suppression of, 178; revival of as an issue, 130-132, 142, 144, 157-164, 171, 176, 181-183, 191; agitation for revival arrested, 185; action of South Carolina legislature with regard to, 131, 143, 144, 159-164, 184-185; map showing geographical distribution of votes in legislature on resolution concerned with, 159; graphs showing relationship between votes in legislature on resolutions concerned with foreign slave trade and proportion of slaves to total population in three groups of state districts, 143, 160, 161, 162, 184

South: question of South Carolina's co-operation with, 16, 19-20, 24, 26-30, 33, 35-36, 39-40, 48, 92, 102, 175 n., 192, 194, 195 n., 198, 215-216, 217, 219, 222-223, 225; economic and cultural independence advocated, 204-205; unity of advocated, 102, 173

South Carolina: comment upon impotency of in 1852, 36; said to be oligarchical, 44; political unity of explained, 97; assailed by Charles Sumner, 115; reputation for extremism, 19-20, 101, 201-202, 219,

224; takes lead in secession movement, 222-226

South Carolina College, influence on political leaders, 8

South Carolina politics, 1850-1860: leadership, 3-25; secession movement of 1850-1852, 26-42; Thirty-third Congress, 42-45; presidential campaign of 1852, 45-49; situation in late 1852, 49-51; first year of Pierce's administration, 52-57; Kansas-Nebraska Bill, 58-64; Kansas events in 1854, 64-66; other proceedings of Thirty-third Congress, 66-67; foreign affairs in 1854, 67; national party affairs, 68-73; situation in late 1854, 73-74; Kansas events in 1855, 75-76; foreign affairs in 1855, 76-78; national party affairs in 1855, 78-79; South Carolina Know-Nothings, 79-83; Southern party proposed, 83-84; advocacy of participation in national party convention, 84-85; situation in late 1855, 85-86; movement for participation in national convention of Democratic party in 1856, 87-105; Kansas events in 1856, 105-113; Brooks-Sumner affair, 113-121; Democratic convention at Cincinnati, 121; presidential campaign of 1856, 121-124; disunion sentiment in 1856, 125-130; advocacy of reviving the foreign slave trade, 130-132; interpretations of popular sovereignty, 132-133; tariff of 1857, 134; Dred Scott decision, 135; Lecompton constitution, 136-138; emigrant-aid movement, 138-139; Buchanan's Kansas policy debated, 139-142; slave-trade agitation, 142-144; Republican party viewed with hostility, 144; dependability of Democratic party considered, 145-147; factional alignments in 1857, 147; Senatorial election of 1857, 147-149; Thirty-fifth Congress, 150-152; Lecompton constitution rejected and English Bill passed, 152-156; slave-trade agitation in 1858, 157-164; prospects for Republican party and secession in 1858 considered, 164-167; national Democratic party and Douglas criticized, 167-170; factions in 1858, 170-175; Senatorial election of 1858, 175-177; foreign affairs in 1859, 178-179; question of slavery in territories, 179-181; slave-trade issue, 182-185; continuation of hostility to Republican party and doubts about reliability of Democratic, 185-189; reaction to John Brown raid, 189-198; Memminger mission to Virginia in 1860, 200-203; situation in Alabama and Mississippi, 203; agitation for Southern cultural and economic independence, 204-205; Thirty-sixth Congress, 205-209; waning confidence of moderates in survival of Union, 209; preparations for state Democratic convention and its proceedings of April, 1860, 210-214; national Democratic convention at Charleston, 214-216; preparations for state Democratic convention and its proceedings of May, 1860, 216-219; Richmond convention, 219-220; campaign of 1860 and the question of secession, 220-225; state convention provided for, 225-226; popular excitement, 226-228; election of convention delegates, 228; initial proceedings of convention, 229; ordinance of secession, 230; paramount political issue, 231-233

Southern confederacy, support for in South Carolina, 27, 29-30, 86 n., 125-126, 128-129, 152, 195-198, 220, 222, 226; *see also* Secession

Southern conference: proposed by legislature of 1859, 194; rejected by Virginia and accepted by Mississippi, 202, 203; opposed in 1860, 222

Southern congress, proposed by legislature of 1850, 28; rejected by South, 30

Southern independence, *see* Secession, Southern confederacy

Southern nationalism: conflict with State Rights, 29; conflict with independent state secession, 30; conflict with Constitutional nationalism, 72-73

Southern party: discussed, 69, 71, 83; advocated by South Carolina Know-Nothings, 81; failure to organize, 83; leaders sympathetic toward, 84; Buchanan-led Democratic party as equivalent, 170

Southern Rights Association, 30

Southern Rights Democrats, 72 n.

Southern Rights party, opposes Know-Nothings in 1855, 81; advocated, 214 n.

Spartanburg *Carolina Spartan*, on Rhett, 14; on fire-eaters, 18; on Kansas aid, 110, 111; on Kansas policy, 141; on slave code, 180; on John Brown raid, 190

Spartanburg *Express*, on fire-eaters, 18-19

Speakership: James L. Orr elected to, 150; election in Thirty-sixth Congress, 205-206

Spratt, Leonidas William, leads movement for revival of foreign slave trade, 130, 142-143, 158-164, 182-184

Squatter sovereignty, 62 n.; as issue in Democratic national convention of 1860, 214 n.; *see* Popular sovereignty

State Rights: early advocacy of in South Carolina, 8; continuation of arguments and slogans for, 9-10; paramountness of state allegiance, 29; and ordinance of 1852, 41; referred to in message of 1853, 55; advocated by Know-Nothings, 81; reaffirmed by state Democratic convention of 1856, 103; and foreign slave trade, 159-164; and nominating conventions, 212

State Rights Democrats, party of advocated, 214 n.; *see* Irreconcilables

State issues, 49, 55, 73

Statesmanship: regard for in South Carolina, 3-5; Spartanburg *Carolina Spartan* on, 6

Sumner, Charles: and A. P. Butler in 1854, 113; speech on Kansas in 1856, 113-115; caned by Preston Brooks, 117

Sumter *Banner*, on antislavery agitation, 64

Sumter *Black River Watchman*: on state convention of 1852, 36; on *Uncle Tom's Cabin*, 50

Sumter *Watchman*: sympathizes with Southern party, 83; on Kansas events, 110, 138; on Northern Representatives, 120; on disunion, 125; on Republican party, 144; on Douglas, 188

Supreme Court of the United States, opinion in Dred Scott case, 135

Tariff, South Carolina views on, 8, 10, 55, 67, 134

Texas, rumors of slave insurrection in, 226

Thompson, Waddy, retirement from public office, 11

Thornwell, James H., view of statesmanship and citizenship, 4

Toomer, A. V., resolution in convention of 1852, 39 n.

Trade, Charleston merchants seek to expand in up country, 204-205

Tradewell, James D.: attacks Orr, 106; attacks Keitt, 172

Tradition, factor in South Carolina politics, 93

Treaty of Washington, resolution on, 160, 164

Trescot, William Henry: on excessive emphasis on politics, 5-6; on Democratic party, 170 n.

Union district, 191

Unionists, 29, 94, 221

Up country: opposition to extreme measures, 23, 29, 104, 126, 159; attempt of Charleston merchants to expand trade in, 204-205

Van Deusen, John G., *Economic Bases of Disunion in South Carolina*, viii-ix

Vigilance committees, 226

Vermont, resolutions from legislature of, 192

Virginia: commissioner to, 194; willingness of South Carolina to cooperate with, 198 n.; reception of Memminger, 201-203; dependability of questioned by *Mercury*, 203

Walker, Robert J., criticized, 139-140

Walker, William, 178

Wallace, Daniel: on Southern distrust of South Carolina, 19 n.; in Thirty-third Congress, 43

Whaley, William, disunion resolution, 195 n.

Whigs: urged to become Democrats in South, 69; in South Carolina, 85; co-operate with National Democrats in 1860, 210

Wilkes, Warren D., solicits aid for Kansas emigrants, 109

Williams, H. C., on South Carolina leadership, 4 n.

Wilson, B. H., moves to table secession resolution, 129

Winnsboro *Register*, on Democratic party, 95

Woodward, Joseph A., in Thirty-second Congress, 43

Yeadon, Richard, 210

Yorkville *Citizen*, for Buchanan, 122